# Rising on Our Own: Pathways to Africa Self-Reliance and Growth

Building From Within: Charting a Course for Africa Independent Development

Nakel Nikiema

© **Copyright 2024 - All rights reserved.**

The content contained within this book may not be reproduced, duplicated or transmitted without direct written permission from the author or the publisher.

Under no circumstances will any blame or legal responsibility be held against the publisher, or author, for any damages, reparation, or monetary loss due to the information contained within this book, either directly or indirectly.

Legal Notice:

This book is copyright protected. It is only for personal use. You cannot amend, distribute, sell, use, quote or paraphrase any part, or the content within this book, without the consent of the author or publisher.

Disclaimer Notice:

Please note the information contained within this document is for educational and entertainment purposes only. All effort has been executed to present accurate, up to date, reliable, complete information. No warranties of any kind are declared or implied. Readers acknowledge that the author is not engaged in the rendering of legal, financial, medical or professional advice. The content within this book has been derived from various sources. Please consult a licensed professional before attempting any techniques outlined in this book.

By reading this document, the reader agrees that under no circumstances is the author responsible for any losses, direct or indirect, that are incurred as a result of the use of the information contained within this document, including, but not limited to, errors, omissions, or inaccuracies.

# Table of Contents

INTRODUCTION ..........................................................................................................1

CHAPTER 1: UNDERSTANDING AFRICA: PRE-COLONIAL CONTEXTS ......................5

EARLY AFRICA AND AFRICANS..........................................................................................6
PRECOLONIAL PROSPERITY: THE RISE (AND FALL) OF AFRICAN KINGDOMS AND EMPIRES .........8
    *The Nile Valley Oasis: Ancient Egypt ..................................................8*
    *The Empires of West Africa: Ghana and Mali....................................10*
    *The Kingdom of Kongo .......................................................................13*
INTELLECTUAL CONTRIBUTIONS AND CULTURAL EXCHANGES ...........................................16
    *From Here to Timbuktu .....................................................................16*
    *The Swahili Coast ..............................................................................17*
THE POLITICAL SYSTEMS OF PRECOLONIAL AFRICA ..........................................................19
    *Governance in Kemet .........................................................................19*
    *Acholi Governance in Uganda ...........................................................20*
    *The Role of Women in African Governance ......................................21*
AFRICAN HISTORICAL THOUGHT.....................................................................................22

CHAPTER 2: THE DEVASTATION OF COLONIAL RULE...........................................25

THE SCRAMBLE FOR AFRICA (1880–1900) ....................................................................26
    *The Berlin Conference of 1884...........................................................27*
    *The (Pseudo) Scientific Underpinnings of Colonizing Africa .............29*
EXPLOITATION, VIOLENCE, AND MUTILATION UNDER COLONIAL RULE ..............................30
    *Direct Versus Indirect Rule .................................................................31*
    *Economic Exploitation .......................................................................32*
    *Brutalities in the Congo Free State ....................................................34*
THE HARROWING IMPACT OF COLONIALISM ..................................................................37

CHAPTER 3: REBUILDING THE CONTINENT—REFORMING POLITICS, POLICIES, AND CULTURE ........................................................................................41

THE STRUGGLE FOR INDEPENDENCE ...............................................................................42
    *Resisting Colonial Rule: Influencing Factors ......................................43*
THE VIOLENCE OF INDEPENDENCE: THE CASE OF THE MAU MAU UPRISING .......................46
    *British Colonial Rule of Kenya ............................................................46*
    *A Ruthless Reaction ...........................................................................48*
DECOLONIZATION: SUCCESSES AND CHALLENGES ............................................................49
    *Impeding Decolonization: The Apartheid Regime in South Africa.................50*
    *Radical Reforms (and Reversals) in Ghana .......................................52*
    *Rebuilding a Nation: Burkina Faso Under Thomas Sankara ............54*

GADDAFI'S LIBYA: THE ENDURING FIGHT AGAINST IMPERIALISM .................................... 59
   *The Makings of the "Mad Dog"* .................................................................. 59
   *Radical Reforms in Libya* ............................................................................ 60
   *Tensions With the West* ............................................................................. 62

## CHAPTER 4: THE ISSUE WITH INTERNATIONAL INTERVENTION AND AID ........... 65

NEOCOLONIALISM: THE ILLUSION OF INDEPENDENCE ............................................................ 66
   *Foreign Aid: Neocolonialism in Disguise?* ................................................ 67
   *The Economic Impact of Foreign Intervention* ........................................ 69
   *Foreign Aid and Democratization* ............................................................. 69
   *The Realities of Foreign Aid: Italy-Libya Relations and the Slave Trade* ........ 71
THE DARK SIDE OF HUMANITARIAN INTERVENTION ............................................................. 72
   *Hypocrisy: The Lack of Intervention in the Rwandan Genocide* .................... 73
   *The Role of NGOs in Africa* ........................................................................ 75
THE QUESTION OF REPARATIONS ................................................................................... 76
   *What Do Reparations Look Like?* .............................................................. 78

## CHAPTER 5: THE IMPACT OF GLOBALIZATION ON AFRICA'S PROGRESS ............. 83

GLOBALIZATION AND THE INHERENT IMBALANCES ............................................................... 84
   *Globalization: Marginalizing Africa* .......................................................... 86
   *The Positive Impacts of Globalization* ...................................................... 90
CULTURAL GLOBALIZATION: UNDERMINING AFRICAN TRADITIONS AND COMMUNITIES ........ 91
   *The Commodification and Appropriation of Cultural Products* ............... 91
   *The Loss of Land and Languages* .............................................................. 93
THE ROLE OF MULTINATIONAL CORPORATIONS IN AFRICA ................................................. 95
CAN GLOBALIZATION BE LEVERAGED FOR THE BENEFIT OF AFRICA? .................................... 97
   *Improving the Democratization Process* .................................................. 97
   *Economic Development and MNCs* .......................................................... 98
   *Civic Participation* ..................................................................................... 99

## CHAPTER 6: CONTEMPORARY AFRICA—A LOOK AT SUCCESSES
## AND CHALLENGES ................................................................................................. 101

AFRICA TODAY ............................................................................................................ 102
   *Senegal's Reforms* .................................................................................... 103
   *South Africa: A Beacon of Democracy and Human Rights* ..................... 104
A CASE STUDY OF RWANDA ......................................................................................... 106
   *Colonial Rule Over Ruanda-Urundi* ........................................................ 106
   *From Civil War to Genocide* .................................................................... 107
   *Rebuilding Rwanda* ................................................................................. 110
   *Reforms Under Kagame* .......................................................................... 112

## CHAPTER 7: LEVERAGING INDIGENOUS KNOWLEDGE AND
## WAYS OF BEING FOR PROGRESS .......................................................................... 115

INDIGENOUS KNOWLEDGE AS TOOL FOR ACHIEVING SUSTAINABLE DEVELOPMENT ............ 116

  *Leveraging AIKS for Healthcare* .................................................. *118*
 AIKS AND AN ENDOGENOUS APPROACH TO DEVELOPMENT ......................................... 121
  *African Unity* ............................................................................. *123*
  *Community Capacity Building* ................................................ *125*
 PRACTICAL TOOLS AND FRAMEWORKS ....................................................................... 131

## CHAPTER 8: HOW TO UNLOCK AFRICA'S POTENTIAL—REGIONAL COOPERATION .................................................................................................. 141

 A (NEW) AFRICAN RENAISSANCE? ................................................................................ 142
 REGIONAL COOPERATION: SUCCESSES AND CHALLENGES ................................................ 144
  *Ethnocentrism: The West Does Not Need to Save Africa* ................. *144*
  *The Case of ECOWAS* ............................................................ *145*
  *The African Union: A Manipulation Tool?* .................................. *147*
  *When ECOWAS and the AU Failed Niger* ................................... *148*
 ECONOMIC DIVERSIFICATION AND INTRA-AFRICAN TRADE ................................................ 150
  *Economic Diversification to Mitigate Exogenous Shocks* ................ *150*
  *Examples From Kenya and Tunisia* ........................................... *151*
  *Continental Trade Partnerships: The AfCFTA* ............................. *153*
 PRACTICAL TOOLS AND FRAMEWORKS ....................................................................... 155

## CHAPTER 9: THE ROLE OF THE AFRICAN DIASPORA ............................................. 159

 WHO IS THE AFRICAN DIASPORA? ............................................................................. 160
  *The Transatlantic Slave Trade* ................................................. *161*
 LATER MIGRATIONS ................................................................................................ 165
  *North Africa* ........................................................................ *165*
  *West and Central Africa* ........................................................ *167*
  *Southern and Eastern Africa* .................................................. *168*
  *Searching for a Better Life?* ................................................... *169*
 DRAINING AFRICA .................................................................................................. 170
  *The "Greener Pastures"* ........................................................ *172*
  *The Brain Drain and Remittances as Developmental Assistance* ....... *173*
 THE BRAIN GAIN AND RETURNING TO THE *MOTHERLAND* ............................................... 174
  *Economic Measures* .............................................................. *175*
  *Political Measures* ................................................................ *176*
  *Social and Technological Measures* .......................................... *177*
 LEVERAGING THE AFRICAN DIASPORA ....................................................................... 178
  *The Case of Medics2You* ........................................................ *178*
  *The African Diaspora and Africa's Development* ........................ *179*
 PRACTICAL TOOLS AND FRAMEWORKS ....................................................................... 180
  *Harnessing and Managing Remittances* ................................... *181*
  *Diasporic Partnerships and Engagements* ................................ *182*
  *Intra-African Freedom of Movement* ....................................... *183*

## CHAPTER 10: BUILDING FROM WITHIN—WHY SELF-RELIANCE IS

**THE KEY TO AFRICA'S FUTURE** .................................................................. **185**

  THE POWER OF GOOD GOVERNANCE .............................................................. 186
    *Governance in the African Context*............................................................ *187*
  CIVIL SOCIETY AS A WATCHDOG ...................................................................... 191
    *Protests: A Pillar of Democracy?* .............................................................. *193*
    *The Role of the Media* ............................................................................. *197*
  SELF-RELIANCE IS NOT SELF-ISOLATION ........................................................... 198
    *The Value of Economic Self-Reliance* ....................................................... *200*
    *The Creative Economy* ............................................................................ *203*
  THE INTERNATIONAL COMMUNITY'S RESPONSIBILITY TO AFRICA........................... 204
    *African Solutions to African Conflicts* ....................................................... *206*
    *Bringing an End to Economic Exploitation* ............................................... *207*
  PRACTICAL TOOLS AND FRAMEWORKS ............................................................. 211
    *The Cornerstones of Good and Inclusive Governance* .............................. *211*
    *Civil Society and Holding Governments Accountable* ............................... *212*
    *Reducing the Exploitation of MNCs in Africa*............................................ *214*

**CHAPTER 11: TOWARDS A SOLUTION—AFRICAN UNITY AND ECONOMIC PROSPERITY** ............................................................................... **219**

  THE AFRICAN WAY: PAN-AFRICANISM AND DEVELOPMENT............................................ 220
    *A Brief History* ......................................................................................... *221*
    *Pan-Africanism Today* ............................................................................. *224*
    *Pan-Africanism to Achieve Sustainable Development* .............................. *226*
  THE IMPORTANCE OF CONTINENTAL UNITY ..................................................... 228
    *Identifying the Sources of Conflict*........................................................... *228*
    *Social Solidarity and AIKS for Achieving Peace* ........................................ *229*
    *Re-Instilling a Sense of Ubuntu*................................................................ *231*
    *Solidarity and Ubuntu in the 21st Century* ............................................... *233*
  AFRICA BY AFRICANS AND FOR AFRICANS....................................................... 236
    *Education and Awareness Programs for AIKS and Peace-Building*............. *236*
  AFRICA RISING: BUILDING A RESILIENT CONTINENT ....................................... 237
    *The Post-COVID-19 Recovery* .................................................................. *238*
  PRACTICAL TOOLS AND FRAMEWORKS ............................................................. 241
    *Building a Resilient Africa: Key Strategies* ................................................ *241*
    *Developing a Pan-African Framework for the 21st Century* ...................... *242*
    *Checklist: Promoting Social Solidarity in African Societies*......................... *248*
    *Building Resilience to Pandemics and Climate Change* ............................ *251*

**CONCLUSION** ............................................................................................... **253**

  REWRITING HISTORY ....................................................................................... 253
  NEOCOLONIALISM AND WESTERN INTERFERENCE ........................................... 255
  THE FUTURE IS AFRICAN ................................................................................. 256

  **GLOSSARY** .............................................................................................**257**

**REFERENCES** .................................................................................................**265**
    IMAGE REFERENCES........................................................................................290

# Introduction

In 1971, a project was developed to provide employment to the small, semi-nomadic Turkana tribe in Kenya. Owing to frequent droughts in the region, the Turkana, who are primarily goat, cattle, and camel herders, are vulnerable to starvation—prompting foreign powers to intervene and *save* the Africans. More specifically, the Norwegian government invested 22 million dollars to establish the Lake Turkana fish processing plant and, in turn, increase job opportunities for the Turkana people.

However, since the Turkana are semi-nomadic and have no history of fishing or even eating fish, and are primarily concerned with livestock, it should come as no surprise that the processing plant was operational for only a few days before it was completely shut down. The project's failure was further exacerbated by the high demand for clean water in a desert region and the high cost of operating freezers. To complicate the situation, the processing plant's fish production would have been prohibitively expensive for local consumers.

Following the failure of the project, the Turkana people were left destitute, and their livestock died due to disease and overcrowding. The Lake Turkana fish processing plant is just one of many foreign donor-funded projects that have failed to help African citizens— whether they are city dwellers or pastoral nomads. While the intentions of the project may have been good (the aim was to break the cycle of famine and drought and, instead, turn Turkana into a commercial region that would rely on the renewable resource of fish), donor nations and project developers fail to consider that Africa's pastoral and nomadic peoples depend on the survival of their livestock rather than on high-tech projects. In fact, many of these projects have adversely affected the very people they were meant to help: They have led to environmental degradation, the disintegration of African families and communities, and have forced nomads to turn to begging for a living.

For decades, international organizations, foreign donor nations, and nongovernmental organizations have been developing and implementing development projects across the African continent. While some of these projects have been successful, many have failed. The reasons for these failures vary—from war and conflict to corrupt African governments, dwindling donor funding, and the overexploitation of African resources for the economic prosperity of Western countries. However, we must recognize that far too many development projects do not truly acknowledge the realities of African peoples. This raises the question: What are the true goals or objectives of such projects? We must also consider that foreign intervention, aid, and projects create a sense of dependency in which African nations are vulnerable to further exploitation by donor nations. The reliance on foreign aid also enables African government officials to shirk their responsibilities to their citizens.

With this in mind, African nations—their governments and their citizens—must turn inward to advance sustainable development goals and socioeconomic well-being initiatives. By doing so, African nations can become self-reliant and independent from adverse Western influence and interference. *Rising on Our Own: Pathways to Africa's Self-Reliance and Growth* will explore the recent history of the African continent, including the precolonial and postcolonial political, social, economic, and cultural contexts of various African countries. The advent of European colonial rule devastated Africa: Colonialism spread diseases and famine, dehumanized the African "subjects," led to ethnic tensions and conflicts, and resulted in the brutal killings and mutilations of African bodies. Moreover, European colonial rule also played a significant role in hindering the African continent's political and economic prosperity; colonial nations exploited African natural resources and human labor to bolster their own economies—despite the horrendous human cost to Africans.

By providing this historical context, we can then focus on the issues that exist in contemporary Africa and demonstrate the positive and negative influences and impacts of foreign aid and intervention, globalization, and Western interference on the continent. Indeed, as African nations began rebuilding following the fight for independence, many of these nations were also grappling with Western economic interests, Western-funded domestic conflicts, and several other issues that emerged from the unequal relationships between African and Western nations. Arguably, these unequal relationships became even more blatant with the increasing interdependence and connectedness of global economies and cultures. Termed "globalization," this process leveraged advances in technology and mass communication networks to break down barriers in areas such as culture and commerce. Globalization connected citizens from every corner of the world, but it also exacerbated the inequalities between the Global North and the Global South. So, where do we go from here?

*Rising on Our Own: Pathways to Africa's Self-Reliance and Growth* will demonstrate that African nations can (and should) leverage their Indigenous knowledge systems, their intellectually rich and progressive precolonial cultures, ways of being, systems of governance, and natural resources to achieve self-reliance. Self-reliance and, therefore, independence from foreign aid, intervention, and interference can also promote regional and continental cooperation. The colonial system promoted unequal exchanges between African and Western nations, and these exchanges persisted even in the decades following independence. In the later chapters of this book, we argue that African nations can free themselves from colonial legacies and, instead, develop and maintain strong and mutually beneficial intracontinental relationships. Whether this is achieved by forming economic partnerships with other African nations, harnessing the skills and expertise of the African diaspora, or unlocking Africa's potential through its natural resources, a focus on positive intracontinental relationships will reinforce Africa's self-reliance.

Self-reliance does not necessarily mean self-isolation; instead, it is underpinned by agency for oneself, care for the community, and social or civic responsibilities. Indeed, African nations cannot alienate themselves from the wider international community — especially since they are still expected to compete in the global economy — but they can build their political, economic, and social landscapes from within. Building from within not only fosters unity among African nations but also impacts the changing perceptions of the continent. Improving local and national governance, leveraging innovation and talent, and establishing diverse trade and economic relationships across the continent, to name a few examples, all contribute to building a more resilient, prosperous, and dynamic Africa. We can build an Africa for Africans.

# Chapter 1:
# Understanding Africa: Pre-Colonial Contexts

> *Africa's story has been written by others; we need to own our problems and solutions and write our story.*
>
> –Paul Kagame

In his text *Through the Dark Continent* (1878), American-Welsh journalist, explorer, colonial administrator, and author Henry Morton Stanley coined the term "dark continent" to describe Africa. For many American and European explorers, historians, and scholars of previous centuries, Africa was considered both a mystery and a land inhabited by savage, uncivilized peoples.

It was a harsh area with dangerous terrain and primitive inhabitants. These Europeans conveniently left out the fact that African nations and peoples had sophisticated trade networks that reached states in the Middle East and Asia, as well as prosperous cultural hubs and universities, and had made numerous advancements in the fields of mathematics and astronomy, to name a few examples. Africa, before the advent of European colonial rule, was a region rich in both human and natural resources.

However, to justify their plundering of African lands and the exploitation of natural resources, European explorers and colonizers had to spread the idea that Africans were savages in desperate need of *saving* and *civilizing*. The Western tales of diseased Africans and beastly jungles contradicted the reality of Africa; this was a continent teeming with comprehensive systems of governance, progressive technology, intra- and intercontinental cultural exchanges, and several wealthy kingdoms and empires.

Nevertheless, the Europeans claimed they were bringing light to the "dark continent," and as a result, they arrived on the African shores and spread famine, disease, and conflict among the once-prosperous African states. Before we discuss the horrors of European colonial rule in Africa, let us first examine the sociocultural, political, and economic landscapes of precolonial Africa.

## Early Africa and Africans

Owing to the scarcity of written records from ancient Africa, much of what we understand about this era is derived from archaeological findings—such as graves and bones—and artifacts. What we do know about ancient Africa is that it possessed lands and waters rich in mineral resources, including precious metals and gems.

Africa is also believed to be the birthplace of the Hominidae—the taxonomic family to which modern humans belong—who originated in the eastern regions of sub-Saharan Africa and later spread to Northern Africa and the Middle East.

For millennia, human migration has occurred in and out of Africa, leading to the evolution of African languages, cultures, traditions, and religions, as well as the rise and fall of various African kingdoms and empires. Early Africans adapted to and evolved alongside their environments, playing a vital role in their ecosystems. Due to tropical diseases and the preference for foraging and hunting over farming, these early Africans seldom established permanent settlements or farmed the land. Instead, they lived in small but highly mobile groups until the agricultural revolution. Believed to have originated around 9,000 B.C.E., the era of agriculture saw early Africans domesticating plants and livestock—such as sheep, pigs, goats, and cows—thereby establishing settlements on favorable lands.

It was only a matter of time before clans or lineage groups emerged, and subsequently, clusters of households transformed into small or large villages or towns.

These villages were situated on land suitable for farming and near water reserves; when they were threatened by famine, drought, or other environmental events, they would clear new land and rebuild their settlements.

]As a result, Africans were able to settle in and establish societies, farm the land, and interact with other societies; sophisticated trade routes and networks began to emerge.

For example, camel caravans transported textiles, salt, gold, ivory, and copper from settlements in the Mali Empire to West and North Africa, Egypt, Sudan, and the Mediterranean coast. These flourishing trade networks eventually led to the emergence of wealthy and powerful kingdoms and empires, including the Mali Empire, the Ghana Empire, the Kongo Kingdom, and the Ife Empire.

# Precolonial Prosperity: The Rise (and Fall) of African Kingdoms and Empires

## *The Nile Valley Oasis: Ancient Egypt*

As a civilization that dates back to the 4th millennium B.C.E., Ancient Egypt boasts several achievements in art, science, mathematics, and architecture. This region was an oasis in the northeast African deserts and featured a series of stable kingdoms (with some periods of instability in between), including the Old Kingdom of the Early Bronze Age, the Middle Kingdom of the Middle Bronze Age, and the New Kingdom of the Late Bronze Age.

It was during the New Kingdom that Ancient Egypt was at its most prosperous, and its successes are largely attributed to the Egyptians' ability to adapt to the conditions of the Nile River valley and leverage its resources for agriculture.

The Nile River not only contained mineral deposits and gold but also connected several populations, enabling trade as well as cultural and intellectual exchanges. Agriculture in Ancient Egypt largely consisted of barley and emmer wheat, and the fertility and predictability of the land allowed for highly productive farming.

In fact, Egyptians were able to store large supplies of crops, and as a result, they could protect themselves against crop failures. Importantly, this agricultural productivity also helped transform Ancient Egypt into the greatest empire in the ancient Middle East. Grain crops, however, were not the only abundant resource: Fruits and vegetables were irrigated year-round, fish were plentiful, and papyrus was cultivated to make sandals, rope, mats, and writing materials. The development of a unique writing system and the construction of pyramids demonstrate that while the crops were thriving, the Egyptians were also honing their craft and organizational abilities.

Ancient Egyptians were adept at surveying, quarrying, and building techniques, which enabled them to construct monumental temples and pyramids. In addition, they developed systems of mathematics, medicine, and literature and made advancements in farming techniques, irrigation, and water transport. More specifically, this civilization identified numerous physical threats, such as malaria and parasites from the Nile River, dangerous wildlife (including crocodiles), and the pressures farming and building placed on the spine and joints. Consequently, they found ways to remedy these issues.

Egyptian physicians were highly trained and specialized in certain parts of the body, allowing them to effectively treat specific conditions. Medical papyri also demonstrated that these physicians possessed empirical knowledge of human anatomy and were able to administer practical treatments. Wounds, for instance, were bandaged with raw meat, sutures, white linen, and honey-soaked swabs to prevent infection, while burns were treated with dressings soaked in milk.

Honey and copper salts were also administered to prevent infections at the burn sites. There is ample evidence showing that Egyptian physicians were capable of amputating diseased limbs and setting broken bones.

In terms of mathematics, the Ancient Egyptians had a fully developed numeral system that was used for accounting grain, land, and labor. They were also able to perform addition, subtraction, multiplication, and division; use fractions; calculate the areas of circles, triangles, and rectangles; and determine the volume of pyramids and columns. With these advancements in mind, it is unsurprising that Ancient Egypt's architecture, art, and intellectual projects were copied across the globe.

## *The Empires of West Africa: Ghana and Mali*

Owing largely to the introduction of camels, which provided a means of transport across the Saharan Desert, the trans-Saharan trade network was revolutionized between the 3rd and 5th centuries. This innovation prompted traders from West Africa to become the link between the salt trading of the northern regions of Africa and the gold trading of the sub-Saharan areas of the continent. As a result, West African traders became embroiled in the trade networks of Mediterranean civilizations and leveraged their control over the trans-Saharan trade route to build magnificent and wealthy empires.

### *The Land of Gold*

From the 6th to the 13th century, the Ghana Empire facilitated the trade of important commodities, including gold, copper, ivory, and iron. The empire's easy access to the Senegal River and Niger River, along with its rich deposits of copper and either locally mined or traded gold resources, all contributed to the exceptional prosperity of its kings and people. The kings of Ghana were not only the empire's monarchs and heads of religion and justice, but they also maintained strict control over the empire's gold markets. While the ordinary people and traders of the Ghana Empire traded in gold dust or powder, the kings would stockpile gold nuggets weighing between 25 grams and half a kilogram. The kings were also often adorned with golden bracelets and necklaces, and their regalia was generously decorated with gold.

The Ghana Empire's dominance over West African trade peaked during the 6th and 7th centuries. Muslim traders sent camel caravans carrying salt from the northern regions of Africa, and in turn, the empire's kings provided the traders with ivory, gold, ostrich feathers, and slaves. In addition, these commodities were taxed twice: once when they arrived in the Ghana Empire and a second time when they left. This taxation, coupled with the kings' trading of gold dust (rather than gold nuggets), meant that the kings of the Ghana Empire exercised great control over the gold market and ensured that the value of gold did not decrease by maintaining a limited supply of this commodity in circulation.

It is also significant to note the influence and spread of Islam throughout this region. The Muslim traders or merchants, who were largely Berber, regularly encountered West African traders, elites, and royalty. Several leaders in West Africa realized that adopting Islam, or at least tolerating the religion, led to greater trade relationships with the Muslim merchants.

While there is no evidence that the kings of the Ghana Empire converted to Islam, several mosques were erected for the Muslim merchants and for the local populations who converted. It is also believed that indigenous animist beliefs were practiced alongside Islam, with the former being primarily practiced in the rural regions of the Ghana Empire. Despite its immense wealth, the Ghana Empire began to decline in the mid-11th century.

This decline was sparked when the Almoravids of North Africa plundered the capital of Koumbi Saleh. While there is a lack of concrete evidence regarding the motivations for the attack and its immediate aftermath, the Ghana Empire struggled to recover. The development of competing trade routes, the detrimental effects of the dry climate on agricultural production, and a series of civil wars all served to exacerbate this situation. Recognizing the vulnerability of the central government of the Ghana Empire, local chiefs seized the opportunity to declare their independence from the empire, with some even allying themselves with the Almoravids.

The Ghana Empire collapsed, and once the Almoravids' rule also fell, the Kingdom of Sosso swept in to take control of the once-prosperous empire. However, the Kingdom of Sosso was soon conquered by Sundiata Keita in 1235, and Keita went on to establish the Mali Empire in 1240.

## *The Mali Empire*

Emerging from the ashes of the Ghana Empire, with King Sundiata Keita as its ruler, the Mali Empire boasted a centralized government and an ever-expanding, well-trained army. It is unsurprising that it became the largest empire in Africa at that time. Much of the Mali Empire's wealth came from its trade networks, high taxes on traded goods, and tributes (such as rice and arrows) collected from several small kingdoms and the outlying regions of the empire.

Interestingly, the Mali Empire did not have direct control over the goldfields; instead, it accessed the gold found along the Black Volta and in the Akan Forest. Thus, the empire was still able to dominate the gold trade. Despite being a monarchy, the Mali Empire's state power was assigned to court officials, which played a major role in maintaining stability during times of political unrest and poor leadership. This system of governance was also effective during the reigns of *good* kings. Mansa Musa I (1312–1337), for example, took the Mali Empire's wealth and prosperity to new heights. His reign is infamous not only because he controlled Mali's regional trade networks but also due to his lavish lifestyle and generosity. For instance, Mansa Musa I traveled to Mecca, Saudi Arabia, in 1324 with the aid of 100 camels and 500 slaves to carry his gold.

Throughout the journey, he handed out gold as gifts—so much so that his generosity led to the value of the gold dinar decreasing by 20% in Cairo (Cartwright, 2019). Tales of Mansa Musa I's wealth soon spread across Africa and beyond. Like several other empires and kingdoms, the Mali Empire was not immune to decline, and following a series of civil wars, the emergence of competing trade routes, and the rise of the Songhai Empire, the Mali Empire ultimately collapsed in the 1460s.

## *The Kingdom of Kongo*

In what began as a federation of small polities, the conquering of new peoples and lands, the formation of a royal patrimony supported by numerous provinces, and a peace treaty between the kingdoms of Mbata and Mpemba Kasi all led to the founding of the Kingdom of Kongo around 1390. By the 15th and 16th centuries, this kingdom had significantly expanded its territories, and because it was located at the center of a prosperous trade network, the Kingdom of Kongo traded and manufactured various resources and goods, including pottery, metals, ivory, raffia cloth, and copperware.

The kingdom's governance was also highly centralized, and with most of its population inhabiting the capital, the Kingdom of Kongo was able to transport trade goods, surplus food, and natural resources across its region. The monopoly over trade networks and access to valuable resources established several African empires and kingdoms as wealthy. However, what set the Kingdom of Kongo apart from other rich empires was its encouragement and prioritization of art.

The Kingdom of Kongo boasted many talented sculptors and hosted national festivals to celebrate these artists. Kongo kings were adorned with ornate headdresses and jewelry made from precious metals as well.

By the time Portuguese explorers arrived in 1483, the Kingdom of Kongo had become a powerful state. The African kingdom's wealth, art, and extensive trade connections impressed these explorers, who were seeking political and commercial alliances. This contact with the Portuguese marked the beginning of a new era for the Kingdom of Kongo:

The then-king, Nzinga a Nkuwu, and his son, Mvemba a Nzinga, soon converted to Christianity, were baptized, and received Christian names. Thus, Mvemba a Nzinga became Afonso and ruled as King Afonso I from 1506 to 1543. It is worth noting that King Afonso I's conversion to Christianity may not have represented an acceptance of a new religion but rather a strategic move to strengthen the Kingdom of Kongo's relationship with the Portuguese. Subsequently, some nobles from the Kingdom of Kongo traveled to Portugal to study the country's language and customs, and in turn, Portuguese soldiers, priests, missionaries, and traders began to inhabit the kingdom.

King Afonso I's interest in European culture, however, did not impede his attempts to maintain the Kingdom of Kongo's autonomy. For instance, he sent his son, Henrique, to the Vatican to become a bishop so that upon the latter's return, he would have the power to appoint Kongolese priests within the kingdom. King Afonso I also limited the Portuguese access to the Kingdom of Kongo.

It is unsurprising that the relationship between the Kingdom of Kongo and the Portuguese soon turned sour. The burgeoning slave trade led to a high demand for African slaves, who were then traded for luxury goods such as silk and cotton from Europe or sent to work on the sugar colonies on the Portuguese island of São Tomé.

It is worth noting that prior to the arrival of the Portuguese, not much was known about slavery in the Kingdom of Kongo, and some sources claim that the kingdom's use of slaves was largely motivated by its relationship with the Portuguese. Despite King Afonso I's attempts to curtail the Portuguese exploitation of Kongolese people, his death led to a power vacuum, and several Kongolese factions began vying to replace him.

Internal power struggles, conflicts with neighboring states, civil wars and rebellions, and tense material and diplomatic ties with European nations characterized the following few decades.

By the late 17th and early 18th centuries, the Kingdom of Kongo was further destabilized by the large number of Africans being captured by European slave traders as part of the transatlantic slave trade, and the once strong and highly centralized kingdom was now dealing with internal conflicts and warring factions.

Moreover, in retaliation for being ousted from Luanda, the Portuguese invaded the Kingdom of Kongo, defeated the Kongolese forces, killed the then-king, and seized Luanda.

Historians are still debating the reasons for the rapid decline of the Kingdom of Kongo: some attribute the decline to the pressures of the slave trade and weakened monarchy, while others assign blame to the numerous attacks by the Portuguese military against the kingdom, and some argue that internal conflicts caused the kingdom to collapse.

However, by the 1700s, the Kingdom of Kongo had become decentralized and was only a semblance of its former splendor.

# Intellectual Contributions and Cultural Exchanges

*From Here to Timbuktu*

Despite the rise and fall of numerous African kingdoms and empires, their immense intellectual and cultural influence remains undeniable. The Mali Empire, for example, was home to Timbuktu — a city that garnered its wealth by having access to and controlling the trade routes between the Niger River and North Africa. In fact, Timbuktu's proximity to the Niger River made it a starting point for traders and camel caravans that traveled along the trans-Saharan trade route. This, coupled with strong diplomatic ties to Egypt and Morocco, established

Timbuktu as a cosmopolitan city. Indeed, it was home to several ethnic groups as well as temporary and permanent merchants. The city, however, was internationally revered for its majestic mosques and universities; as such, Timbuktu became an intellectual hub that outlasted both the Mali Empire and the rule of the Songhai Empire, the Tuaregs, and the Moroccan Pashas.

Timbuktu encouraged all forms of learning, and its universities boasted large libraries, students skilled in memorizing and producing texts, and studies in Islam and theology, grammar, law, logic and rhetoric, astronomy, geography, history, mathematics, medicine, and astrology. In spite of the immense influence of Islam and Islamic studies, indigenous animistic beliefs were still practiced, demonstrating how different religious beliefs could peacefully coexist.

Many European explorers remained mystified by the city despite its developing reputation as a center of learning and wealth. Here, European explorers found it difficult to locate Timbuktu, and considering the violence and exploitation unleashed by European colonial powers in Africa, it was fortunate that they could not find the city.

## *The Swahili Coast*

The Swahili Coast is a culturally diverse region in East Africa that thrived in the 15th and 16th centuries. Importantly, the African Bantu peoples, who frequently traded with Persian and Arab populations, lived in this area. This enabled many cultural exchanges, and the use of Arab dhows, in turn, allowed for easier, faster, and longer-distance travel across the sea – reaching all the way to India and China.

Here, the predominantly Muslim traders from Egypt, Persia, and Arabia mixed with the African Bantu peoples, and subsequently, the Persian, Arab, and African Bantu peoples living along the coast developed their own language (Kiswahili), traditions, and culture. With a long history of trading with Persia, Arabia, and China, its prime location along the East African coast, and a climate favorable for agricultural production, the people of the Swahili Coast developed an extensive maritime trade network. Along with the Arab dhows, they built small sailing boats and canoes to travel across the calm waters, and the several coastal islands also provided them with time and a place to rest.

The growing maritime trade networks eventually led to numerous settlements being established along the coast. These settlements soon transformed into city-states that thrived due to maritime trade. The Swahili city-states produced several goods, such as pottery and cloth, which they traded for products from China, India, and Southeast Asia. Like other trading regions, these city-states were home to temporary and permanent merchants, religious rulers, governors, and craftspeople. They were also home to many mosques and palaces featuring large courtyards, domed ceilings, pools, and audience halls.

As in the case of the Kingdom of Kongo, the rich history, wealth, and unique cultures of the Swahili Coast were threatened by the arrival of the Portuguese. More specifically, the Portuguese explorer Vasco da Gama arrived on the Swahili Coast in the late 15th century, and despite facing resistance from the Swahili people, the Portuguese seized control of the maritime trade networks and routes. Any city that stood in the way of Portuguese greed would be destroyed, and the once-vibrant Swahili city-states were left devastated. Despite the sudden end to the prosperity of the Swahili city-states, this region demonstrates the incredible impact of cultural exchanges.

The Swahili peoples and cultures have a mix of African and Arab origins, and their extensive trade networks also facilitated many more cultural exchanges and influences with nations like China and India. It is crucial to keep in mind the artistic and intellectual contributions, the agricultural and technological advancements, and the sophisticated governance structures of various African nations—as well as how the emergence of European colonialism impeded prosperity and progress.

# The Political Systems of Precolonial Africa

In ancient Africa, systems of governance were largely formed to protect the states from external invasions as well as internal coups and conflicts. Even in times of political destabilization, African states would adapt and establish new forms of governance. Given the diversity of ancient Africa, governance structures and practices varied from one state to another; however, there is evidence demonstrating the practice of democracy in traditional African governments. For example, the chief, king, and/or queen would rule over the state and its people as long as they fulfilled the needs and aspirations of their subjects. If they faltered, processes were in place to remove the leader from political power.

## *Governance in Kemet*

In Kemet (modern-day Egypt), for instance, the government was developed and operated as a highly centralized and participatory institution. Provincial governors addressed more localized issues and conflicts and then reported back to the central authorities, whereas the centralized authorities largely consisted of the royal court and the office of kingship. Indeed, when the many communities of the Nile Valley unified into one polity, it was decided that there would be one ruler to govern both Upper and Lower Kemet.

Kingship or queenship was determined by divine right, and according to related mythology, the king or queen was believed to be a direct descendant of the gods or goddesses. Similar to other systems of governance in ancient Africa, and despite the close link between kingship or queenship and divinity, there were checks and balances in place should the king or queen reign irresponsibly. In such cases, the king or queen would be removed. Importantly, Kemet had several laws that supported the civic participation of its people.

When laws were drafted, the everyday needs of the populace were considered, and various government stakeholders were consulted. Additionally, this implied that all three tiers of government would have to support the overthrow of a king or queen. Pyramid construction serves as the foundation for much of what we know about the political power wielded by kings or queens. The number of pyramids constructed by a ruler signified the extent of their political power and influence. Ultimately, a ruler in Kemet had the main responsibility of ensuring the well-being of their people, maintaining peace within the state or region, and remedying any external conflicts that might arise.

## *Acholi Governance in Uganda*

According to oral histories and traditions, the Acholi people in the East African state of Uganda had a strong and organized democratic system of governance in which power rested in the hands of the *Rwot*, or head of government, as well as the judicial, legislative, and executive branches of government. A council of chiefs and elders supported the Rwot, who was both a political and religious figure, serving as a bridge between the spiritual and material worlds. Moreover, Acholi chiefdoms comprised several fenced villages, where lineage played a vital role in political representation.

For example, the rights to hunting and agricultural land and the organization of production (and the use of the proceeds from that production) were granted to each localized lineage, enabling the lineage leader or head, along with lineage elders, to be responsible for their own internal affairs. This decentralization of power, in turn, allowed village or lineage leaders, elders, and council members to hold the Rwot accountable for any poor or irresponsible governance. When it came to smaller or more localized tensions and conflicts, the Rwot would work alongside the council of chiefs and elders to resolve disputes between the involved parties.

Through a system of *mato oput* (an approach to justice that sought to repair the relationship between the conflicting parties), the root causes of the conflict would be identified and addressed. The participation of chiefs and councils in political processes closely demonstrates a parliamentary system in Acholi, Uganda, as issues or conflicts of national concern were deliberated and resolved through consensus. As seen in Kemet, the Rwot ruled over the Acholi people, and should his leadership not reflect the needs or will of the Acholi people, he would be removed from office. If the Acholi people were satisfied with the Rwot's leadership, his rule would only come to an end upon his death, at which point his son would assume office.

## *The Role of Women in African Governance*

In ancient West African states, the social power and status of men and women differed. For men, their status stemmed from material wealth, such as land, houses, livestock, and wives. In contrast, women's wealth and status were derived from having children, operating successful farms and households, and managing livestock. As such, it was possible for West African women to attain the same social status and power as their husbands. In cases where women accumulated significant wealth through trade, they could actually enhance their own position as well as that of their husbands.

Of course, women in urban areas enjoyed advantages due to the increased opportunities they had to sell their crafts and weave in markets. While men held much of the political power in West Africa, women still had a voice in political practices, discussions, and institutions. As a result, women were able to attain chieftainship. Here, the Omu (female chieftain) and her cabinet had the power to make political decisions, and although such decisions could be vetoed by the Obi (or male leader), the Omu was also empowered to challenge the authority of the Obi. In some West African societies, the Omu also served as a spiritual leader who not only meted out punishment for crimes but also set and controlled market prices. The markets, in this context, were hubs of economic activity and religious spaces, granting the Omu both spiritual and economic authority. However, the gender dynamics present in many African cultures and communities were forever changed when European colonial powers took control.

## African Historical Thought

African historical thought is a relatively new development, as 20th-century African scholars sought to respond to the overwhelming misrepresentations of Africa and its peoples by colonists. One prominent African scholar and thinker is Senegalese historian and anthropologist Cheikh Anta Diop, who has attributed significant importance to African history, a level usually reserved for Western countries. As such, Diop continues to be regarded as one of the most prominent Afrocentric scholars.

Born on December 29, 1923, in Diourbel, Senegal, Diop developed an interest in African history by experiencing the nationalist movements of that time. His academic fame emerged in the 1940s when Diop translated Albert Einstein's theory of relativity into a Senegalese language, making Einstein's work accessible to the Senegalese people and demonstrating the ability of African languages to convey scientific knowledge. Diop also published several books on African history, culture, and philosophy—many of which undermined the prevailing ideas, stereotypes, and misrepresentations of Africa and its peoples. Indeed, colonial writers and historians focused on the contributions of

Europeans to African development, while Diop promoted a nationalist approach to African history and asserted that Africa had a history before Europeans arrived. Diop argued and maintained that Africans were not simply observers of their own histories; rather, they were the makers. Their intellectual and artistic contributions, as well as their sophisticated governance structures and trade networks, are a testament to the many accomplishments and innovations of precolonial Africa. Diop also advocated for the development and use of an independent methodology to explore and understand African history.

This is because existing Western sources are imbued with colonial racism, while original sources, such as artifacts and oral traditions, present a more accurate and balanced view of Africa's history. Importantly, Diop stressed the need for a prominent African language to be used in educational institutions and governments to replace Western languages. He argued that the use of a unifying African language would also help to ease international relations.

Cheikh Anta Diop's writings illustrate an interesting insight: He noted that in the postcolonial era, African nations are still politically, economically, socially, and morally under the control of European countries. As such, postcolonial leaders depend on the former colonial powers for financial support. In turn, European countries (and the West in general) take advantage of this dependency and impose their own agendas and interests on African nations.

This not only quells revolutionary thought and movements in Africa but also turns nationalist African leaders into puppets or executive committees for Western countries. The significance of Diop's work cannot be overstated: he was a controversial figure who dared to suggest that Black people were the first to achieve civilization and that Western countries modeled their own societies after them. Yet the well-organized political, economic, and social structures of precolonial Africa were deliberately destroyed upon the arrival of European explorers and colonists. It was through the establishment of the slave trade, colonialism, and capitalism by the Europeans that African societies were both destroyed and underdeveloped. As we will explore in the next chapter, European colonial rule devastated African lands, resources, and populations while building the wealth of European colonial powers.

# Chapter 2:
# The Devastation of Colonial Rule

> *When the missionaries came to Africa they had the Bible and we had the land. They said 'Let us pray.' We closed our eyes. When we opened them we had the Bible and they had the land.*
>
> –Desmond Tutu

To understand the extent of European colonialism's harrowing impact on the African continent, we first need to examine the systems of governance that existed in precolonial African kingdoms, empires, and states.

Contrary to the widespread belief that precolonial Africa had primitive political systems, many African states had robust systems of democratic and despotic governance, economic policies, and social unity.

In fact, it was through these functional systems of governance and strong policies that wealthy kingdoms and sophisticated trade networks emerged.

Of course, the well-being and progress of African nations, economies, and their people came to a sudden halt when the European colonial powers wreaked havoc on the continent.

# The Scramble for Africa (1880–1900)

There were only a few regions in Africa under European rule in the 1880s, but this soon changed when European powers gathered to discuss, carve up, and take control of the continent. The Scramble for Africa was a two-decade period that saw the rapid colonization of Africa by European powers, including Great Britain, France, Spain, and Belgium. Interestingly, the motivations for this "scramble" were largely rooted in the socioeconomic and political contexts of Europe.

When European explorers initially traversed African terrains, they were motivated by curiosity; they sought mysterious lands, such as Timbuktu, and hoped to publish texts about the so-called dark continent.

However, in the latter part of the 19th century, these explorers became more concerned with Africa's flourishing trade networks and goods, hoping to secure them for the wealthy philanthropists funding their expeditions.

Henry Morton Stanley, the explorer who popularized the term "dark continent," for example, traveled in Africa on behalf of King Leopold II of Belgium. Here, Stanley was hired to negotiate and establish treaties with local chiefs in the Kongo region and to assess this region's potential as a Belgian colony. Stanley's mission also prompted several other European explorers to follow suit.

During the 19th century, Europe gradually shifted away from the trade of slaves; however, capitalists still needed profitable trade to bolster the economies of European countries. Based on the accounts of European explorers describing vast natural resources and sophisticated trade routes and networks on the African continent, Europeans regarded Africa as both a figurative and literal goldmine.

Africa was a place from which Europeans could extract many raw materials, enriching their own countries in the process, and it also represented a market for European nations to sell their manufactured goods. If Europeans could establish colonies in Africa, they would monopolize the extraction of natural resources and the exploitation of human labor. It is also worth noting that Europe's advancements in weaponry, such as faster-loading and quick-firing guns, provided them with an edge in their quest for control over Africa.

## The Berlin Conference of 1884

On Saturday, November 15, 1884, an international conference took place in the newly formed German Empire. Here, representatives from all European countries (except for Switzerland) and the United States gathered to divide the African continent for their own political and economic interests.

The 104-day-long conference transformed the African continent into a playground for white European colonial powers—a playground where these powers could establish their own free trade networks, use the land as a battleground for their conflicts and wars, and exploit it for their benefit. In other words, the Berlin Conference of 1884 was a discussion on the effective occupation of foreign lands. In the year of the Berlin Conference, around 80% of Africa was under the control of traditional and local governance systems (Gathara, 2019). The remaining 20% was primarily along the African coast, where Europeans had already established their colonies, trading posts, and geographic boundaries. Yet, after only 20 years, Liberia and Ethiopia were the only African countries that remained outside of European colonial rule.

It is worth noting that many Africans attempted to resist colonial rule and subjugation; however, given the dehumanizing, discriminatory, and brutal nature of colonialism, combined with the European colonial powers' arsenal of weapons and products from the Industrial Revolution, their efforts were largely futile. As such, Great Britain established control over East Africa (notably Kenya and Uganda),

Rhodesia (modern-day Zimbabwe), South Africa, and Gambia, among many others; Belgium took control of the Congo; and France colonized Algeria, Chad, Sudan, the Ivory Coast, Morocco, and Senegal, to name a few examples. Additionally, Germany established colonies in German East Africa, German South-West Africa, Togoland, and others, while Portugal seized Angola, Cape Verde, Mombasa, Tangier, and Zanzibar. These are only some of the many regions or states in Africa that came under European control.

One of the countless problems associated with the Scramble for Africa is the European colonial powers' lack of consideration for existing African communities, ethnicities, and tribes. When the European colonial powers carved up the African continent for their taking, they also separated certain ethnic groups. For instance, the Maasai peoples were divided between Kenya (62%) and Tanzania (38%); the Malinke peoples were dispersed across six different countries; and the Nukwe were split among Namibia, Zambia, Angola, and Botswana (Michalopoulos & Papaioannou, 2016).

The arbitrary drawing of borders by the European colonial powers had a devastating impact by fragmenting ethnic groups and communities and sowing tensions among these groups—tensions that persist even today.

## The (Pseudo)/cientific Underpinnings of Colonizing Africa

The exploitation of natural and human resources in Africa was brutal; thus, European colonial powers needed a justification for the subjugation of and violence inflicted upon African bodies. While it is now debunked or considered a pseudoscience, scientific racism is an ideology that argues for the natural or inherent superiority of white Europeans and, likewise, for the inherent inferiority of non-white and non-European peoples. The misappropriation of advances in medicine and Charles Darwin's theory of evolution led to the increasing popularity of scientific racism among Western scientists, academics, and scholars during the 18th and 19th centuries. Different from but intricately linked to scientific racism is the theory of eugenics.

Eugenicists argued that through planned breeding, (involuntary) sterilization, and social exclusion, humans could improve the quality of the human gene pool. In other words, people with traits deemed desirable would be encouraged to reproduce, while those with traits considered undesirable and inferior would be deemed unfit for reproduction.

Eugenicists also believed that biological and behavioral characteristics were fixed; as a result, some groups or populations were naturally superior to others. It is unsurprising that eugenicists linked undesirable and inferior traits to non-white people, individuals with disabilities, and many others. Several countries in the Western world, including Canada, the United States, and Germany, adopted policies based on scientific racism and eugenics, leading to many so-called undesirable individuals being forcibly sterilized or subjected to discrimination and violence. In German South West Africa (modern-day Namibia), for example, a horrific genocide was perpetrated against the indigenous Herero and Namaqua peoples. As a German colony from 1884 to 1919, this region saw German soldiers massacring Herero and Nama men, women, children, and the elderly to the extent that German forces wiped out around 75% of the Herero population and 50% of the Namaqua population (Nebe, 2021). Many of the remaining Herero and Namaqua people were sent to death and concentration camps, where they were killed or forced into labor. Moreover, the remains (such as the skulls) of some of the Herero and Namaqua victims of genocide were sent to German scientists to further develop the theories of eugenics and scientific racism. In turn, theories of scientific racism and eugenics drew support from colonial powers to justify the brutalities they inflicted upon African peoples. Indeed, the European colonial powers portrayed themselves as brave heroes willing and ready to *save* and *civilize* the African *savages*.

## Exploitation, Violence, and Mutilation Under Colonial Rule

European colonial rule devastated the African continent in countless ways. Defined as the domination of one country by another, with political and economic power resting in the hands of the foreign power, colonialism involves the political domination and exploitation of the colonized country. European colonial rule in Africa took place between 1800 and the 1960s and formed part of a larger imperialist process—one that served only the interests of the colonial powers. The colonization of the African continent emerged from the Industrial Revolution's high demand for raw materials and a drastic increase in production. In this context, European countries also needed a new and extensive market (namely, Africa) to which they could sell their manufactured goods. Coupled with the abolition of slavery in the

Americas and Europe, the colonial powers decided to utilize African labor in Africa (rather than shipping African slaves across the oceans). As such, the European colonial powers seized existing African systems of governance, markets, natural resources, and human labor to serve their imperialist objectives.

## Direct Versus Indirect Rule

While European colonial powers had similar goals of plundering the African continent of its natural and human resources to strengthen their own economies, some European countries differed in their colonial policies. Britain, for example, implemented a system of indirect rule, whereby it exerted power and control over the colonized peoples through their own traditional institutions. The British utilized existing power structures to achieve their imperial goals and employed indigenous tribal chiefs as political intermediaries.

Indirect rule was regarded as cheaper — incurring no costs related to colonial administration — more practical and more convenient. In the Sokoto Caliphate (northern Nigeria), for instance, military and tax control were managed by the British, while local affairs were left in the hands of local, indigenous Africans who had allied with the British either during or after Britain's conquest of the Sokoto Caliphate.

Indeed, when the British conquered the Sokoto Caliphate in the early 20th century, they recognized that they could leverage the existing and highly developed administrative system of the emirs to control both the emirs and their people.

In contrast to Britain, France's imperialist project included the policy of assimilating African peoples into French culture, traditions, and norms. Thus, France's direct rule aimed to weaken or dismantle existing indigenous institutions and systems of governance, replacing them with new institutions and systems modeled on European ones.

This exertion of power and control also extended into the sociocultural sphere of French colonies in Africa: French colonial rule sought to erase African cultures and impose the process of "Frenchification" on African men and women. An integral part of this process was the French government's—and the Catholic Church's—control over the media and educational institutions; as a result, any news material that criticized or challenged French authority was banned or systematically censored.

## *Economic Exploitation*

The European colonizers faced significant resistance from African chiefs and peoples, and the existing structure of African economies did not permit a large and steady supply of natural resources, which was necessary to meet the colonizers' demands. Therefore, it was crucial for the European colonial powers to exert direct and complete control over African political administrations and economies, reorganizing these systems to suit their needs and serve their economic interests. As a result, the African economies, originally based on the barter system, were transformed to conform to international trade and market standards. The colonizers' direct control over African economies had another sinister underpinning: they sought to prevent African peoples from manufacturing their own natural resources and potentially competing with European countries at that time. Consequently, it was in the colonizers' best interests to underdevelop African political systems and technology to keep both these systems and African peoples under control.

African labor was needed to meet the demands of the colonizers, and considering the scale of the imperialist project, this labor was coerced. Moreover, why would an African individual willingly or voluntarily work in a job that benefited the economies of European countries? The complete control over African political systems and economies allowed the colonizers to also dominate African peoples and their bodies—forcing them to submit to the colonial administration and its demands. In this context, the colonizers employed several tactics to ensure that their exploitation of African human labor was met with minimal resistance or violence. First, the colonizers politically, socially, culturally, and economically conquered and occupied new territories and peoples across the African continent. Armed with guns and motivated by the prospect of wealth, the colonizers systematically intervened in the sovereignty and internal affairs of African states. In doing so, they would assist political factions in unseating political leaders and installing their own leaders who were amenable to colonial interests. African traders were also displaced, and the colonizers imposed treaties that served their own interests. If African rulers, chiefs, or traders resisted, they faced violence and trade wars.

Another tactic of exploitation was the use of forced African labor on colonial plantations, in mines, and in industries. This was achieved by occupying and taking control of African lands and natural resources. From gold and copper mines to wool, rubber, and cotton plantations, European colonizers confiscated lands rich in such resources, and the now-dispossessed Africans had to work for the colonizers to ensure their own survival and that of their families. In some cases, colonialists imposed legal measures to secure the supply of forced African labor.

For example, the hut tax was established in Sierra Leone, where African peoples had to sell their labor to the colonizers to pay this tax. The collection of this tax was violently enforced, and as a result, the colonizers effectively destroyed the economic strength and sense of community among African peoples. When colonialists, who were frequently violent, dehumanized people, it became increasingly difficult to resist such legal measures.

The hut tax was not the only tactic used to maintain control and dominance over African lands and peoples. In fact, Africans were forced to pay taxes in the currencies of the colonial countries, which compelled them to work in colonial plantations or industries to earn wages in colonial currency to subsequently pay these taxes. Thus, Africans were no longer using livestock, palm oil, and yams to pay taxes to their African rulers; instead, they were forced to adhere to European currencies and economic standards. For the colonizers, such taxes ensured a steady source of labor on the colonial plantations and guaranteed that African laborers bore the cost of the colonial administration. The colonized peoples were effectively paying for the operational costs of the very system that dominated, oppressed, and dehumanized them. Coupled with the comprehensive and strict system of tax collection, African peoples were unable to evade these taxes.

Relatedly, by making the raw materials produced by African laborers cheap and raising the price of manufactured goods, the colonizers intentionally made it difficult for African laborers to earn enough in colonial currency. Clearly, this system resulted in the colonizers and their home countries growing richer while African laborers became poorer. Indeed, African laborers were often paid exceedingly low wages for their arduous work. Because these wages were insufficient to support the laborers and their families (wives, children, and elders), this forced the laborers' families to make their labor available to the colonialists.

### *Brutalities in the Congo Free /tate*

The Congo Free State (modern-day Democratic Republic of the Congo) was an absolute monarchy privately owned by the Kingdom of Belgium, under the rule of King Leopold II. During the Berlin Conference of 1884, King Leopold II convinced the other European colonial powers that he was involved in humanitarian work in the Congo Free State region; as such, he was able to lay claim to and seize much of the Congo Basin. By the end of the conference, King Leopold II had declared his new possession the "Congo Free State" and privately ruled over the land and its peoples—despite never actually visiting the region. Nevertheless, it was under King Leopold II's rule that this region and its people experienced extreme violence, abuses of human rights, and bodily mutilations. In addition to plundering the Congo Free State of its natural resources, King Leopold II and the Belgian colonial administration regularly repressed, tortured, and arbitrarily killed the state's African inhabitants. The dehumanization of the people of the Congo Free State began when King Leopold commissioned Henry Morton Stanley (and his men) to persuade the Congolese kings to relinquish their lands in exchange for alcohol and pieces of cloth.

This was a very unequal exchange, demonstrating that Stanley, on behalf of King Leopold, was successful in fraudulently dispossessing the Congo kings and their peoples of their lands. Considering the Congo Free State was rich in ivory and rubber (the latter being in high demand for the manufacturing of cars), King Leopold II built immense wealth from these natural and human resources. Congolese laborers were under pressure to meet the rubber trade quotas and ensure a steady supply of this resource. To achieve this, King Leopold II's soldiers and colonial administrators enacted a reign of terror against the native populations.

This involved the use of a potentially fatal whip (made from dried hippopotamus hide) on the Congolese people, the destruction and slaughter of entire villages and their inhabitants, and the amputation of the hands of those who resisted the colonial regime or who were unable to meet the rubber quota.

Indeed, the severed hands were presented as trophies to the representatives of King Leopold II, and soon, severed hands became synonymous with the Congo Free State. The mutilations, torture, and massacres of African bodies were met with protests; however, this resistance did little to inhibit King Leopold II's brutalities.

His reign of terror garnered an international backlash, and following a commission of inquiry, he was forced to relinquish his control and power over the Congo Free State. Nevertheless, King Leopold II's violence resulted in the deaths of an estimated 10 million Africans (Tunamsifu, 2022).

Before handing over his colony, King Leopold II destroyed all records and documents detailing his reign of terror and financial activities.

Even without King Leopold II as the ruler of this region, the Congo Free State (now the Belgian Congo) remained under the control of a colonial power from 1908 to 1960. Despite the Belgian Parliament passing the Colonial Charter law to prevent labor exploitation, forced labor continued in the Belgian Congo, and Congolese people were banned from engaging in political activity.

Consequently, a small European elite controlled all political and economic power in the Belgian Congo, while Congolese laborers were still exploited and economically deprived. The Congolese laborers were pushed into poverty and famine while also being racially segregated from the so-called superior European elites.

This apartheid regime also meant that Black Congolese people were excluded from higher education, as well as from white or European-only residential areas and social spaces.

The political subjugation of the Congolese people (and other Africans) by European colonial administrators was accompanied by restrictions imposed on Congolese education. As part of their civilizing mission, the Belgian colonists sought to morally educate the Congolese population and lead them to Christianity.

Of course, this version of Christianity served the economic interests of the colonial administrations, and as such, the colonial missionaries were tasked with teaching students to read (but not to reason or think critically), to see the colonists as heroes, and to ignore the many natural resources of the Belgian Congo.

The colonialists understood that their operations and exploitation would be threatened should Africans become empowered through education.

## The Harrowing Impact of Colonialism

European colonial rule in Africa not only destroyed existing systems of governance, trade routes and networks, cultures, traditions, and languages, but it also underdeveloped the continent in terms of economics, education, technology, and industry. Colonial education, for example, aimed to support colonial administrators in their exploitation of natural resources, while traditional African education focused more on meeting the technological needs of African communities and states. Indeed, prior to colonial rule, many Africans were skilled carvers, miners, weavers, blacksmiths, and sculptors, and they were able to meet the technological needs of their people. Colonial education, however, forced Africans to abandon their skills and expertise to work for colonial industrialists. The long hours and harsh working conditions did not benefit African laborers or their families and communities, as the exploitation and production of Africa's natural resources were used to bolster the economies of European countries. African laborers were not allowed to manufacture their own raw materials into goods; instead, the fruits of their labor were exported to European countries.

Yet, even when African laborers sought to purchase manufactured goods, their meager wages were insufficient to afford the high prices of such goods. Traditional or precolonial African markets and trade routes operated according to the needs of local communities, but European colonial rule rendered such operations irrelevant.

This not only led to the end of most traditional African marketing hubs but also distorted the continent's pattern of urbanization and socioeconomic development. Under colonial rule, African markets were characterized by an export-import orientation, in which Africans rarely saw or benefited from the profits of their labor.

Even the transport routes during the colonial era were designed to help the colonialists remove raw materials from the African continent in a faster and more convenient manner. Again, African peoples did not benefit from these transport routes. There are countless ways in which European colonial rule erased the rich histories, traditions, religious beliefs, arts, and cultures of African societies. Significantly, colonialism also imposed a strict class-based hierarchy among Africans.

The class divides, and classifications that emerged included the colonial, or European, comprador bourgeoisie (as they represented colonial power and interests), the petty bourgeoisie, the proletariat, and the peasants. Interestingly, the African petty bourgeoisie served as middlepeople or facilitators in the colonialists' exploitation of African labor.

Here, the African petty bourgeoisie and the European comprador bourgeoisie had similar interests, so it was no surprise that the former group rose to leadership positions during the period of political independence.

# Chapter 3:
# Rebuilding the Continent—Reforming Politics, Policies, and Culture

> *These divisions, which the colonial powers have always exploited the better to dominate us, have played an important role—and are still playing that role—in the suicide of Africa.*
>
> –Patrice Lumumba

While resistance to European colonial rule emerged with the advent of colonialism in Africa, the immediate aftermath of World War II marked a foundational moment for large-scale, Pan-African social and independence movements.

These movements included newly formed political parties, media platforms, and unions that were predominantly composed of educated and skilled African political elites, and they were part of the global socialist and labor movements.

The leaders and important figures of the African independence and socialist movements had similar objectives; however, their means of achieving those goals differed.

For example, Tanzania's Julius Nyerere and Ghana's Kwame Nkrumah were Western European-style socialists who promoted peaceful approaches to resistance and mass mobilization.

In contrast, Algeria's Frantz Fanon and Cameroon's Ruben Um Nyobé adopted a more radical approach and supported violent rebellion in the struggle for independence.

Whether anti-colonial leaders and activists followed a peaceful approach or opted for more violent forms of resistance, the struggle for liberation emerged from the urban regions of African nations and soon spread to smaller rural towns, where it ultimately united Africans in the fight against colonial rule and for decolonization.

## The Struggle for Independence

Anti-colonial sentiments and organizations existed in the early 19th century and were largely composed of a few highly educated African elites. Although they did not constitute mass movements, these organizations planted the seeds for later large-scale anti-colonial movements.

Importantly, the anti-colonial movements of the 20th century successfully bridged the gap between African urban elites and nonliterate Africans living in rural areas.

By actively including the latter group in the anti-colonial resistance and liberation movements, Africans were able to stand united against the tyranny of European colonial rule.

## *Resisting Colonial Rule: Influencing Factors*

### *Nationalism*

Nationalist sentiments that arose in opposition to European colonial rule in Africa served as the foundation for the independence struggle. Indeed, many Africans grew resentful of the colonial administrations in their countries, and, bolstered by an array of young and charismatic leaders such as Jomo Kenyatta and Patrice Lumumba, many channeled this resentment into anti-colonial, liberation, and nationalist movements.

Most of these movements were initially reformist in nature, seeking to change certain socioeconomic and political aspects of African society rather than replacing existing structures. However, toward the latter half of the 20th century, these movements became increasingly revolutionary. This shift entailed the complete dismantling of the colonial state in African nations.

This sense of African nationalism not only called for the unification of the continent but also aimed to transform the concepts of African identity and culture. European colonial rule employed a divide-and-conquer strategy to carve up the African continent and to separate or splinter different ethnic groups and communities. The colonial administrators emphasized racial or ethnic identities based on the territories divided by the colonial powers and instilled a political, social, economic, and cultural hierarchy that deemed Africans as savage and uncivilized. The colonial regimes in Africa were dehumanizing, discriminatory, oppressive, and violent; as such, the African nationalist movements sought to rehumanize themselves and their fellow Africans.

## Economic Policies

The economic policies of the colonial states imposed unfair taxes, forced labor, and various other strategies that benefited only the economies of European countries. Additionally, these policies led to the displacement of Africans and caused economic hardships for them. In the former instance, the Europeans who settled in the African colonies displaced the indigenous populations from their arable lands and homes. This, in turn, led to further racial segregation, malnutrition, and poverty among African peoples, as well as the decimation of African cultures, traditions, and rituals.

This was especially problematic in cases where important rituals were tied to ancestral lands. The trade between European colonial powers and their African colonies was also impacted by the First and Second World Wars. As the wars in the Western world intensified, welfare and development policies in the African colonies were neglected, while the export of raw materials (such as palm oil, coffee, and cotton) from African colonies to European countries significantly decreased. Consequently, the demand for African raw materials declined, leading to a drastic fall in the prices of these commodities. With African traders and farmers experiencing significantly reduced incomes, coupled with various boycotts and strikes, and the formation of trade unions, the situation became ripe for anti-colonial and nationalist movements to garner mass support.

### Greater Communication Netmorks

While the transport and communication networks throughout Africa benefited the colonial powers, the increase in African towns and cities in the early 20th century helped establish a sense of community among Africans. This also enabled the greater spread of information, including anti-colonial sentiment and resistance, among different African populations—turning several African cities into hubs of activism and resistance art.

The transformation of African cities and towns was accompanied by inadequate housing and sanitation, high unemployment rates, and other hardships, which encouraged Africans to place further pressure on the colonial authorities and administrations.

### 7he Role of Religion in Resistance

Christianity was used as an oppressive tool by colonial administrators and missionaries; however, the narratives of oppression in the Bible resonated with many colonized Africans. For instance, some churches, such as the "Ethiopian Churches," encouraged independence from European missionaries and missions, incorporating African songs, practices, and rituals into their services. These churches played an integral role in anti-colonial protests and movements through their assertion of African pride and nationalism.

*International Factors*

The aftermath of WWII saw the return of African soldiers who had served in the colonial armies. Coupled with the economic hardships of the war and the post-war years, this created an increased incentive to support the objectives of African liberation and nationalist movements. Moreover, the United States and the Soviet Union emerged as global superpowers in the post-WWII years, coinciding with the declining influence and power of European empires. Indeed, Britain and France lost much of their global power and influence, further enabling the rise and spread of African nationalist movements.

The independence movements in Asia, particularly in India and Pakistan, as well as the civil rights movement in the United States, also inspired African independence movements. Thus, by the 1950s, most African colonies had some form of an anti-colonial movement or political party. By the 1960s, the fight for independence was in full swing across the African continent. In 1957, for example, Ghana declared independence from Britain; the Republic of Congo gained independence from Belgium in 1960; and Algeria declared independence from France in 1962. By 1966, most African nations had been liberated from European colonial rule.

# The Violence of Independence: The Case of the Mau Mau Uprising

*British Colonial Rule of Kenya*

The Mau Mau uprising (1952 to 1960) was a conflict in British Kenya between the Kenya Land and Freedom Army (KLFA), also known as the Mau Mau, and the British colonial authorities. The uprising, which was an armed rebellion, was a cumulative response to British colonial rule in Kenya, characterized by significant violence and land eviction. While there had been much resistance to colonial rule since the onset of British occupation, many of these efforts were unsuccessful in combating the power and resources of the British. Coupled with forced labor and low wages, the brutalities inflicted by British troops, along with the seizure of Kenyan land by the colonial government and settlers, led to mounting grievances against colonial rule. Kenyan workers were often flogged by their white employers for petty offenses, and the colonial legal system did little to protect workers from labor violations and floggings.

In the meantime, the Mau Mau were working toward political representation and liberation in Kenya. Former soldiers who had served in the British Army in Ceylon, Burma, and Somalia during World War II were largely responsible for organizing this militant wing. When these soldiers returned to Kenya, they were not paid for their service in the army, nor did they receive any recognition, in contrast to their British counterparts.

In fact, the British soldiers were awarded medals and, more significantly, land that had been seized from native Kenyans. The Mau Mau initially struggled to implement reforms, and they soon turned to the younger, more militant Kenyans, who were also members of trade union movements, as well as Kenyan women, to fight against the colonial regime. The Mau Mau's various guerrilla attacks against the colonial regime were well organized, brutal, and made use of propaganda strategies.

Here, they leveraged the expertise and platforms of African intellectuals and newspaper editors to garner more supporters for their cause. We also cannot overlook the integral role that Kenyan women played in the Mau Mau organization and in the larger anti-colonial movements. The women of the Mau Mau were initially able to evade suspicion from the colonial authorities, travel through colonial spaces and Mau Mau strongholds without being caught, and deliver supplies such as ammunition, information, medical care, and food to their fellow guerrilla fighters.

## A Ruthless Reaction

In response to the Mau Mau's attacks, the British colonial authorities portrayed the guerrilla fighters as savages, irrational forces of evil, and beasts engaged in perverted and cult-like tribalism. The British also retaliated by declaring a state of emergency in Kenya, detaining alleged Mau Mau leaders, imposing internment on thousands of suspected Mau Mau members and sympathizers, and enacting torture upon those detained or interned. The British colonial authorities aimed to punish the Mau Mau and undermine their support by confiscating land, property, and livestock, imposing collective fines, and sending Mau Mau suspects to forced labor camps.

Subsequently, they implemented the villagization program to diminish support for the Mau Mau in certain regions and to eliminate their supply lines. This entailed a large-scale forced resettlement program in various districts and resulted in the establishment of over 800 "protected" villages. The "protected" villages functioned in a manner akin to concentration camps, surrounded by barbed-wire fences and deep spiked trenches.

It is unsurprising that many of those in these villages suffered from starvation, malnutrition, and diseases, while the British colonial authorities blamed the parents for not providing enough food for their children. However, it was also the adults in these villages who suffered from malnutrition, all while being forced into labor. The villagization program ran until 1962, and it is estimated that around 1.5 million Kenyans were forcibly resettled and detained in these villages (Anderson & Weis, 2018). Consequently, this program dealt a severe blow to the Mau Mau and their supporters, and by the end of the Mau Mau rebellion, around 95 Europeans and at least 11,000 Mau Mau fighters and other Kenyans had been killed (Mwangi, 2010). Many Mau Mau sympathizers and fighters were also detained.

Despite suffering a defeat when the Mau Mau senior military and spiritual leader, Dedan Kimathi Waciuri, was captured and executed in 1956 and 1957, the Mau Mau were an essential and radical part of the fight for freedom from colonial rule, dehumanization, and oppression. On December 12, 1963, Kenya finally gained independence, was renamed the Republic of Kenya, and had anti-colonial activist Jomo Kenyatta serving as its Prime Minister and later as President. However, the road to decolonization in Kenya and many other newly independent African countries was paved with several challenges.

## Decolonization: Successes and Challenges

The colonization of Africa was brutal and exploitative, severely hindering the progress and development of the continent. The once-prosperous kingdoms and empires were destroyed; significant African art and artifacts were looted; libraries containing sophisticated knowledge systems were burned to the ground; African bodies were mutilated, tortured, affected by diseases, and slain; and entire ethnic groups and communities were separated.

Moreover, colonial rule disarticulated African trade networks, economies, education, transportation, and social institutions. Coupled with the dehumanization and oppression of African peoples, European colonialism prevented the industrialization of the continent and plundered its lands and peoples in the interest of strengthening European economies. Colonization was physical, psychological, and cultural in determining who held power and who was oppressed, exploited, and dehumanized.

As such, decolonization refers to the process of former colonies seeking and achieving independence from colonial rule, fostering self-governance and self-determination, and challenging colonial notions of white or Western superiority. In essence, decolonization is an ongoing process of undoing colonization in the spheres of politics and governance, economics, society, and culture.

## *Impeding Decolonization: The Apartheid Regime in South Africa*

The Netherlands (from 1652 to 1795 and 1803 to 1806) and Great Britain (from 1795 to 1803 and from 1806 to 1961) were the two European powers that occupied South Africa. European colonialism in South Africa brought with it slavery and a system of forced labor.

While the colonizers encountered some resistance, many indigenous peoples were ultimately dispossessed of their land and absorbed into colonial society as slaves or low-status servants. As was the case with other European colonies in Africa, colonial authorities in South Africa exploited natural resources, implemented labor and class structures that subjugated native South Africans, established several European settlements, and eroded the authority of many local chiefs and leaders.

By 1910, colonial South Africa had become a mining and industrial hub of the subcontinent—at the expense of African natural and human resources. The Native Lands Act of 1913, for example, allocated around one-eighth of the land to native South Africans, while the rest of the land was given to European/white colonial administrators and settlers. South Africa became a union with a white government in 1910, while it remained a colony of Britain until 1961. The decolonization process in South Africa, however, is vastly different from that of other African countries.

Indeed, the National Party came to power in South Africa in 1948, marking the beginning of white-minority Afrikaner rule and racial segregation.

Known as Apartheid, the racial segregation laws and policies imposed by the all-white government dictated that all non-white South Africans (including Black, Indian, and Colored individuals) were required to live in separate areas from white people, use separate public facilities, and have limited contact with white individuals.

Interracial relations were banned, access to certain areas was based on Apartheid's rigid racial classifications, and millions of Black South Africans were forcibly removed from their homes and lands. Furthermore, Black South Africans were barred from participating in politics and voting, and their education systems, employment opportunities, movement, and freedoms were severely restricted.

Thus, even though South Africa gained independence from British colonial rule, the country was still grappling with white authoritarianism and supremacy in its economic, political, and sociocultural spheres.

The apartheid regime was marked by brutal violence, torture, political and economic oppression, and human rights abuses enacted upon Black South Africans. It was only in 1994 when the apartheid regime came to an end and Black South Africans gained political and human rights, that the country could finally begin the decolonization process — decades after other African countries had gained independence.

Considering the hundreds of years under foreign and then apartheid rule, the decolonization process in South Africa is particularly multifaceted and challenging, and the majority of Black South Africans continue to face structural barriers and discrimination.

## Radical Reforms (and Reversals) in Ghana

The postindependence reconstruction of Ghana's economy was radical in terms of its scope and ambitions. Under the leadership of Kwame Nkrumah, the Convention People's Party (CPP) developed and implemented concrete plans for genuine economic independence, aiming to free its industrial and agricultural sectors from European domination and capital. Although Nkrumah was deposed following a coup d'état in 1966, he is still regarded as one of the leading figures in Africa's decolonization process.

Indeed, his administration was predominantly nationalist and socialist, funding nationwide energy and industrial projects, establishing a strong national education system, and promoting a Pan-Africanist culture in Ghana. Throughout Nkrumah's rule, approximately 150 new industries were established based on an economic model of self-sustaining growth. Additionally, Nkrumah's administration resisted the international specialization imposed by Western countries, which dictated which countries should grow crops and mine ores, and which should manufacture goods, develop commerce, and dominate industries, as well as later pressures from the International Monetary Fund. State control over trade also meant that surplus profits from exports went to the government, which, in turn, funded the expansion of domestic industries, production, and the formation of modernized agricultural cooperatives. Nkrumah and his administration developed and implemented the Seven-Year Development Plan for Economic Reconstruction and Development, which outlined ambitious production and revenue targets, as well as investment goals.

For example, this plan allocated 49.8% of the nation's total investment to productive sectors, including mining, industry, and agriculture — demonstrating the benefits of ambitious, comprehensive plans and economic structures based on self-reliance. Another integral part of Ghana's plan was the construction of the Volta Dam, which, following its completion in 1966, provided a significant boost to the country's industry. The Volta Dam supplied large amounts of cheap electricity to the surrounding heavy industries, making Ghana the only nation in West Africa — and one of the few African countries — to invest in heavy industry. As a result, Ghana reduced its reliance on machinery and equipment imported from Western countries.

Ghana's rapid industrialization and economic development coincided with its efforts to strengthen diplomatic and economic ties with other African nations, establishing an integrated economic zone on the continent to facilitate the free movement of labor among African countries.

This also prevented Western countries that were operating businesses in West Africa from forcing African laborers to accept very low wages. Unsurprisingly, Ghana's radical economic reforms garnered negative reactions and backlash from Western countries, particularly the United States of America. Nkrumah's commitment to African independence and self-reliance, along with his ambitious reforms and policies, made him an adversary to American interests. The coup that deposed Nkrumah in 1966 was supported by the CIA, and in the years that followed, many of Nkrumah's initiatives were reversed (Hecht, 2020). Indeed, state enterprises were privatized and became amenable to the demands and interests of the United States. The overthrow of Nkrumah, however, was not the only example of how Western nations interfered in African countries and impeded the decolonization process.

## *Rebuilding a Nation: Burkina Faso Under Thomas Sankara*

Burkina Faso, a country in West Africa, was part of French West Africa when France colonized it in 1896. By 1958, Upper Volta became a self-governing colony within French West Africa, and only two years later, Burkina Faso gained independence from its colonial rulers. The postindependence years, however, were marked by political instability, corruption, famine, and drought; the country was reeling from the trauma of colonial rule while also experiencing several attempted coups. In 1983, a successful coup d'état led to Marxist and Pan-Africanist revolutionary Thomas Sankara being appointed as the President of Burkina Faso—an event that Sankara and his colleagues labeled a democratic and popular revolution rather than a coup.

A Marxist since his military days, Sankara was fiercely anti-imperialist, supported the liberation movements of his fellow African nations, and was unafraid to criticize the foreign policies of Burkina Faso's former colonizer, France. Like Nkrumah and other anti-imperial, anti-colonial, and anti-West African leaders, Thomas Sankara became an enemy of Western powers and their African allies.

### *Cultural Diversity and Pride*

Sankara also promoted Pan-African unity across the African continent while supporting efforts to build and modernize Burkina Faso. This entailed instilling a sense of nationhood among the people of Upper Volta (a region that was rather neocolonial and extremely underdeveloped) and developing and implementing several sociocultural reforms. It is important to remember that French colonial rule sought to impose French values, norms, and traditions on the colonized Africans.

As a result, Sankara's reforms in Burkina Faso were acutely aware of the need to transform the country's culture and meet the needs of its diverse population. For example, news broadcasts on television screens were only delivered in French; however, under Sankara's rule, the news was delivered in French and other local languages, while radio broadcasts were delivered in 11 indigenous languages. In addition, large rallies and conferences often featured musical and dance performances by artists from different ethnic groups to foster interethnic exchanges and enrichment. Through such celebrations of cultural diversity and richness, many Burkinabé developed a sense of pride in their African identity.

*/ocioeconomic Reforms and Projects*

Sankara and his administration also initiated a series of revolutionary and ambitious socioeconomic reforms and programs, including improvements in infrastructure, boosting domestic agricultural production and consumption, enabling mass vaccinations, and advancing women's rights, to name a few examples. Subsistence agriculture and a lack of industries dominated Burkina Faso's economy when Sankara came to power. Similar to other formerly colonized African countries, Burkina Faso was reliant on external market relations, illustrating the need to rebuild a national economy that was self-sufficient and based on domestic interests and markets. To generate funds for socioeconomic reforms, Sankara's administration froze the salaries of civil servants and forced government officials to cede their allowances. The administration also prioritized spending on education, healthcare, and other social welfare programs, as well as investments in productive projects and infrastructure. This also entailed a stronger focus on Burkinabé people in the rural countryside.

Here, Sankara's administration provided greater public services, price incentives, and better irrigation systems to impoverished livestock herders and farmers. The increased access to healthcare and education in the countryside resulted in over two million village children being vaccinated against major diseases and all villagers being taught basic literacy. In fact, Sankara and his administration developed and implemented a national literacy campaign and equalized access to education for all citizens of Burkina Faso. Moreover, forced marriages and female genital mutilation were outlawed, and the land was redistributed to the peasant class.

### /ocial Mobilization and Community Labor

Another key aspect of Sankara's administration was the promotion of social mobilization and local self-help projects. By tapping into the nation's deeply rooted sense of community and social solidarity, the administration encouraged the formation of village assemblies, cooperatives, youth groups, farmers' organizations, and other civil associations.

The Committees for the Defence of the Revolution (CDRs), for example, mobilized people from urban areas and villages to help clean schools and hospitals, build schools and small dams, gravel roads, and construct community centers, theaters, and other public facilities or gathering places. Local communities were, of course, consulted in the CDRs' projects. The CDRs largely consisted of the rural and urban poor, and their inclusive nature enabled these groups to be represented in the political and economic spheres. The youth, who had little power and status in their local communities, were among the first and most enthusiastic participants in the projects of the CDRs. This youth mobilization initially alarmed the socially conservative authority figures, such as chiefs and elders in the villages, but the fruits of the youth's labor benefited all.

*The Advancement of Women's Rights and Freedoms*

Through the CDRs and other socioeconomic reforms and projects, Burkinabé women were actively engaged in rebuilding the nation, with some even rising to prominent leadership positions. Sankara greatly encouraged the emancipation of women, which was reflected in his administration's pro-women measures and programs, such as aiding in the formation of local women's cooperatives, providing literacy classes targeted at women, and implementing a family code that established the minimum age for marriage, allowed for mutually consensual divorces, granted widows the right to inherit, and banned bride prices. These measures were accompanied by public campaigns against polygamy, forced marriages, and female genital mutilation. Sankara also appointed women to several cabinet and governmental positions, enabling them to become ministers of culture, health, budget, and family affairs.

*The End of the Sankarist Revolution*

Sankara's radical reforms and Pan-Africanist approach to development came at a cost: his anti-corruption efforts exposed many illegal dealings among political and governmental actors, while his anti-imperialist and anti-West stance angered Western powers and their allies in Africa. There was immense pressure from France and its African ally, Côte d'Ivoire, on Sankara to ease his anti-Western orientation, and there remains much speculation that France either directly or indirectly played a part in the coup that overthrew him.

Indeed, on October 15, 1987, a coup led to the assassination of Sankara and many of his allies, resulting in the collapse of the Sankarist revolution. As a result, many progressive programs, measures, and policies of Sankara's administration were reversed, and the new regime, under the leadership of Blaise Compaoré in Burkina Faso, strengthened its relations with the governments of France, Côte d'Ivoire, and several Western nations.

The financial aid from France also allowed the new regime to violently quell any domestic political rivals and enforce a formidable authoritarian rule that lasted for 27 years. Compaoré was able to retain political power and control for almost three decades through electoral fraud, manipulation of the constitution, corruption, and, most importantly, support from France.

While Sankara's rule was not without its flaws, he successfully implemented strong and progressive reforms, mobilized many Burkinabé, including women and the youth, and fostered a sense of community and African pride.

However, the assassination of Sankara is part of the larger project of targeting anti-imperial, anti-Western African leaders (and activists) who were not welcoming to Western interests and exploitation. As Murrey (2018, p. 78–79) writes, "Sankara's assassination is the norm within the historical geopolitical context of imperialism in the South," and he had "the 'madness' to pursue a radical revolutionary agenda that placed mental emancipation, agrarian justice, and people's agency front and center."

Sankara, however, was not the only anti-imperialist African leader to be labeled as "mad" by Western powers; thus, he was only one of many who were overthrown and/or assassinated, directly or indirectly, by such powers.

# Gaddafi's Libya: The Enduring Fight Against Imperialism

*The Makings of the "Mad Dog"*

Western countries and the media have long labeled Muammar Gaddafi as the "Mad Dog of the Middle East" and as a totalitarian leader and dictator. Muammar Gaddafi was a complex political figure who resisted Western dominance, exploitation, and intervention for more than four decades while in power in Libya, despite the fact that his rule was characterized by political repression, extrajudicial killings, and corruption. Gaddafi and his legacy are also quite divisive in Libya, but he remains one of the most influential leaders of the postindependence era and in political history.

Born in a tent in the deserts of Tripolitania (in Western Libya) to a nomadic Bedouin family, Muammar al-Gaddafi was the youngest of four children. Despite being born into a poor family that survived by herding goats and camels, Gaddafi received an education, and his incredible work ethic and exposure to diverse political ideologies at school turned him into a graduate who espoused the ideals of socialism and Arab nationalism. Importantly, Gaddafi's early childhood involved witnessing firsthand the adverse effects of European colonial rule.

Indeed, Libya was an Italian colony when Gaddafi was born, and the country hosted numerous major conflicts and desert campaigns between Western powers during World War II. Following World War II, both British and French forces occupied Libya. By the 1960s, Gaddafi was receiving military training while being politically active: he led a demonstration opposing Syria's secession from the United Arab Republic and organized a revolutionary group named the Central

Committee of the Free Officers Movement. The conditions in Libya were also ripe for a revolutionary and radical leader; despite having gained independence in 1951, Libya was under the rule of a pro-Western monarch, King Idris. King Idris and his pro-Western orientation were incredibly unpopular among Libyans, and while the King was abroad, Muammar Gaddafi and his colleagues began occupying police stations, government offices, airports, and other major institutions. Known as the One September Revolution, the 1969 coup d'état forced the Crown Prince to relinquish his control of the government, and soon, Gaddafi was appointed Prime Minister of the Libyan Arab Republic.

## *Radical Reforms in Libya*

With an emphasis on unity, freedom, and socialism, Muammar Gaddafi's early years as a ruler saw him consolidating his political power, transforming the Free Officers Movement into the Revolutionary Command Council (RCC), and dodging two coup attempts. Similar to other postindependence leaders, Gaddafi developed and implemented several radical and progressive reforms in Libya's political, economic, and sociocultural spheres. For example, Gaddafi sought to move Libya away from Western influence and control; in this effort, he closed down the British and American military bases in the country. His Arab nationalist and socialist policies also led Gaddafi and his administration to support liberation movements and strengthen diplomatic relations with other African countries.

However, it was Gaddafi's "Green Revolution" that significantly transformed Libya. This initiative entailed the construction of farms and the installation of irrigation systems along the Libyan coast to boost the country's economy, compelling the oil industry to contribute more of its revenue to the Libyan government. Around 51% of the operations of foreign oil producers in Libya were nationalized, and the subsequent revenues were allocated to fund social welfare programs. The Green Revolution also included expropriating land from Italian settlers, which was either redistributed or used to enhance agricultural productivity. In the latter case, Gaddafi's administration aimed for Libya to decrease its reliance on imported food and, instead, become self-sufficient in its food production.

Thanks to the increase in oil revenues, Gaddafi's administration developed and funded numerous important social welfare programs and projects. Firstly, compulsory education was expanded, adult literacy programs were offered, university education became free, existing universities were expanded, and new universities were constructed. This led to the poorer classes of Libyan society becoming integrated into the country's education system. Secondly, the healthcare sector was transformed; more hospitals were built, and the number of doctors in the country drastically increased. As a result, malaria was eradicated, and the rates of other major health conditions, such as tuberculosis, were greatly reduced. Thirdly, urban development programs included the construction of housing to eradicate homelessness and to cater to Libya's growing population. These programs were closely linked to the introduction of major rent reductions, the doubling of the minimum wage, and the implementation of statutory price controls.

Fourthly, Gaddafi's administration paid particular attention to women's rights and equality. Gaddafi sought to reverse the social restrictions placed on women during previous regimes, and his administration subsequently established the Revolutionary Women's Formation to assist in this endeavor. Thus, in the 1970s, a wage parity law was enacted, the marriage of females under the age of 16 was criminalized, and education and employment opportunities specifically targeting women were introduced. It is no surprise that these policies and programs made Muammar Gaddafi a popular and beloved figure among many Libyans during this time.

## Tensions With the West

Like Kwame Nkrumah, Muammar Gaddafi pushed for the political integration of Africa and revived interest in creating an African Union in the mid-1990s. For Gaddafi, African unity was not just rhetoric; however, his attempts at achieving African unity and independence from Western control and influence were met with considerable anger from Western nations. Coupled with Libya's implication in terrorist attacks and its economic decline, Gaddafi faced increasing pressure to mend his and Libya's relationships with the West on several fronts. Throughout the 1990s and early 2000s, Gaddafi attempted to improve relations with European nations while still championing African unity, including a military alliance among African nations, and continuing his anti-United States rhetoric. Yet, he also reversed some of his previous economic reforms, leading to the privatization of several industries in Libya.

By 2011, revolts were spreading across several Middle Eastern countries, resulting in the removal of the leaders of Egypt and Tunisia. In response to these revolts, collectively known as the Arab Spring, Gaddafi violently quelled the protests, but this did little to prevent the rebellion from turning into a civil war. Gaddafi's brutalities alienated him from other countries and even from some members of his own administration. Coupled with allegations of committing war crimes and sanctions imposed on Libya, the North Atlantic Treaty Organization (NATO) launched an airstrike that killed one of Gaddafi's sons as well as three of his grandchildren. Eventually, on October 20, 2011, NATO bombed Gaddafi's convoy, and shortly afterward, rebel forces killed Muammar Gaddafi.

Muammar Gaddafi's legacy is a complicated one: he implemented several successful reforms and policies, but his suppression of political rivals and brutal response to protests have marked him as a dictator to some, especially those in the West. It is also worth noting that NATO allegedly sought to prevent Gaddafi from unifying Africa and establishing the African gold dinar—two projects that would have further threatened the West's interests in Africa and the Middle East.

If former French spy Jean-François Lhuillier is to be believed, a 2011 campaign led by France and Britain to overthrow Gaddafi was shortsighted. Indeed, France and Britain struck Gaddafi at a time when he was trying to improve Libya's relations with the West. Compounded by the fact that the West's pretext for intervening in Libya was based on cherry-picked information and that there were almost no plans for stabilizing Libya after overthrowing Gaddafi, the political consequences of this campaign have been devastating.

Since Gaddafi's death, Libya has faced a civil war, warring militias vying for political power, a public slave trade, and worsening socioeconomic conditions.

# Chapter 4:
# The Issue With International Intervention and Aid

> ...for we cannot be conscious of ourselves and yet remain in bondage...
>
> –Steve Biko

As African nations began gaining independence from the oppressive, exploitative, and brutal European colonial powers, several countries in the West scrambled to maintain their diplomatic and trade relations with these African nations. Of course, these relations heavily relied on violence, forced and low-wage labor, and unfair taxation systems, and now that African nations were free, there was a fear among Western countries that the neocolonial relationships they had in Africa would no longer favor Western interests.

For instance, Britain's attempt to maintain its relationship with its former colonies occurred through regional formations such as the Commonwealth, which in turn, served as a means to maintain and create new economic and political alliances. These alliances disproportionately favored the interests of Britain. The fact that many prominent figures of the anti-imperial and anti-colonial liberation movements were now presidents or prime ministers of these recently independent African countries exacerbated the fear of losing influence and control over their former colonies. Indeed, these anti-imperialist African leaders posed a major threat to Western countries and their interests, so it is unsurprising that these Western nations played a key role in overthrowing anti-imperialist leaders and installing rulers who were more amenable to Western interests.

## Neocolonialism: The Illusion of Independence

The concept of neocolonialism can be traced back to the first postindependence leaders of African nations, such as Kwame Nkrumah and Nnamdi Azikiwe. These leaders soon realized that foreign control, particularly by Western powers, continued to influence African nations well into the postindependence years. As stated by Nkrumah (cited in Amoateng, 2022, para. 4), the "essence of neocolonialism is that the state which is subject to it is, in theory, independent and has all the outward trappings of international sovereignty," but in reality, "its economic system and thus its political policy is directed from outside."

Neocolonialism can be observed in the ways that former colonial powers, such as Britain, Italy, and France, have continued to undermine Africa's political stability and socioeconomic development through well-funded coup d'états. The overthrow of Kwame Nkrumah, for instance, was financially supported and spearheaded by Britain and the Central Intelligence Agency of the United States.

In another example, France has allegedly played a role in the assassinations of at least 22 African presidents, including the assassination of Thomas Sankara. Of course, neocolonialism also involves portraying staunchly anti-imperial or anti-West political leaders as tyrants or dictators. While we cannot ignore the role of local actors in executing military coups in Africa, we can still argue that Western powers have kept many African countries in a subjugated state. Because neocolonialism emerged during the moment of independence, it is incredibly challenging for formerly colonized African countries to resist it. Indeed, some African nations can be considered neocolonial as they rely on external economic and military aid for their survival. Such aid, however, comes with certain terms and conditions that disproportionately serve the interests of the former colonial powers. Neocolonialism is also evident in the sociocultural spheres of former colonies: In the former French colony of Cameroon, for example, the French continue to maintain a strong military presence and have institutionalized cultural and linguistic links between themselves and Cameroon. This means that there is still a reinforcement of French ideology, culture, and language in Cameroon.

## *Foreign Aid: Neocolonialism in Disguise?*

Western nations can advance their neocolonial objectives through indirect means, such as the International Monetary Fund (IMF) and the World Bank. Foreign aid to and investments in Africa often come with strict financial conditions, rendering the African nations at the mercy of the economic and political will and interests of the foreign, usually Western, donors. Foreign aid exists in the form of physical items, financial grants and loans, and skills; since the end of World War II, most foreign aid to so-called developing countries has been multilateral.

That is, the donor governments provide aid to international organizations, such as the World Bank or the United Nations, which, in turn, seek to alleviate poverty and promote economic development in the receiving countries. Moreover, foreign aid falls into three key categories: humanitarian aid, which is dispensed following natural disasters or major conflicts; systematic aid, sent directly to the receiving governments; and charity-based aid, provided by charitable organizations.

So, who are these donor countries? Usually, countries in North America, Western Europe, the Middle East, and Scandinavia provide aid either directly or indirectly to the receiving nations. More recently, however, countries such as India, South Korea, China, Turkey, Brazil, and South Africa have emerged as donor countries. Regardless of where this aid comes from, it frequently carries explicit and implicit goals to advance vested interests.

Foreign aid, whether direct or indirect, enables Western countries to exert power and control over the former African colonies while facing little to no resistance or accountability. It can, therefore, be argued that true liberation has not yet been achieved, as the economic and political policies of many African nations are still influenced by foreign countries and/or multinational corporations.

Should these African nations attempt to break free from these shackles, they will face severe economic hardships. This also raises the following question: Is foreign aid truly effective in boosting economic growth in African countries?

While foreign aid can support economic development and advance the socioeconomic well-being of African citizens, even well-intentioned foreign aid programs have often failed to implement successful or effective economic policies. Additionally, there are internal factors to consider.

There are many cases where the aid does not actually filter down to benefit the citizens of the receiving African country. Instead, financial aid remains available from corrupt government officials and the ruling elite. Zambian economist Dr. Dambisa Moyo is highly critical of the effectiveness of foreign aid in Africa and highlights the fact that foreign aid creates a cycle of aid dependency, which hinders the economic development of the receiving countries. She also states that this cycle can, in turn, foster corruption.

## *The Economic Impact of Foreign Intervention*

In the immediate aftermath of independence, many African countries experienced rapid industrial expansion and export diversification; however, such economic progress did not last long. The lack of skilled labor and capital in these countries led them to rely on their former colonizers for financial and technical support and policy advice. Since the 1970s, Africa has received significant aid from Western countries. By the 1990s, approximately 31 African countries received 10% of their Gross Domestic Product (GDP) from Western aid (Fentahun, 2023).

Africa soon became aid dependent in terms of government expenditure and GDP, and despite being the largest recipient of foreign aid, African economies became increasingly stagnant. Indeed, the rates of inflation, poverty, and unemployment significantly increased in many African countries in the second half of the 20th century. Coupled with rapid population growth, oil embargoes, civil wars, and other political upheavals, domestic revenue in African countries was constantly under threat, forcing these countries to accept the oppressive concessions and conditions of the World Bank and the IMF. The conditions that accompanied foreign aid also played a major role in hindering the development of small local industries and businesses in African countries and, ultimately, destroying local manufacturing industries. Under the guise of soft power relations and the pretext of alleviating poverty and boosting development, foreign aid led to the reintegration of African economies into the global market along colonial lines, imposing liberal economic interests and values on these economies.

## *Foreign Aid and Democratization*

The links between foreign aid and democratization are problematic. Many bilateral and multilateral donors have long stated that their agenda for providing aid is to establish democracy in African nations. However, it can be argued that this agenda is largely based on the self-interests of Western donors, their colonial pasts, and the economic potential of the receiving countries. This is evidenced by the fact that democratization processes in numerous African countries, including Rwanda, South Sudan, North Sudan, and Somalia, have not only failed but have also been marked by violence and political unrest.

African countries have struggled to maintain political stability due to colonial legacies and the oppressive nature of neocolonialism. The shackles of colonial modes of governance, slave trades, and dehumanization are challenging to remove when the former colonial powers still exert control over African nations.

Furthermore, even in cases of political stability and successful socioeconomic reforms in African countries, the West has been quick to overthrow progressive governments and instead install authoritarian regimes. The dependency on foreign aid creates a vicious cycle, as African governments are more compelled to consider the interests of their donors rather than those of their own peoples. This cycle enables the West to use systematic aid as a tool to keep the African continent underdeveloped.

This occurs under the façade of promoting human rights and democratization in what are deemed "backward" and "savage" African nations. Moreover, if democracy were to truly benefit African peoples, it must consider their needs and living conditions—not just the interests of Western countries.

This is where contradictions emerge: Western liberal democracy, which promotes self-interests and individuality, is incompatible with the communalist orientation of African peoples, making this type of democracy rather alien to their beliefs, norms, and values.

## The Realities of Foreign Aid: Italy-Libya Relations and the Slave Trade

By providing significant aid to its former colony, Italy leverages its historical links and geographic proximity to Libya to promote its own national interests. For instance, Italian companies in the energy sector have economic interests in Libya since Italy lacks internal energy sources. More importantly, the Italian government has been attempting to limit the flow of refugees from Africa into Europe.

The geographical proximity between Italy and Libya may have been beneficial during colonialism, but in more modern contexts, Libya serves as a vital transit point for African migrants.

Here, migrants and refugees travel to Libya to traverse the dangerous Mediterranean Sea to (hopefully) arrive in Europe. Since 2017, Italy has been trying to stem the flow of many African migrants and refugees accessing Europe from Libya. Using foreign aid as a tool, Italy (either directly or via the European Union) has poured millions of euros into strengthening Libya's border security and naval capabilities.

However, the ramifications of Italy's interests in and close supervision over Libya are horrendous. In late 2017, a special report by CNN exposed that African migrants using Libya as a transit point to enter Europe were being sold as slaves. Local criminal organizations and European criminal organizations operating in Libya frequently control this slave trade. In the latter case, African migrants were recruited to work on Italian farms—their cheap labor was exploited, and their bodies were at the mercy of harsh working and living conditions.

The Italian government's response was to ignore this exploitation of labor, as they deemed it a deterrent to African migrants hoping for a future in Italy. In response to the special report, protests erupted across the globe to condemn this slave trade, and some African governments, such as Nigeria, launched rescue missions for their nationals. While we should hold African leaders, especially the Libyan government, accountable for this slave trade and human rights violations, we also need to acknowledge that Italy's interests and interventions in Libya have enabled this trade. The Italian government's funding of Libyan warlords (in exchange for keeping African migrants out of Europe) has not only turned African bodies into commodities but has also had very little success in stopping the flow of migrants into Europe. Instead, migrants have become increasingly vulnerable to human rights abuses, slavery, rape, starvation, and torture at the border and in detention camps.

## The Dark Side of Humanitarian Intervention

The concept of humanitarian intervention largely emerged in the aftermath of the Cold War as the United Nations sought to advance a universal understanding of human rights. The 1990s were considered the "humanitarian decade," but the optimism for a more equal future soon dissipated when humanitarian groups and organizations were faced with reality. Humanitarian intervention involves the use of armed forces by a state or group of states to protect and preserve the lives of citizens from the horrendous actions—such as war crimes, genocide, and human rights abuses—of their governments. The lines, however, become blurred when these armed forces cause the accidental (or even intentional) deaths of those they are meant to protect. Indeed, the collateral damage from humanitarian intervention demonstrates the challenges that arise when foreign armed forces exert power and control in a nation. Of course, we must also question the motivations behind the governments that send their armed forces abroad as part of humanitarian intervention: Are these governments fulfilling their responsibility to protect oppressed populations, or are they basing their interventions on their own material self-interest?

## *Hypocrisy: The Lack of Intervention in the Rmandan Genocide*

In the case of the Rwandan Genocide in 1994, foreign governments and powers failed to provide significant humanitarian intervention and aid. While the United Nations assembled a force of 5,000 peacekeepers to intervene, this effort did not achieve its mandate nor prevent the deterioration of the humanitarian situation in Rwanda.

The international community and key state actors turned a blind eye to the situation in Rwanda, and the lack of funds from foreign governments, especially Belgium, resulted in a full-blown genocide in which hundreds of thousands of Rwandans were slaughtered. So why did no foreign governments or organizations provide meaningful humanitarian intervention in Rwanda? Some countries, such as the United States, had no national interests in Rwanda and, therefore, did not intervene. However, even a country with national interests in Rwanda, France, did little to prevent the genocide. In fact, France actively contributed to the genocide. This lack of intervention from major political players—namely the United States, Belgium, and France—is rooted in a lack of political will, as these countries were aware of the nature of the slaughters and had the capacity to stop or even prevent the genocide.

Indeed, the United States has been a leading political actor in taking humanitarian action and is a dominant member of the UN, yet it failed to label the slaughters in Rwanda as a "genocide," which prevented mass public outrage and nongovernmental organizations (NGOs) from pressuring major political players. Moreover, then-President Bill Clinton, who was more focused on his poll ratings, outlined several factors that needed to be met for the United States to approve peacekeeping missions by the UN. Unfortunately for the victims of the genocide, Rwanda did not qualify for United States-funded peacekeeping operations.

In addition to the fact that the United States did not have any national interest in Rwanda and that the genocide received very little global media coverage, there is a lack of understanding of African conflicts by international and primarily Western governments. Instead of viewing the killings in Rwanda as out of the ordinary, the international community and Western governments perceive conflict as an inherent part of post-colonial Africa's nature. In doing so, the United States avoided using the term "genocide" and instead labeled the killings as "ethnic violence."

However, the latter term does not account for the nuances of the Rwandan genocide, nor does it explore the roles of Belgium and France in paving the way for the killings. Indeed, France has a long political and military history in Rwanda and actively contributed to the genocide by providing political and military support to the interim government. France was aware of the massacres, and while it did send some troops to Rwanda, the French embassy was abandoned just a few days after the genocide began. In fact, at least 70 French soldiers remained in Rwanda and primarily distributed firearms, trained the local militia, and controlled the checkpoints. Arguably, France mainly intervened to ensure that Rwanda remained francophone, and while it had some national interest in Rwanda, its intervention did little to protect human lives.

## *The Role of NGOs in Africa*

While nongovernmental organizations are intended to serve as vehicles for humanitarian aid and development in Africa, they face increasing challenges associated with this type of aid. In mid-2024, for example, a Belgian-Portuguese consultant for the United States NGO FHI 360, Martin Joseph Figueira, was arrested in the Central African Republic on allegations of supplying arms to and funding militant groups, as well as espionage. This arrest led to increased scrutiny of NGOs in the Central African Republic and other regions in Africa, as Figueira's actions not only undermined state security but also actively contributed to terrorism. Other NGOs, such as World Vision, a

Christian relief and development organization, have also faced allegations of directly or indirectly supporting militant groups under the guise of humanitarian aid.

Meanwhile, many African governments lack the capacity to effectively monitor and manage the foreign NGOs operating in their countries, leading to significant oversights that threaten political stability and the well-being of the people in these nations. The reputations of NGOs operating in African countries are also at risk due to the exposure of clandestine activities by Figueira and others like him. NGOs operating in conflict zones in Africa are often crucial for providing support when government capacity is limited; however, these organizations can easily be misused to exacerbate violence in these regions. According to Msimang (2024, para. 8), the distinction between humanitarian assistance and political interference is becoming increasingly hazy. Despite the numerous issues that can accompany NGOs operating in African countries, their influence continues to grow—especially in the age of globalization.

## The Question of Reparations

While we know that the Western world seldom has altruistic intentions when it comes to sending aid and humanitarian relief to African countries, we also need to consider what the West may owe to Africa. Reparations are measures that address and seek to remedy past wrongdoings and human rights violations by providing the victim(s) with symbolic or material benefits. Such measures should be effective, adequate, and proportional to the severity of the harm suffered.

Considering the transatlantic slave trade, European colonial rule, neocolonialism, and the adverse impacts of globalization, the West arguably owes quite a bit to Africans. Indeed, the slave trade decimated African families and communities and led to a "brain drain" on the continent; colonial rule spread diseases, damaged the environment, enacted violence and torture, exploited African bodies, seized ancestral lands, and devastated all spheres of African life, including culture, traditions, solidarity, and beliefs. The colonists also looted Africa for its natural resources, art, and artifacts. The natural resources were leveraged to build and strengthen European economies, while the art and artifacts are still displayed in museums and galleries across the Global North.

Even in the postindependence era, the United States and the former colonial powers of Europe have continued to interfere in African political systems and affairs, directly or indirectly toppling entire governments and installing their own West-friendly authoritarian leaders. The idea of reparations has been discussed, debated, and negotiated for years, and while there has been some surface-level progress—such as museums loaning artifacts to the formerly colonized countries—it is challenging to demand reparations from nations unwilling to admit their past exploitation and violence and from countries that continue to exploit the nations in the Global South. In the context of Africa, the process of reparations includes three key stages:

First, the perpetrator country must fully and publicly acknowledge its historical and current harm; second, the perpetrator country must apologize. This apology must demonstrate that the perpetrator country takes seriously the suffering of the victim country or countries. Third, the perpetrator country must provide compensation to the victim country or countries to help rebuild the latter's infrastructure, economies, societies, cultures, and histories. In doing so, the perpetrator country provides reparations to compensate for its past mistreatment of the country or countries and attempts to restore a sense of equality between itself and those it has harmed. The reparations question often leads to numerous other inquiries: Who bears the responsibility for providing reparations? What kinds of reparations are needed? Is foreign aid not enough? In response to the first question, for example, the former colonial powers that exploited and dominated African countries are responsible for the reparations. This also raises the following question: Do religious organizations and Christian missionaries also owe Africans reparations for the part they played in colonialism?

Furthermore, in terms of international organizations such as the IMF, World Bank, and MNCs, it may be difficult to hold them responsible, as they are deeply integrated into global economies and markets. Additionally, many African nations do not have the status or power to demand reparations from international organizations and MNCs. In response to the second and third questions, one could also argue that foreign aid is, in itself, a form of reparation. However, once we start to look at this more closely, it becomes clear that foreign aid often serves Western interests and seldom truly benefits African nations and peoples.

## *What Do Reparations Look Like?*

Reparations can take on many forms, but they usually require financial compensation. This compensation would then be directed to alleviate the consequences of colonialism and neocolonialism, namely underdevelopment, material deprivation, and socioeconomic issues in African countries. Compensation can also be used to boost social services, such as education and healthcare, and to reduce poverty.

This, of course, heavily depends on whether the government or state channels the compensation into social services or development efforts rather than securing the money and keeping it within the circle of the political elite. Another form of compensation is the cancellation of debt for loans from international financial institutions, such as the IMF and World Bank. Moreover, African countries cannot participate effectively in global markets if they are burdened with debt and loans.

In addition to financial compensation, reparations can also include efforts to restore African cultural identity and pride through the establishment of museums, monuments, and galleries, as well as the return of looted art and artifacts. Such efforts would help African peoples understand and internalize their own culture and history rather than primarily valuing Western culture and norms.

Museums, for instance, offer Africans a space where the past can be mourned, studied, and remembered. Additionally, the return of looted artifacts and artworks can contribute to the tourism industries of African countries, while the return of important documents regarding African history can aid in preserving and maintaining cultural and intellectual legacies. There are ongoing debates about which form of compensation should take priority, as a museum or monument may not be as beneficial as financial compensation that addresses poverty and malnourishment. Indeed, there appears to be a hierarchy in which people's basic needs must be met before cultural reparations can be truly appreciated.

Colonialism did not occur solely at the symbolic level; as such, reparations need to be practical and pragmatic. While the prevailing argument seems to advocate for the allocation of financial compensation to policies and social services that serve the collective good, we cannot completely dismiss the value of cultural reparations. Africans should not have to choose between financial compensation and the return of looted artifacts in the context of reparations.

Instead, Africans can (and should) demand both financial compensation and cultural reparations from the former colonial powers. This is especially important, as the underdevelopment and exploitation of Africa and Africans occurred on systemic, institutional, and cultural levels. Therefore, because the exploitation was multifaceted, the reparations should also be diverse and benefit Africa in political, economic, social, and cultural spheres.

## A Case for Cultural Reparations

In 1906, a group of around 170 British soldiers launched a punitive expedition against the town of Chibok in northern Nigeria. What was the reason for this expedition? Well, the small farming community of Chibok had performed one of the greatest acts of resistance against British colonization. Here, the people of Chibok had been carrying out raids along the British trade routes, and in response, the British soldiers annexed Chibok and starved its people over the course of around three months. The people of Chibok had initially fought back by shooting poisoned arrows at the soldiers, but the British ultimately won the battle.

Upon their victory, the British soldiers collected the arrows and spears that the Chibok people had used against them and sent the weapons to London. The spears and arrows are part of the almost 73,000 artifacts stolen from Africa and placed on display or stored away at the British Museum. The museum conveniently leaves out the origin story of these artifacts.

In 1897, Britain enacted another punitive expedition. This time, around 1,200 naval soldiers and 5,000 colonial troops carried out a 10-day massacre in Benin—a self-sustaining nation with street lighting (one of the first places in the world to have such lighting), a majestic palace, and large earthwork walls. The once-prosperous nation was reduced to ashes in less than two weeks, but the British justified their actions by claiming that the troops were saving the Bini people from barbarism, slavery, and human sacrifices. The allegation of human sacrifices was based on the British troops finding numerous deep holes filled with corpses. Yet, it is likely that prior to fleeing, the villagers had hastily buried the bodies of those who had died at the hands of the British troops.

The death toll in Benin remains unknown, but the British troops took care to steal at least 3,000 artifacts from the royal palace and from the surrounding homes (Gbadamosi, 2021). As the British and American press celebrated the capture and burning of Benin, the looted goods were being auctioned off to private galleries and collectors from across the Western world. The Benin Bronzes, a collection of brass, bronze, and ivory sculptures and plaques, were exhibited at the British Museum only a few months after Benin was destroyed. The looting at Benin came at a human cost, but the stolen artifacts fetch millions of dollars per piece at auction houses.

Countless Western curators defend the collections of African artifacts by claiming that they are universal and represent the art of the world. But, as we know, we cannot rely on the victor's account of history because when we dig deeper, we see the devastating human, environmental, and cultural cost of what the British did in Africa (and South Asia). Western museums contribute to the ongoing legitimization of colonial conquests and atrocities, and while several African governments are actively demanding or seeking the return of their looted artifacts, Western museums and authorities are ready to offer a myriad of excuses and/or argue that no one can determine the true origins of the artifacts in question. In line with colonial ideas of Africans being uncivilized or not as advanced as Western peoples, curators and authorities also claim that Africans do not have the capacity, skills, knowledge, or technology to preserve the artifacts.

While France and Germany returned some of the looted artifacts, much of the negotiations with Western museums reached an impasse. There have been a few bills passed by Western parliaments outlining promises to return looted artifacts, but it was mainly after the murder of George Floyd in the United States and the subsequent Black Lives Matter protests across the world in 2020 that the repatriation of African artifacts gained widespread momentum. Since then, Germany was one of the first countries to state that it would return a number of the Benin Bronzes by 2022 and invest in research on the looted items and the guidelines for their return. Interestingly, the British Museum agreed to loan a few Nigerian artifacts to Nigeria—a rather superficial form of acknowledging past atrocities. Some museums offer programs on restitution while still refusing to repatriate any of their looted items.

As more and more Western governments, galleries, and museums decide on whether they will return or loan out the looted artifacts, African curators and artists remain steadfast in their aims to bring back African artifacts—even when restitution processes do not translate into action or are commodified. We may not want Western countries to interfere or intervene in African political affairs or exert their power and control via foreign aid, but they can (and should) return the looted art and artifacts rather than continuing to profit off them and, therefore, profit from colonialism.

# Chapter 5:
# The Impact of Globalization on Africa's Progress

> It turns out that globalisation, while promising sameness through brand-name consumption, was fostering, through uneven economic growth, an intense feeling of difference.
>
> —Pankaj Mishra

Owing to advancements in communication networks, transport, and technology, the world has become increasingly interconnected. Indeed, globalization has broken down the barriers between communication, culture, and commerce to integrate economic, political, social, and cultural landscapes from across the globe. While scholars continue to debate the true origins of globalization, we cannot deny that the late 19th and early 20th centuries saw a drastic increase in the connectedness of the world's cultures and economies. This connectedness slowed down with the advent of the First and Second World Wars, but following the Cold War, there was a rapid period of liberalization and interconnectedness. The United States emerged from the Cold War as the world's political superpower, policeman, and leading advocate of a free market economy.

The process of globalization was also marked by the movement and migration of people from various countries but, most significantly, the migration of those from the Global South to the Global North. Some migrants were searching for a better life or more fruitful education and employment opportunities in the Global North, but physical migration was not truly necessary to be part of this interconnected world. People from all parts of the globe were connected by the proliferation of digital technology and the Internet: a simple button click could connect someone from Australia to their relatives in South Korea in less than a minute. In another example and as seen during the Arab Spring, the citizens of one country can be inspired by protests in another country and consequently leverage social media platforms to mobilize others for their protests. But as with many major events in recent history, globalization is not without its challenges and inequalities.

## Globalization and the Inherent Imbalances

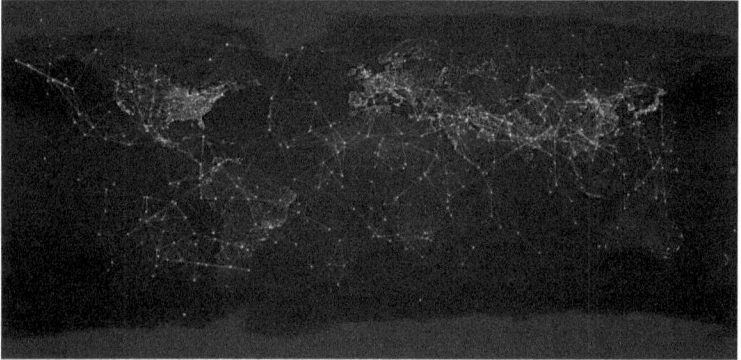

Globalization is multidimensional and, as such, impacts all aspects of life, including sociocultural, economic, and environmental landscapes. The rapid increase in international trade, the flow of foreign direct investment, information technologies, and liberalization has not only promised the governments and citizens of the world economic growth and development, but it has also led to or exacerbated existing instabilities, unequal power dynamics, and marginalization.

Indeed, how can a country like the Democratic Republic of the Congo compete with Canada on the international market when the former is still reeling from its colonial past and still experiencing massive exploitation of its natural and human resources? How can meaningful cultural exchanges occur between two countries that are ideologically and culturally so different? The growth and wealth of several countries have significantly increased thanks to globalization, but such growth and wealth are not equal across countries and continents.

In countries that are overexploited, have high poverty and unemployment rates, and that have experienced significant obstacles to their development, the fruits of globalization remain to be seen. Instead, the political, economic, and sociocultural marginalization of these countries is reflected in their tiny position on global markets.

African nations (and other formerly colonized countries) are having difficulty leveraging globalization for their own prosperity due to external debt, problematic foreign aid, and a lack of capital or financial support. The process of globalization also entails the homogenization of cultures, values, norms, ideas, and lifestyles, and considering the inequalities and systematic oppressions of the past (and their legacies), it is unsurprising that Western values, ideas, and so on dominate this homogenization. In fact, we could go so far as to say that globalization has directly and indirectly enabled the assimilation to Western ideals.

Globalization has paved the way for the formation of an international community in which the interactions among diverse groups of people resemble the interactions among village members — giving rise to terms such as "villagization" and "one world." This increasing interdependence between countries across the globe has also led to economic decisions being made as a collective whole:

Markets matter more than countries, and countries must adapt to international norms and the homogeneity of interest rates, products, and prices. To conform to such norms, these countries must adapt their sociocultural and political spheres accordingly. For example, the countries must be democratic in their political processes and systems and capitalist in their economic systems.

## *Globalization: Marginalizing Africa*

### *Political Considerations*

Given their recent colonial pasts and subsequent political instabilities and rise of authoritarian regimes, African countries are lagging in the race for economic and human development. Globalization was born from the Cold War, in which the two blocs, the Soviet Union and the United States, tried to keep African nations in their respective ideological camps. As a result, the 1960s and 1970s saw a significant rise in authoritarian rule (largely military or one-party regimes) in Africa—reducing the continent's negotiating power on the international stage.

The aftermath of the Cold War, too, did little to benefit the economic development and democratization process in African countries as the IMF, World Bank, and the World Trade Organization's policies and models of development were imposed on these countries. Globalization reinforces the marginalization of African economies and exacerbates income inequality, as the demand and prices of Africa's raw materials are dependent on external factors.

That is, African economies remain at the mercy of international market demands—turning them into enslaved economies that serve the interests and needs of external powers.

## Westernization/Americanization

In terms of sociocultural impacts, globalization and its inherent Western cultural dominance not only prevent Africans from reclaiming their cultural identities but also do not allow Africans to interact with other, and especially Western, cultures on an autonomous and equal basis. A paragon of the cultural domination of the West and, more specifically, the United States, is the widespread popularity of Hollywood entertainment in non-Western countries.

Here, globalization has enabled Hollywood products, including films and television series, to reach a more global audience. While Hollywood can provide entertainment for audiences in many countries, this American media machine tends to misrepresent racial and ethnic groups and reinforce colonial-era stereotypes about non-Western countries and peoples.

This is especially nefarious when we consider the ways in which Hollywood films about African nations or African peoples tend to focus on the suffering or abject poverty of Africans. Indeed, these films seldom include shots of skyscrapers and bustling cities in African countries but instead use only shots of dusty villages, haphazard huts, naked, dancing African women, or weird 'African' accents (even though Africa has diverse languages and dialects). In fact, African cultures and peoples are seen as unchanging, homogenous entities, and because these stereotypes and clichés dominate Hollywood films, audiences who are none the wiser are susceptible to believing these misrepresentations.

In essence, Africa remains a "dark continent" to many Westerners and given the far-reaching nature of Hollywood, African people, too, are exposed to these stereotypes about themselves. Relatedly, African cinema (and especially films made by Africans for Africans) remains on the periphery of global film industries and struggles to reach as wide an audience as Hollywood. Hollywood, however, is only one branch of American-dominated global mass media, yet its role in shaping cultural practices, norms, and values on a global scale should not be underestimated. As more and more media corporations grow their reach and influence, they advance a homogenized and standardized idea of culture. Unfortunately, this culture trumps local and non-Western cultural practices and expressions—leaving non-Western peoples very little room to express themselves and their cultures. The diffusion of Western cultural lifestyles, practices, and values by the global mass media is often referred to as "Westernization" or "Americanization" and permeates across industries and disciplines. Indeed, music styles and genres, consumer habits, fashion and style, cuisine, and jargon, to name a few examples, have all undergone the Americanization process.

### Indigenous Knomledge /ystems and Democratization

Because globalization imposes Western knowledge systems and Western technological development, precolonial Africa's advances in technology, education, art, science, and literature are deliberately erased from mainstream history and narratives. From burning down libraries or looting Africa's art and artifacts, European colonial rule disrupted the indigenous development of production, science, and technology in African countries.

Globalization has followed suit by imposing Western knowledge systems, science, and production on non-Western nations—further undermining the potential of indigenous ways of being, thinking, and bettering the world. As seen in many other cases, this Western imposition also makes African countries reliant on Western manufacturers and engineers should their technology fail or malfunction.

To compete in international markets and trade, African countries must conform to Western democratic and capitalist principles and processes. But this conformity is especially challenging to achieve when African governments have little capacity to control and determine the events in their countries. Here, the political processes and economies of many African countries largely depend on the terms and conditions of foreign aid, the privatization of industries, external donors, and multinational corporations. As such, African governments focus more on appeasing Western donors and corporations rather than prioritizing the needs of their peoples. In turn, the social welfare of African peoples becomes the responsibility of local and foreign NGOs — undermining the already-little power and legitimacy of African governments.

### *The Lack of African Representation in International Organizations*

Moreover, the political marginalization of African countries is demonstrated in their lack of veto power in international organizations. The United Nations' Security Council is responsible for maintaining peace and security across the globe, but the lack of representation of African countries on the council is reflected in the double standards and imbalances in the UN. In September 2024, the United States, a dominant member of the UN, declared that it would support the two new and permanent seats on the council for African countries. The caveat, however, is that these two seats will not have the power of a veto vote.

The nations with permanent seats and veto power, including the United States, the United Kingdom, France, China, and Russia, are reluctant to share veto power — lest they lose some of their own influence over the Security Council and its operations. This also raises the question of how Africa will choose its two future representatives on the council: Which two African countries are deserving? Which countries will be able to represent all the interests of the incredibly diverse African continent? Considering the existing imbalances in the UN Security Council, there is also the fear that the two new African representatives will be co-opted by the more politically influential countries on the council. That is, will these African newcomers be expected to serve Western peace and security efforts, even if it comes at the expense of Africa's political stability, development, and human well-being?

Of course, we must also acknowledge the motivations behind these two new permanent seats (albeit without veto power): Arguably, co-opting Africa into this Western organization can be seen as an attempt at curtailing the growing influence of China and Russia in global affairs and security matters.

## The Positive Impacts of Globalization

While the adverse impacts of globalization on African countries far outweigh the positive, we cannot be dismissive of the ways in which globalization has helped some African states and citizens. African countries have emphasized good governance, accountability, and transparency due to the proliferation of democratic systems and processes.

While Western democracy is not the ultimate political system, African leaders and government officials can adhere to several democratic values and principles to enhance their responsiveness to the needs of their peoples. The faster, more convenient, and more accessible information and communication networks have also connected people of various cultures, ethnicities, nationalities, and beliefs. This has greatly aided in fostering positive cultural exchanges and facilitating the flow of indigenous knowledge systems and ideas.

The global village can be leveraged for good as well as for the process of decolonization. If we see decolonization as part of the process of globalization, then we can argue that the widespread dissemination of Western norms, values, and practices can work in tandem with the resistance to and challenging of Western norms, values, and practices.

# Cultural Globalization: Undermining African Traditions and Communities

Cultural globalization is a phenomenon in which everyday life is influenced by the values, ideas, and commodities that are standardized across the globe. Given the disproportionate dominance and influence of Western cultures on the rest of the world, there is a trend towards homogeneity based on the values and cultures of the West and, more specifically, the United States.

These standardized commodities, ideas, and values are underpinned by Western democracy, individualism, and free market economics. The homogenization (and commodification) of culture is rife in our globalized world but has also undermined or eroded the diversity of local cultures and traditions. In many cases, non-Western or nondominant cultural products, practices, and expressions have even been commodified and reduced to material things that can be purchased anywhere and by anyone.

### *The Commodification and Appropriation of Cultural Products*

African cultural products and practices were already marginalized or outright banned during European colonial rule and as a result, valuable traditional and multi-generational knowledge and traditions have been lost or deliberately erased. In cases where these cultural practices and products are persisting, they may even be appropriated as part of the process of globalization.

Here, cultural exchanges do not always occur on equal footing and marginalized cultural products and practices can be appropriated and commodified — much to the detriment of those from these marginalized cultures. Whether African musical styles are appropriated by Western musicians or African artworks and artifacts enrich the experiences of the visitors at the British Museum, the appropriation and commodification of African cultural products and practices seldom benefit actual African peoples. Cultural appropriation refers to the imitation, adoption, or borrowing of cultural products and practices from one culture by those of another culture. Unlike cultural appreciation, appropriation occurs when this imitation or borrowing disregards the cultural significance of the product or practice and instead turns the product or practice into profitable merchandise or goods. The profits, of course, do not go to the original culture or community.

An example of this is *tā moko* (Māori tattooing that has spiritual significance) being inked on non-Māori peoples who may not understand or respect the cultural significance of the practice. Māori symbols are even appropriated and used in fashion designs with very little consideration of the cultural value of these symbols and to no benefit of the Māori people. Cultural appropriation can lead to the further exploitation, marginalization, or erasure of the African cultures from which these products and practices originate, and it can also enable the misrepresentation and stereotyping of these cultures.

When corporations seek to cater to consumer demands through the production and retailing of cultural products from marginalized groups, these corporations often simplify or dilute the original cultural significance or meaning of the products. Instead, the corporations offer a stereotypical, simple, or standardized version of the culture they are appropriating. Here lies another imbalance: Corporations have ample resources, extensive distribution networks, marketing strategies, and global target markets, whereas traditional handicrafts and arts lack such capacities and resources. It is almost impossible for local and indigenous artisans and business owners to compete with these corporations — further enabling the corporations to have a monopoly on the production and sales of cultural products (albeit simplified and standardized products).

## The Loss of Land and Languages

While cultural products may be commodified, simplified, and appropriated to garner profits, land, too, can be commercialized for tourism, conservation, and other purposes. Boosting African tourism and conservation efforts is not inherently negative, but such efforts often entail the displacement of African peoples and the seizure of their ancestral lands and homes.

The Maasai peoples of East Africa have a rich cultural heritage and a unique pastoralist lifestyle. But, following the expansion of commercial agriculture, tourism in East Africa, and conservation efforts, the Maasai peoples are facing land dispossession, the erasure of their traditional way of life, and cultural marginalization. This has forced the Maasai into buckling to economic pressure and performing wage labor to survive.

Moreover, in 2021, the Tanzanian government developed a plan to relocate 82,000 Maasai people from their ancestral lands and homes to the Ngorongoro Conservation Area (NCA). The British colonial government originally established the NCA in the 1950s as a permanent homeland for indigenous peoples, the majority of whom were Maasai. But, even today, the Tanzanian government forcibly relocated Maasai peoples to the NCA — a place with little to no public and social services and an action taken with no consultation with or the consent of the affected Maasai.

Indeed, the NCA lacks adequate schools, healthcare centers, and grazing sites, and the single, three-room houses provided for the Maasai do not take into consideration the needs of the Maasai's large, multi-household, and multi-generational families. The affected Maasai have lost their ancestral lands, their communities, their cultural sites, traditional knowledge, their livestock and means of living, and in some cases, their families.

In terms of language, globalization has facilitated the spread of global languages, namely English, as the default or standard language of trade, business, media, education, and employment. As such, many indigenous languages have been pushed to the periphery, significantly declined, or have gone extinct. Language is a cornerstone of a culture or community, as it serves as a vehicle for the transmission of cultural and historical knowledge, values, and identity.

The global dominance of English and the erosion of indigenous African languages have several consequences: This erosion means that unique cultural and linguistic expressions are lost, histories are forgotten, and intergenerational communication is stunted. This is especially problematic for African communities that have relied on oral traditions and storytelling for education and record-keeping purposes.

As the younger generations of Africans adopt English, they may feel disconnected from their cultural heritage and identity, their elders, their ancestral traditions, and their own families and communities. Yet, this adoption of English is pivotal for any young African seeking education and employment opportunities—giving them very little choice but to adapt and assimilate. Moreover, those unable to adapt often face barriers to accessing employment opportunities, education (and especially tertiary education), and sociopolitical participation.

Kenyan academic and author Ngũgĩ wa Thiong'o (quoted in Agbolo, 2022, para. 12) explains the erosion of indigenous African languages as a consequence of colonial rule and as self-enslavement: "The colonisation of a people's language is to colonise their minds and the knowledge and history carried in that language," and it is "self-enslavement if you know all the languages of this world but not your mother tongue." Africa is the most linguistically diverse continent and accounts for one-third of the globe's languages. We cannot lose such rich histories, diversity, and unique cultural expressions and assimilate to Western cultural values and languages for the sake of development and growth. Indeed, we can still be global citizens or part of the global community without this erosion of our own histories and heritages.

## The Role of Multinational Corporations in Africa

There are countless, multi-faceted economic issues that plague modern-day African countries and African governments, too, are under immense pressure by foreign powers and actors to open themselves to the inflow of capital and foreign investments. Here, multinational corporations (largely from the West) are eager to extract from and/or operate in African countries.

This becomes problematic when multinational corporations (MNCs) do little to benefit the local communities or, in many cases, exploit Africa's human and natural resources. Of course, the responsibility falls on African governments to not be jaded by the promise of foreign investment if it comes at the expense of their citizens and instead, these governments must put the needs and interests of their own citizens first and challenge the foreign corporations that wish to operate in their countries. The rise in MNCs comes as a result of globalization and owing to the immense economic power of larger MNCs, they are able to undermine the policies and political sovereignty of African nations. Indeed, the revenue of some MNCs far exceeds the revenue of entire countries, enabling these corporations to leverage their resources and exploit African natural and human resources for their own profits.

The threat of exploitative MNCs in African countries is exacerbated when the policy and development goals of the government clash with the activities of the MNCs. As such, the government may struggle to influence the decision-making capacity of the MNC or hold them accountable for any clandestine or exploitative activities. Unfortunately, African governments that are burdened by debt, high poverty and unemployment rates, and low commodity prices have little choice but to accede to the demands of the MNCs operating in their countries. Multinational corporations may serve as foreign direct investment in African countries, but many of them represent the interests of their predecessor colonial companies. Coupled with the fact that postindependence African governments retained the colonial model in their legal system, there is very little legal resistance to MNCs' continued exploitation of African natural resources.

Moreover, African citizens are excluded from the management of natural resources and, as a result, have no say in the contracts or deals between their governments and foreign MNCs. This is especially worrisome when we consider that many Africans' livelihoods depend on the activities of MNCs.

The financial and technological superiority of foreign MNCs makes it incredibly challenging for local, African companies to thrive in their own countries. In the competition for raw materials and market dominance, foreign MNCs are far more likely to be the victor — leaving local industries or companies to crumble.

Furthermore, the MNCs may remove African raw materials and export them to the country of origin of the MNCs and consequently, the MNCs deprive African workers of additional employment and income in the processing of raw materials. The exploitation and export of raw materials from African countries by MNCs can also have detrimental effects on the environment. MNCs operating in African countries often contribute to air and water pollution, deforestation and desertification, to name a few examples. Once again, African governments have a weak bargaining position and are usually unable to hold MNCs accountable for their contributions to environmental degradation.

## Can Globalization be Leveraged for the Benefit of Africa?

Because globalization is a multi-faceted and ongoing process, it can be rather challenging to not only mitigate its negative consequences, but also to leverage it for the benefit of African states and peoples. That is, globalization can be used for the betterment and empowerment of African countries and citizens without compromising on local or indigenous cultural values, products, expressions, and practices. So, let us take a look at how we can leverage globalization for our own benefit.

### *Improving the Democratization Process*

Firstly, many African nations struggle with the process of democratization. But it is also important to note that even Western countries do not always work in democratic ways and given the different historical contexts and unequal power dynamics between the Global North and the Global South, Western democratic principles and values should not be imposed onto African nations. Democracy does not have to be accompanied by individualism and free markets; instead, the basic principles of democracy can be indigenized to serve the context, interests, and needs of African peoples. An important part of this is the active political and civic participation of African peoples and strong African governments that do not buckle under the pressure of globalization players, such as the IMF.

Democracy needs to serve African peoples, and therefore its core principles and values can (and should) be shaped by such peoples. In fact, some precolonial African communities had systems of governance that were democratic in nature: The African leader (a king, queen, or chief) would rule over their peoples, but if they no longer fulfilled the needs and aspirations of their peoples or if they faltered, they would be removed from political power. In essence, the process of democratization in Africa should not come with terms and conditions outlined by foreign powers and organizations and should rather focus on the needs and interests of African peoples and their representatives. In doing so, African governments will not only be seen as legitimate in the eyes of African peoples, but their power will be on full display when these governments come face-to-face with those who seek to undermine them. This power can be further expressed through regional or continental alliances or partnerships in which African countries can look to each other for help instead of looking to the West.

## *Economic Development and MNCs*

Economic development strategies need to be clear, realistic, and locally responsive instead of being uncritically imposed upon African nations by foreign powers as a condition for foreign trade, investment, political support, or aid. Unsurprisingly, these conditions serve the interests of the donor countries, and as such, African governments should question the ownership, allocation, utilization, and general nature of the conditions and policies that accompany foreign aid. MNCs, too, need to be critically questioned on their operations in African nations. This is to ascertain exactly how the MNCs and their activities may benefit or harm African lands and peoples, and how or if their activities contribute to growth in local innovations and development. This also needs to be accompanied by stricter and more comprehensive policies and regulations that can be imposed on MNCs to enhance accountability and transparency and to promote the participation of local individuals and communities. That is, African governments must outline clear and realistic plans to ensure the participation of local communities in natural resource management and decision-making processes.

## *Civic Participation*

To enhance engagement between African sociopolitical powers and actors and local industries and communities, African governments need to serve their citizens by ensuring human rights and freedoms, a clean and healthy environment, and the eradication of poverty and other economic ills for all African peoples. This must coincide with accountable and transparent leadership and systems of governance that can be adjusted or adapted to the needs of local communities.

Oftentimes, the interests of the private sector and MNCs are prioritized over the needs of African people and here, the interests of the former usually come at the expense of the latter. When this becomes the norm, African people are less likely to engage in civic participation, which, in turn, undermines the strength of African democracies. Addressing local needs and improving civic participation entails African governments implementing measures to educate African peoples on their social, economic, cultural, and civic rights and responsibilities so that Africans can defend their rights and interests. In doing so, Africans can contribute to the socioeconomic development of their countries on their own terms and with their own interests in mind.

Secondly, we must work towards increasing the representation and voice of African governments in international organizations, such as the United Nations, to alleviate some of the pressures and conditions imposed by global actors and foreign aid. This will also enable African governments to be proactive in terms of addressing the adverse impacts of globalization so that these impacts can be planned for and mitigated. For example, addressing the consequences of cultural globalization can prevent the further loss of cultural products and practices and the erosion of indigenous languages. Here, measures can be developed to preserve declining languages and to advance the revitalization of cultural diversity. These are only a few ways in which African governments can alleviate the adverse impacts of globalization, but more comprehensive solutions and frameworks will be explored in the following chapters.

# Chapter 6:
# Contemporary Africa—A Look at Successes and Challenges

> *I am not African because I was born in Africa but because Africa was born in me.*
>
> -Kwame Nkrumah

Western (and even non-Western) news media tends to depict Africa as a monolithic continent of warfare and conflicts, violent elections, and authoritarian rule, but in reality, Africa is teeming with remarkable stories of democratic strength and success. South Africa and Botswana, for example, serve as beacons of civil and political rights and can teach us about the strengths and sustainability of democracy. While strong democracies are underpinned by free and fair elections, civic participation, and a transparent and accountable government, they are also bolstered by national unity and an economy that supports both political stability and the welfare of the nation's citizens.

Interestingly, apart from South Africa, Africa's democratic nations entered into multi-party politics with high levels of unemployment and poverty and with low GDPs per capita. These countries were also severely underdeveloped and overexploited thanks to colonial rule, and later the authoritarian rule; yet, they were able to rise from the ashes to build themselves.

Of course, the continent is still facing numerous socioeconomic issues, conflicts, and political instability, but in this chapter, we will focus on success stories across the African continent. Indeed, we must acknowledge that there is more to Africa than authoritarian rule, poverty, and conflict.

## Africa Today

European colonial rule and Apartheid (in the case of South Africa and Namibia) were white regimes that embedded race- and ethnicity-based divisions, hierarchies, and hostilities. Against this context, one would assume that these nations would have collapsed into authoritarian and oppressive regimes in the postindependence and postapartheid years, but this has proven to be the opposite for several African nations. As the United States and numerous European countries are being swept up in the rise of right-wing populism and discriminatory politics, Africa's democratic countries continue to be resilient in the face of global issues and anxieties. The fact that foreign intervention (via aid or indirect support of regime changes) in Africa has resulted in some of the most repressive and authoritarian regimes further demonstrates that Africa's strong democracies are internal creations.

## /enegal's Reforms

Additionally, we must acknowledge the significant role that African citizens who have fought for democracy and civil rights in their nations have played. In a time when many people around the world are questioning the value of democracies, African people show that they are prepared to fight for free and fair elections, human rights, and civil liberties and to fight against the return of one-party, authoritarian, or military rule

In Dakar, Senegal, for example, several small-scale, traditional fishermen of Ouakam Beach have been disenfranchised by the country's previous political leaders' lack of action against dwindling fish stocks. Here, traditional and artisanal fishing along the West African coast is constantly under threat by foreign boats or trawlers, largely from China and European countries, that export the fish away from Senegal and, as a result, leave traditional fishers with empty nets. The decrease in fish stocks also led to local fish prices soaring — adversely affecting Senegalese fishers' livelihoods and Senegalese people's nutritional intake.

The appointment of a new president, Bassirou Diomaye Faye, however, has renewed hope for many traditional fishers: In 2024, Faye proposed a review of the fishing agreements Senegal has signed with foreign countries and entities to ensure that these agreements do not enable overfishing and instead positively impact local, traditional, and small-scale fishers. As a former tax inspector, Faye has also promised to audit fisheries licenses and regulations to increase the voice of small-scale fishers in the country's fishing industry—much to the chagrin of the European Union (EU) that has been renewing its exploitative fishing deal with Senegal since the 1970s. While it is still the early days of Faye's administration, several Senegalese fishers are hopeful.

In an interview with Al Jazeera (Popoviciu, 2024, para. 43), Moussa Gueye, a Senegalese fisherman, spoke of both his faith in and cynicism of the new administration's promises regarding the fishing industry: "We've woken up as a society," and if Faye "doesn't do the job well, he won't last more than one term." Indeed, African citizens are ready to hold their leaders accountable for their promises and take action should their leaders fail them.

## *South Africa: A Beacon of Democracy and Human Rights*

In April 1994, South Africa transitioned from a white supremacist Apartheid regime to a democracy in which South Africans of all races were provided with human and civil rights and freedoms. With anti-apartheid activist, Nelson Mandela, appointed as the first democratic president, South Africa ushered in a new era and a comprehensive constitution.

The Constitution of South Africa is the supreme law of South Africa and serves as the legal foundation for the rights and duties of South African citizens and the structure of the South African government. Since its implementation in February 1997, the Constitution has been amended by 18 amendment acts, and it is still considered one of the most progressive and internationally acclaimed constitutions across the globe.

These are only a few of the provisions and rights outlined in the chapters of the Constitution:

- The Republic of South Africa is a sovereign, democratic nation that upholds the values of constitutional supremacy, human rights, the rule of law, and universal adult suffrage.

- The Bill of Rights entails the political, economic, social, civil, and cultural human rights of all South Africans. Except for the right to work, right to vote, and right to enter the country, these rights apply to people in South Africa, including immigrants and refugees.

- In response to the discriminatory and oppressive laws of Apartheid, the Bill of Rights prohibits discrimination on the basis of race, sex, gender, marital status, ethnic or social origin, pregnancy, color, age, disability, sexual orientation, conscience, belief, religion, language, culture, and birth.

- The Bill of Rights explicitly ensures the freedom of speech and expression, including the freedom of the press and the right to protest, as well as labor rights that enable South Africans to unionize and strike.

- Importantly, Chapter Nine institutions include several offices and commissions dedicated to the support and protection of human rights and democracy. Examples of these institutions are the Public Protector (an ombudsman), the Commission for the Promotion and Protection of the Rights of Cultural, the South African Human Rights Commission, the Commission for Gender Equality, the Independent Electoral Commission, Religious and Linguistic Communities, the Independent Communications Authority, and the Auditor-General.

It is owing to these rights and freedoms that South Africa was able to pursue "dignified development" (as termed by political scientist, Evan Lieberman) to transform its unjust society into one in which human rights and freedoms are enshrined in a robust constitution.

Here, "dignified development" refers not only to economic growth but also to being treated like human beings in all aspects of everyday life.

## A Case Study of Rwanda

### Colonial Rule Over Ruanda-Urundi

During the Berlin Conference of 1884, the Rwandan territory was assigned to the German Empire and, as such, formed part of German East Africa. Just three years later, Germany had established its presence in Rwanda, and while this colonial power did not significantly modify the social structure of the Rwandan colony, they did exert power and influence through their alliance with the Rwandan ruler and by delegating power to the local chiefs. However, Belgian forces invaded both Rwanda and Burundi in 1916 and again in 1922 and began to rule these two territories under the Ruanda-Urundi mandate. Here, Belgium exerted a more direct form of colonial rule: The Belgian colonizers centralized political power, implemented large-scale health, education, and agricultural projects, and promoted Tutsi supremacy.

While Tutsi and Hutu identity before colonialism was fluid and mainly based on wealth, the Germans and Belgians considered the Hutu and the Tutsi as different races, and the Belgians used the Tutsis as proxies in their rule over Rwanda. The Belgians also imposed an identity card system that labelled the Rwandan peoples as either Tutsi, Hutu, Twa, or Naturalized.

These identity cards further divided the peoples of Ruanda-Urundi, and even after Rwanda gained independence in 1962, tensions between the Tutsis and Hutus persisted. There were several significant events that preceded the Rwandan Genocide of 1994:

Firstly, Hutu activists killed Tutsi's and destroyed their houses in the 1959 Rwandan Revolution—forcing many Tutsis to flee and seek refuge in neighboring African countries. The Tutsis were forced or voted out of positions of power, and anti-Tutsi sentiment increased.

Secondly, in 1961, the Belgians suddenly switched allegiances to Hutu majority rule and enabled the separation of Rwanda from Burundi. In the immediate aftermath of independence, the exiled Tutsis began their attacks from Rwanda's neighboring countries, and in response, the Hutus increased their repression and slaughter of the Tutsi.

Thirdly, there was a notable increase in Rwanda's population in the latter part of the century, and as a result, the competition for land intensified. Fourthly, a rebel group of Tutsi refugees, the Rwandan Patriotic Front (RPF), invaded northern Rwanda from their base in Uganda.

Thus began the Rwandan Civil War in 1990, and here, the RPF challenged the Hutu-dominated Rwandan government and their leader, Juvénal Habyarimana, for their failure to democratize the country and their inability to address the issues being experienced by refugees.

## *From Civil War to Genocide*

The Rwandan Civil War not only displaced thousands of people but also weakened the political authority of the Rwandan government and forced them into signing the Arusha Accord with the RPF. But the cease-fire soon came to an end on April 6, 1994, when Habyarimana's plane was shot down near Kigali airport. While it is still unclear as to who shot down the plane (the Hutus or the RPF), the Rwandan media blamed the assassination on the Tutsi rebels.

Against the backdrop of anti-Tutsi sentiment and propaganda, the Rwandan Genocide began within a few hours of Habyarimana's assassination, and over the course of 100 days, the Hutus slaughtered an estimated 800,000 Tutsis, moderate Hutus, and Twas (Lawal, 2024). With the support of the police and civil authorities, the militia forces carried out their vicious attacks against the Tutsis and forced Rwandan civilians (via fines, bribery, propaganda, and intimidation) to also enact violence against the Tutsis.

These civilians used machetes and clubs to hack at Tutsis (and Hutus, who offered Tutsis refuge), looted the homes of their neighbors and community members, raped women, and herded the victims into schools and stadiums to massacre them. The Tutsi RPF was quick to respond to the attacks, and by mid-July, they had seized control of the country — leading to around two million Hutus fleeing Rwanda in fear of the RPF's retaliation. By capturing government-controlled territories, the RPF effectively ended the genocide. In November 1994, the International Criminal Tribunal for Rwanda was established in Arusha, Tanzania, by the United Nations to seek justice for the victims of the genocide.

Here, the leaders of the genocide were tried, and around 61 people were convicted for inciting, aiding, and failing to prevent the genocide. Just two years later, Rwanda also initiated trials to hold accountable those who planned, incited, led, or oversaw the massacres, and 22 defendants were found guilty and sentenced to death by firing squad. However, because judicial infrastructure was destroyed, and legal professionals were killed or fled the country during the genocide, most of the cases were tried in informal community courts. The Rwandan government implemented the traditional gacaca court system — a grassroots-level justice and reconciliation system in which local communities elected judges to preside over the trials. The defendants who were remorseful and who aimed to reconcile with the community were handed lighter sentences, and, in most cases, those who confessed to their less serious offenses were able to evade punishment or merely receive community service orders. Over 12,000 gacaca courts tried more than 1.2 million cases across the nation and allowed the victims and their families to learn the truth about the deaths of their loved ones.

While this process was criticized for exposing survivors to threats and intimidation from the perpetrators and for having judges who participated in the genocide themselves, some have reported that the gacaca system helped communities heal and reconcile. Nevertheless, this court system was closed in 2012.

The recovery and reconciliation process in Rwanda did not end with the community-based court system, as over the next few decades, there was a major focus on reconstructing the Rwandan identity, promoting unity, and balancing justice, security, and peace.

The Rwandan Constitution, for example, states that all Rwandans share equal rights and several laws have been passed to fight genocide ideology and discrimination. In another instance, the National Unity and Reconciliation Commission was established in 1999 to promote peace education (programs to explore Rwandan history and the source of divisions among the Rwandan population), leadership programs (based on Rwandan values), training of community and political leaders, women, and youth in conflict resolution and mitigation; summits on human rights, justice, and good governance.

Hundreds of thousands of Rwandans have participated in and benefited from these initiatives.

## Rebuilding Rmanda

As a result of the genocide, most Rwandans were forcibly displaced within the country or to a neighboring African country. Within the next few years, however, the largely Tutsi Rwandans who had fled the country from 1959 onwards started re-entering the country and claiming their land and property. This coincided with the return of those who had fled the country in the immediate aftermath of the genocide.

The second group of returnees were largely Hutu, and they, too, submitted claims of ownership of buildings, farms, and other lands and properties. While many returnees were willing to share land and resources, local land disputes prompted the government to implement a number of land policies. When Paul Kagame became the president of Rwanda in 2000, he assumed leadership of a country that had been torn apart by a genocide and that was still reeling from the immediate aftermath of such violence.

Many in the international community doubted Kagame's ability to rebuild the country, but with the help of uneducated guerrilla fighters and cadres, he proved many of his critics wrong. Over the course of two decades, Paul Kagame's administration built a stable, unified, and prosperous nation in which social services, such as healthcare, education, and housing, were provided to all Rwandans—regardless of their ethnic identity or region of origin.

Nevertheless, political leaders and human rights groups outside of Africa still labeled Kagame, an authoritarian leader who restricted political freedoms and the press in Rwanda. Key criticisms also pointed to Kagame's changing of the Constitution to allow him to remain Rwanda's president beyond the legal term. While there are many aspects of Kagame's rule that can be described as repressive, we also need to note that Kagame and the people of Rwanda established freedoms in a country that lacked freedoms for much of its recent history. Indeed, a political leader cannot take away rights and freedoms from their citizens if their citizens did not have these rights and freedoms to begin with. Kagame was keenly aware of this lack of rights and freedoms.

Following anti-Tutsi violence, Kagame's parents fled the country when he was just two years old. He was raised in refugee camps in Uganda and was exposed to the oppression and violence enacted upon his people. Kagame later studied at Makerere University and joined the National Resistance Army, a guerrilla movement in Uganda that helped install Yoweri Museveni as Uganda's president.

Here, he served as Museveni's chief of intelligence and gained quite a reputation for his enforcement of a strict code of behavior. Kagame returned to Rwanda as the leader of the RPF and led around 10,000 to 14,000 RPF soldiers against the Hutus perpetrating the genocide. As a result, RPF forces were able to mitigate the casualties of the genocide and seize Rwanda's capital, Kigali. The RPF forces then installed their own government, with Pasteur Bizimungu as the country's president. However, true political power lay in the hands of Kagame, who had since assumed the positions of vice president and minister of defense.

## Reforms Under Kagame

When Paul Kagame was appointed the president of Rwanda in 2000, he set out on an uncompromising plan to eradicate populism, corruption, and divisive speech in the government and in Rwandan society. His tough style of ruling led to the imprisonment of politicians who employed hate speech and hate-charged rhetoric, as well as an adaptation of democratic systems to suit the needs of Rwanda and its people.

Indeed, Kagame tailored democracy to address the issues faced by the Rwandan people and, in doing so, sought to unify a country in which the perpetrators of violence and their victims were expected to live among each other in peace. These attempts at national unity were bolstered by several socioeconomic programs: Kagame's Vision 2020 plan was ambitious in nature and sought to improve transport systems and infrastructure, agricultural production, good governance, the health and education sectors, and turn Rwanda into a middle-income country. In one such example of improving healthcare, Rwandan mothers received extensive antenatal and postnatal healthcare, and as a result, the maternal mortality ratios decreased by 77% from 2000 to 2013, and all newborns were vaccinated (Ruhumuliza, 2019).

Since 2000, Rwanda's economy has grown rapidly owing to Kagame's liberalizing of the economy, boosting the private sector, and turning the country's agriculture-based economy into a knowledge-based one. Because Rwanda has few natural resources (compared to other African nations), Kagame's administration has significantly improved its service sector, including wholesale and retail trade, transport, broadband and telecommunications, finance and banking, real estate, insurance, restaurants and hotels, and public administration. This, in turn, helped Rwanda develop into a tourism hotspot and an information and communications technology (ICT) hub. In terms of education, the government has offered free education in state-run schools for 12 years and has built several more universities—increasing the literacy rate in Rwanda from 58% in 1991 to 78.76% in 2022 (MicroTrends, 2024). The healthcare sector has seen similar improvements: The prevalence and mortality rate of communicable diseases, such as pneumonia, HIV/AIDS, and malaria, has seen a sharp decline; maternal and neonatal tetanus has been eliminated, and during the COVID-19 pandemic, the government's quick response to the virus saw Rwanda having one of the lowest infection and mortality rates in the world. In fact, by April 2022, Rwanda had fully vaccinated over 60% of its population against COVID-19 (AfricaNews, 2022).

Here are just a few more of Rwanda's successes under Paul Kagame (Gage, 2022):

- The poverty dropped from 77% in 2001 to 55% in 2017.

- Life expectancy went from 26 years in 1993 (owing to the Rwandan Civil War) to 69 years in 2019.

- Rwanda ranks alongside Norway, Finland, Sweden, and Iceland in terms of gender equality, and as of November 2021, the Rwandan parliament consists of 61% women, and the Rwandan workforce boasts the participation of 84% of women.

- The maternal mortality rate has seen a decrease of 23% since the 1990s, and this is largely owing to innovations in the healthcare sector and medical field.

- Launched in 2012, the Green Fund encourages rural communities to engage in reforestation and agroforestry. This initiative also led to the creation of over 10,000 jobs.

- Historically, Rwanda had some of the highest rates of inequality in terms of wealth and income, education, social identity, space, health, and nutrition, but over the past two decades, there have been significant improvements in terms of access to services and utilities.

- Rwanda has a universal healthcare system, and as of 2019, around 96% of the population is covered.

- Due to a quick response to the COVID-19 pandemic, Rwanda saw a 3.4% increase in its GDP in 2020.

While Rwanda faces major socioeconomic challenges, such as a high unemployment rate, it still scores well on the Human Development Index, and Kagame's economic policies continue to be praised by many. Of course, some international analysts and critics have condemned Kagame's unusual approach to democracy and economic growth, but assessing Rwanda's development through a Western lens undermines the nuances of rebuilding a post-genocide country. The fact that the majority of voters support the constitutional amendments allowing Kagame to run for re-election weakens even the criticisms of his extended term as president.

Besides, not many Western nations can boast a cabinet with an average age of 40 and a women-led parliament (Ruhumuliza, 2019). Rwanda's rebuilding and prosperity since the genocide in 1994 make the country one of Africa's greatest success stories. Under the leadership of Paul Kagame, an indigenous approach to justice and reconciliation, and a keen focus on dismantling discrimination, hate speech, and social inequalities, Rwanda continues to develop its sociocultural, economic, and political spheres. We can also argue that this nation's success largely stems from its endogenous approach to complex issues.

# Chapter 7:
# Leveraging Indigenous Knowledge and Ways of Being for Progress

> *In African systems of thought, the ontological position emphasizes that to understand reality is to weave a holistic view of society, that is, to accept the need for harmonious co-existence between nature, culture and society.*
>
> –Njoki Nathani Wane

African Indigenous Knowledge Systems (AIKS) have existed for centuries, but science disciplines only acknowledged these systems a few decades ago. Arguably, this recognition emerged at a time when African peoples were given political recognition and rights, when early development efforts failed the African continent, and when Africans grew more and more disillusioned with the promises of Western sciences, economic systems, and development strategies. The term "indigenous" refers to a specific group of people occupying a particular geographic area for several generations. This group possesses, practices, protects, and teaches the skills and knowledge based on their belief systems, meanings, ways of being and living, and cultural expressions—factors that distinguish the group from others.

As such, AIKS shape and are shaped by the group's environments and domains of life and usually operate on two intertwined levels: The empirical level that includes the natural (biodiversity, agriculture, and medicine), the sociocultural (social welfare, music, and arts), and the technological and architectural (buildings, textiles, and food processing). The second level is cognitive and refers to the conceptualization of all perceptions of and theories related to culture and nature. In other words, AIKS operates on the coevolution of the natural, human, and spiritual worlds, and all Indigenous knowledge, the knowledge holders, and the technologies used for the application of this knowledge are bound to a worldview. African Indigenous Knowledge Systems are often community-based, preserved through oral traditions and collective memory, and are influenced by practices, proverbs, customs, and rituals—making AIKS fluid and dynamic and perhaps a means to address and even remedy contemporary challenges in Africa.

## Indigenous Knowledge as Tool for Achieving Sustainable Development

Given the nature of AIKS, European colonial rule subjugated existing systems of knowledge in Africa and instead replaced them with Western-driven knowledge and belief systems. This not only led to the erasure and stigmatization of AIKS but also trapped African peoples in a cycle of perpetuating their own subjugation through the valorization of Christianity, Western education, and the undermining of traditional African economies and structures of governance.

The colonial authorities exacerbated this subjugation by seizing lands, imposing arbitrary political borders, and dividing kin groups and communities. As with almost all other elements of colonial rule, the undermining of AIKS continues in the postindependence era—to the extent that Western knowledge systems dominate in African education and academic spheres.

Traditional knowledge or wisdom on wellness, governance, morality, justice, and conflict resolution remains on the periphery. This is especially problematic as AIKS have historically been used to remedy various forms of conflict, to impart morals, beliefs, and knowledge to the younger generations, and to promote a sense of community well-being and unity. As part of the decolonization process, several previously colonized countries, such as South Africa, India, Argentina, and Brazil, have all implemented policies to aid in an indigenous knowledge systems (IKS) renaissance of sorts and to encourage education institutions to include IKS in their curricula.

African countries can (and should) incorporate AIKS in their policies to highlight the importance of such knowledge systems *and* to find endogenous ways to address relevant socioeconomic, political, and environmental issues. Indeed, AIKS can be integrated into existing sources of knowledge to correct historical (and current) misinterpretations and to challenge lingering colonial beliefs and ideals.

One of the many strengths of AIKS is that it has a long history of practical or tangible application: AIKS was used to preserve past and collective memory, pass down knowledge and skills to the younger generations, resolve conflicts within the community, and help treat ailments. AIKS can provide modern-day Africa with theoretical and empirical ways to use, value, and manage natural resources, maintain the balance of their ecosystems, cope with natural disasters, and form traditional structures of governance and associated institutions that prioritize the protection of citizens, nature, and resources. For example, AIKS can be used to restore and preserve the ecosystems devastated by or vulnerable to capitalist exploitation, as well as provide realistic sustainability benchmarks for African governments. Some African youth have dismissed AIKS and related practices as they associate them with scarcity, poverty, and a lack of material wealth. This view of AIKS is part of the colonial legacy as the European missionaries and colonizers denigrated African religious beliefs and spirituality, knowledge systems, and cultural traditions and practices. Instead, the missionaries and colonizers positioned themselves as the epitome of civility and the experts on food production, agriculture, and infrastructure. What resulted for colonized Africans was spiritual, cultural, and intellectual poverty (along with violence and exploitation).

More recently, however, globalization has blurred geographical, cultural, political, and intellectual borders, but given the dominance of Western values, systems, and beliefs, modern-day Africans are at risk of recolonization. This makes it all the more pivotal to reposition AIKS, challenge its colonial devaluation and denigration, and leverage it to address the political, sociocultural, spiritual, and economic realities of everyday Africans. Before we outline the ways in which AIKS can be leveraged to address socioeconomic, political, and environmental issues in contemporary Africa, we first need to acknowledge that Africans are culturally diverse, but some common elements exist among them. African indigenous knowledge systems and traditions have also been disrupted due to various forms of colonialism and neocolonialism and, as a result, may not be identical to precolonial AIKS. Nonetheless, AIKS is fluid and dynamic rather than being frozen in time, and as such, African governments, institutions, and organizations can adapt AIKS to address contemporary needs and issues. This is especially relevant when we consider that AIKS emerged from African peoples' relationships with nature and the environment and, therefore, consists of hands-on experience and holistic and non-linear ways of thinking.

## *Leveraging AIK/ for Healthcare*

African Indigenous Knowledge Systems provides a holistic framework for how we, as Africans, should live in and interact with the people, environments, and worlds around us. The merging of ideas and practices, too, is holistic across disciplines, such as law, the arts, and economics, and this type of knowledge is produced and reproduced within relationships between human beings and within humans' relationships with nature. Medicine and healing are salient aspects of AIKS, and according to the World Health Organization (Moeti, 2022), around 80% of Africans make use of traditional medicine for their basic health needs. Since the advent of African Traditional Medicine Day in 2003, around 40 African countries have developed national policies focused on traditional medicine, the training of traditional health practitioners, and collaborations between traditional and Western medicines.

As of 2022, 34 research institutes in 26 African countries are dedicated to researching and developing traditional medicine, and 25 countries have integrated traditional medicine into the curricula of their health science field. Considering that Africa is home to around 45,000 species of plants, it is no surprise that around 5,000 of these species are used for medicinal purposes (Mahomoodally, 2013). For instance, gum Arabic, or Acacia Senegal, is often used in North Africa and West Africa to treat infections, bleeding, typhoid fever, and leprosy, and serves as a natural alternative to chemical binders used in organic products and in soft drinks and candy. Aloe ferox, or Xanthorrhoeaceae, is native to South Africa and Lesotho and has anti-inflammatory, antioxidant, and antimicrobial properties. It has since been adapted into numerous commercial applications in the food, cosmetics, and pharmaceutical industries, and in doing so, has led to the formation of trade agreements and cooperatives that benefit many local and rural communities.

In another example, Centella Asiatica (also known as wormwood) has been used for medicinal purposes since prehistoric times. Owing to its healing effects on burns, wounds, and ulcers and its ability to help treat tuberculosis, asthma, epilepsy, hypertension, and inflammation, wormwood is an important plant in Chinese traditional medicine, Japanese traditional medicine, Ayurvedic medicine, and African traditional medicine. These are only a few of the many medicinal uses of plants in Africa, but they remain an important pillar for the healthcare of African peoples. This is especially relevant for poorer people who may not have access to Western and pharmaceutical drugs and treatments, but who can use the diverse fauna and flora of their ecosystems to treat their medical conditions or ailments. While there is a need for further clinical explorations into the medicinal properties of lesser-known or lesser-researched plants, the AIKS regarding plants is robust and has centuries of empirical evidence.

The current phytomedicine industries in African countries must advance their efforts towards validating traditional knowledge and ensuring quality control standards—for the health and safety of African peoples and international consumers. Many Africans used traditional medicine in the early days of the COVID-19 pandemic, but this was accompanied by poor documentation and validation of the effects of these medicines in treating the coronavirus. This is worrisome as most Africans embrace traditional medicines, and proper documentation and validation would have had incredible potential in identifying ways to control or prevent the outbreaks of infectious diseases. Progress has been made in terms of empowering traditional medicine industries and practitioners, but African governments can (and should) allocate more resources to the formal study of traditional and herbal medicines.

The COVID-19 pandemic sparked new and ongoing clinical trials of various herbal medicines in Ghana, Nigeria, South Africa, Uganda, Tanzania, the DRC, Guinea, and Burkina Faso. Yet, African governments, institutions, and the private sector should not wait for an outbreak of a virus to prioritize traditional medicine in their healthcare policies and strategies and to strengthen the capacity of their regulatory authorities. In Asian countries, for instance, traditional medicines and formulations are meticulously recorded and evaluated at national and international levels, and consequently, Asia's phytomedicine industries reap the rewards (and profits). Placing value on AIKS and traditional medicine enables African nations to dismantle dangerous colonial beliefs and allows these nations to truly and fully leverage their rich biodiversity and the associated medicinal uses. Like Asia, Africa can integrate traditional medicine into its healthcare systems, research, and curricula for the health, safety, and well-being of its citizens.

## AIKS and an Endogenous Approach to Development

The term "endogenous development" refers to development efforts or strategies that already exist and are active in local communities. In other words, advancing the development of a community should come from within or from that particular community. Various African communities have long pursued development and, in doing so, have amassed sophisticated indigenous knowledge that has shaped their cultural identities and world views. While this knowledge is subject to constant change, it can also be employed to boost African nations' sustainable development goals—without the influence or interference from Western countries and exploitation.

Importantly, the endogenous approach to development and the use of AIKS do not entail the isolation of African nations and communities from the rest of the world, but rather, these nations and communities can draw strategies from local knowledge, resources, cultures, institutions, and initiatives. An endogenous approach will prioritize AIKS and values, especially when it comes to addressing pertinent socioeconomic issues and environmental degradation and ensuring the well-being of all Africans. Arguably, many postindependent development strategies in Africa have failed to meet the needs of African citizens because they are not endogenous.

That is, these strategies are not locally rooted, nor do they significantly integrate local contexts, values, needs and priorities, and worldviews. When development strategies come from external sources or foreign countries (and are prioritized owing to foreign aid and its accompanying terms and conditions), they usually fail to meet the needs of the most marginalized in Africa.

Moreover, we cannot simply impose foreign development goals, strategies, and efforts into African contexts and peoples. Consequently, when development is driven by external or foreign donor funding, endogenous methods and AIKS fall to the wayside or are completely forgotten, and instead, the foreign donors are rewarded for their 'investments' and 'innovations' in Africa. When we consider an endogenous approach to development in Africa, we should focus on the underpinning values associated with traditional political, economic, and sociocultural systems, institutions, and practices.

For example, agroforestry (or the integration of trees into animal and crop farming systems for the benefit of society and the environment) is rife across Africa, and African farmers have for years amassed a wealth of knowledge on the potentials and limitations of combining crops and trees. This knowledge is inspired by ancient traditions among African farmers and garnered by practical experiences with local ecosystems.

The specialized knowledge of the classification and management of trees enables African farmers to know which tree species are always available for use, which are seasonal, and which trees are preserved for spiritual uses.

In Uganda's Balamogi County, for example, researchers found that the local people were able to identify 315 different plant species and had extensive knowledge of the plants' ecological relevance.

## *African Unity*

The endogenous approach also highlights the need for intra-African partnerships, especially when it comes to human resources development. That is, instead of importing technology and skills from abroad, African nations can look within to create employment opportunities for local people and leverage their skilled labor force for economic growth. Nigeria and South Africa have recognized the potential of the endogenous approach to human resources and labor, as both countries have become hubs for the training of postgraduate students in the areas of applied sciences and medicine. Intra-African partnerships can also benefit African nations when it comes to trade.

Why should an African country continue to import food products from a European country when they can instead import the same products from fellow African countries? The reliance on imports traps African countries in the cycle of underdevelopment—hindering local exchanges and putting African countries at a further disadvantage in global markets. African nations' overreliance on foreign goods is closely linked to their reliance on foreign aid. African governments become more accountable to their donors rather than to their own citizens, and this can severely impede these governments from drawing from their local sources or even identifying the potential of their own citizens. Besides, a government that focuses more on pleasing its donors may not even realize that its citizens may hold the key to sustainable development and progress. The overlooking of local resources, however, is not the only challenge when it comes to the endogenous approach to development.

In addition to buckling to external, largely Western, pressures and aid, some African governments struggle with strong, accountable, and transparent political leaders. The early years of independence boasted numerous strong and passionate African leaders, but with foreign interference in African politics, rampant corruption, and other political issues, Africa lacked united and committed leadership.

Unfortunately, foreign aid often provides immediate relief, but it also has long-term adverse effects. Should African governments shift from foreign aid to leverage local and available resources, this would require the governments to focus more on local production and national product rather than on foreign investments and GDPs. African peoples, too, will have to work harder and go beyond the documentation of validation of AIKS and local practices.

This shift can be quite challenging in a continent that is significantly influenced and consumed by foreign products, media, values, and worldviews. In what Frantz Fanon describes as the "Black Skins, White Masks syndrome," the average African and the elite groups veer away from their African cultural identities to assimilate or adapt to Western contexts. This is especially evident when African students and workers must compete against those from the Global North.

Moreover, these foreign tastes or preferences for Western goods and services can prevent African peoples from critically engaging with local resources and AIKS.

## *Community Capacity Building*

Communal solidarity is a vital aspect of African indigenous ways of organizing, as traditional African societies and communities would work together to preserve their cultural memory and traditions, protect their resources, and lend physical or moral assistance wherever needed. In Kenya, for example, both men and women would work together in clearing lands, assisting in childbirth, comforting each other in times of stress or grief, and caring for each other in times of sickness.

That is, there was (and still is) a sense of collective responsibility in African societies or communities. Considering the barriers to employing an endogenous approach to development, it is all the more important for all African peoples and communities to contribute to capacity building and preserve a sense of collective responsibility. Healthy people and families make up healthy communities, which in turn, create healthy environments with good economies, sustainable development, and general prosperity.

It takes the capacity to create and maintain the healthy functioning of these communities and countries, and leaders, too, need to emphasize the importance of capacity building in their nations. This can be described as a union of African political leadership and local communities: The latter has capacities stored in their everyday lives and their everyday interactions with other humans and with nature, and African leaders can leverage this endowed knowledge and provide the local communities with further skills, clear plans for development, and access to what is needed to build African communities from within.

When African governments turn their priorities away from pleasing foreign donors, they will have the time, energy, resources, and sense of commitment to recognize the knowledge and skills of their local communities, identify the basic needs and services of these communities, and implement strategies for long-term development. Community capacity building, like AIKS, is fluid, dynamic, and natural, so it should be adaptable to the changing needs of African people.

*Individual and Community Participation*

While AIKS values the community over the individual, communities are made up of individuals and, as such, need the active participation of these individuals to ensure sustainable growth and well-being. Individual engagement requires a bottom-up approach where members of a community are proud to be endowed with traditional knowledge but are still respectful towards different interests, beliefs, and cultures within that community.

For instance, these individuals or members of the community should be aware of different styles of communication (and the misunderstandings or miscommunications that may arise) and the specific needs of fellow community members who may have disabilities or need extra services. It is only when this respect, support, and pride is present that communities can mobilize, actively participate in development efforts, and foster a sense of self-reliance. There are various branches of community participation:

Firstly, we have individuals and their families (this includes extended families); second is the community in which all its members are stakeholders; third is the social amenities in the community, including schools, healthcare facilities, and places of worship; fourth is small to medium local businesses; and lastly are the laws, policies, and administration systems that (should) ensure the well-being of the community and beyond. These branches must synergize to become a key resource for individual and indigenous knowledge as well as international knowledge.

Whether the community is small and rural or it is large and urban, it must center AIKS in its development efforts by:

- Acknowledging AIKS as cultural methodologies and values (rather than as 'primitive' or 'backward' ways of thinking and doing).

- Recognizing the ongoing significance and relevance of AIKS in terms of addressing community and cross-cultural issues.

- Ensuring that AIKS can be effectively transferred (ethnographically and symbolically) and preserved (through oral traditions and storytelling, videos, texts, and tapes).

- Disseminating AIKS to the wider or other communities, so the exchange of knowledge can be national or even continental.

- Adapting technology to meet the community's specific needs.

When most African peoples still rely on traditional medicine, agriculture, and other local practices, it is futile for official development efforts to try to formalize these informal systems. For instance, modern techniques and products (like farming machinery) and foreign aid are seen as the best (or only) means to enable small-scale farmers to participate and compete in global markets.

This, however, has an adverse effect: The small-scale farmers become indebted to the donors for their so-called innovations, and the foreign products and machinery may contribute to environmental degradation. As a result, the increased marginalization of small-scale farmers further impedes their ability to compete in national and global markets—leading to some of these farmers losing their lands or migrating for better economic opportunities. The ability to compete in global markets should not be the be-all and end-all of development, as the global market economy seldom benefits rural residents and workers.

*Examples of AIK/ in Action*

Endogenous development can support the populations that do not benefit from the global market economy by enabling them to explore opportunities that are local and within their span of control. Here, the benefits are more likely to directly and positively impact African peoples, be disseminated within their communities, improve their livelihoods and overall well-being, enhance the community's capacity for sustainable development, and enable the community to solve their own problems. For example, the Centre for Indian Knowledge Systems (CIKS) discovered through their endogenous development efforts in India that traditional seed varieties tend to be more drought-resistant than the hybrid yet high-yielding seed varieties promoted by the country's Department of Agriculture. This finding is especially significant as modernized and mechanical agriculture often fail during periods of drought. By using traditional seed varieties and indigenous technologies, the Indian farmers (and their broader communities) were able to maintain food security and secure their incomes during droughts.

Prior to the introduction of artificial pesticides, farmers in Ghana used products from local plants to control and prevent harmful insects on farm produce. These methods were effective in repelling insects, preventing the spread of harmful viruses, increasing crop yields, and protecting the plants. Similarly, Rwandan women continue to use African indigenous knowledge to cultivate beans and, as a result, have greatly contributed to the process of adapting modern cultivation techniques. A couple of studies (Olaopa & Ayodele, 2021) have confirmed that the bean varieties selected and planted by Rwandan women using AIKS produced a far higher yield than the bean varieties chosen using non-AIKS methods.

A recent study (Kom et al., 2024) in the Vhembe district, Limpopo, South Africa, explored the way in which rural communities used indigenous knowledge methods to improve their food security. From a survey with 200 randomly selected indigenous farmers, it was revealed that AIKS was used to manage the impact of climate change on crop production, preserve food via sundrying processes (in cases of food shortages), improve soil quality and fertility (through mixed cropping, intercropping, crop rotations, and the use of livestock manure), and predict rainfall and other negative weather conditions. More specifically, indigenous farmers and their communities focused on the form of the crescent moon, the behavior of certain animals, and the changes in wind direction to predict the imminent weather conditions. The use of AIKS, therefore, enabled these farmers to prepare for the negative weather conditions and minimize the risk of crop loss. While this demonstrates the value of AIKS for rural, indigenous communities, we must still remember that in South Africa, the recognition of AIKS is lacking on a national level. That is, South Africa favors Western and scientific modes of crop production in their national strategies, policies, and plans. This disconnect not only undermines AIKS, but also hinders the potential of endogenous development.

AIKS is also employed by indigenous Africans to assist with wildlife management and conservation: In some East and Central African countries, for example, there are community forests (such as the Busaga and Buhanga forests in Rwanda) that demonstrate the local communities' close engagement with sustainable forest management processes and the protection of various animal species.

The local Maasai community in the Loita Forest and Loima Forest regions has conserved and protected their rich and diverse ecosystems and environments—without the intervention of the government or NGOs. Before the era of globalization, these community forests offered the local communities' food, medicinal plants, and a space for sociocultural meetings, and this sacred view of the community forests, in turn, ensured that the local communities would protect, preserve, manage, and conserve these ecosystems. Perhaps this care for the environment and sacred view of nature is key to addressing climate change issues in these regions (and beyond).

In fact, this is where intra-African partnerships are significant, as African communities can exchange knowledge on climate change issues and ensure the holistic protection of the continent's rich biodiversity and resources.

## Practical Tools and Frameworks

| Leveraging and Implementing AIKS Priorities/Checklist | Areas of Innovation | Done |
|---|---|---|
| 1. Identify key sociocultural, economic, and political issues within the local community. | • Agriculture<br>• Environmental protection (and mitigating natural disasters)<br>• Medicine and healthcare (including maternal care and childbirth)<br>• Intra-community tensions<br>• Economic mobility and opportunities | |

| | | |
|---|---|---|
| 2. Identify and explore the AIKS of the local community. | Answer the following questions:<br><br>• What forms of AIKS are present in the local community?<br><br>• How have these forms of AIKS contributed towards development?<br><br>• What resources are lacking in the implementation of AIKS in the local community? | |

| | | |
|---|---|---|
| 3. Communication with the local community. | Answer the following questions:<br>• Are the relevant community leaders and/or members involved in the communications on and processes of sustainable development?<br>• Is the youth engaged in AIKS processes and practices?<br>• Who in the community holds and shares the wisdom of AIKS? | |

| | | |
|---|---|---|
| 4. Explore key barriers to AIKS. | • Cultural barriers (such as lack of African pride and unity or a sense of cultural inferiority).<br><br>• Obstacles in the sharing of AIKS (including the possible indifference of the youth, issues concerning language and translation, or the migration of the youth away from the community).<br><br>• Environmental barriers (this entails NGOs and other local or international organizations intervening in protection and conservation | |

|  |  | efforts). |  |
|  |  | • The involvement of political or government leaders. That is, has the government introduced any policies or measures to acknowledge, support, and protect AIKS? |  |

| | | |
|---|---|---|
| 5. Resource allocation. | This includes identifying, addressing, and alleviating any and all obstacles to the implementation of AIKS, such as:<br><br>• Foreign interventions<br><br>• Poverty and scarce resources<br><br>• Issues with infrastructure<br><br>• Lack of education and employment opportunities<br><br>• The erosion of indigenous languages | |

| | | |
|---|---|---|
| 6. The formal integration of AIKS. | AIKS can (and should) be introduced in the following institutions:<br><br>• Primary and secondary education curricula.<br><br>• The curricula of tertiary education institutions, including universities and technical colleges.<br><br>• Community resource centers. | |

| | | |
|---|---|---|
| 7. Community capacity. | • Identify and address any barriers to unity and tensions within the local communities.<br><br>• Ascertain the education and employment potential of the community members.<br><br>• If needed, establish community resource centers to mobilize community leaders and members and promote the exchange of AIKS wisdom.<br><br>• Identify local governance and administration structures. | |

| | | |
|---|---|---|
| 8. Identify similarities in AIKS across the continent. | • Create a database of the current use of AIKS across African nations.<br><br>• Compare the forms of AIKS and identify any similarities or common threads among African communities. This aids in building and fostering intra-African partnerships.<br><br>• Identify the African communities that can benefit from the AIKS of other African communities. | |

# Chapter 8:
# How to Unlock Africa's Potential—Regional Cooperation

> *I am an African. I owe my being to the hills and the valleys, the mountains and the glades, the rivers, the deserts, the trees, the flowers, the seas and the ever-changing seasons that define the face of our native land.*
>
> –Thabo Mbeki

During the Constitutional Assembly of South Africa on May 8, 1996, the then-Deputy President of South Africa, Thabo Mbeki, delivered his seminal "I Am an African" speech in which he hinted at an African Renaissance project. Here, he suggested that the African continent would undergo a political, social, and economic renewal and would be integrated into the global economy.

Thabo Mbeki also encouraged Africans to adapt democracy to suit their own contexts and conditions (without compromising on the values of accountability and representation), to create a sense of their own self-confidence, to take pride in their African identity, and to determine their own future. In essence, the African Renaissance sought to establish an inspiring vision of Africa's rebirth in which the continent's foreign debt was canceled, its trade conditions were improved, development assistance was expanded, and the positive aspects of globalization could be leveraged to develop African economies. Thabo Mbeki referred specifically to challenge the negative perceptions of Africa, the failures of one-party regimes, and the hope for stable democracies; the remnants of European racism and tyranny; the emancipation of African women; liberation from underdevelopment, oppression, and foreign aid and dependence; and the immense 'brain drain' from Africa and the hope for the return of the African diaspora.

It has been a few decades since Thabo Mbeki's passionate speech, the formation of the African Union, and the occurrence of several African Renaissance festivals, but many Africans are still waiting on the promises of the continent's rebirth. From skeletal policies that have not been translated into action and the lack of support and promotion from governmental officials to the fact that the African Renaissance has largely been confined to the borders of South Africa, there has yet to be large-scale, grassroots support for an African Renaissance across the continent and in the African diaspora.

This is coupled with persistent interethnic tensions and conflicts, civil wars, genocides, and overexploitation across African nations, so it is unsurprising that an African Renaissance has fallen to the wayside of African policymakers and politicians' list of priorities. Despite the failure to translate it into tangible policies, strategies, and efforts, we can still learn from the key elements of the African Renaissance (and perhaps renew the call for the continent's rebirth).

## A (New) African Renaissance?

The conceptual origin of the African Renaissance can be traced to the Senegalese historian, Cheikh Anta Diop, who, in the mid-20th century, penned a series of essays on the development of Africa. Diop, however, argued that because African elites and writers had abandoned African languages, they could not be the authentic agents of the African Renaissance. Despite this, Diop's work formed the blueprint of Thabo Mbeki's call for an African Renaissance — a process that was supposed to emerge after decolonization and the spread of democracy across the African continent. The African Renaissance entailed a number of different initiatives and movements, including Pan-Africanism, African humanism, and the Black Consciousness Movement (BCM), as well as regional partnerships, such as the New Partnership for African Development (NEPAD), the Economic Community of West African Countries (ECOWAS), and the Southern Africa Economic Development Community (SADC). The BCM, for example, was a restorative movement in the sense that it sought to restore Black people's resistance to colonial and apartheid oppression while simultaneously affirming themselves as the makers of their own histories.

The hopes for social cohesion, economic growth, democracy, and the establishment of Africa as a prominent play in geopolitical affairs were short-lived as the Eritrean-Ethiopian War and the Second Congo War in 1998 ravaged many African nations. Despite the colonial inheritance of rampant corruption, disease outbreaks, and the persistence of one-party regimes, the average African seemed unable to achieve the African Renaissance. Indeed, the African Renaissance can only occur once African unity is achieved — something that was greatly impeded by various conflicts and socioeconomic issues in the late 20th and early 21st centuries.

The initiatives of the African Renaissance, too, have been met with significant criticism: NEPAD was portrayed as the pathway to a better future for the continent but focused more on the partnerships between poorer African countries and the wealthier countries of the Global North. NEPAD, which has the open support of the G8 nations, promotes specific partnerships that are arguably neocolonialist and see good governance in Africa as a conduit for increased foreign aid. If anything, Africa needs social, institutional, and human capacity rather than foreign aid and capital to boost its sustainable development.

Moreover, NEPAD's criticism comes largely from human rights organizations, civil society groups, and labor unions, as NEPAD's main economic goal is to integrate Africa into the global economy and center the IMF, World Bank, and the G8 countries in this effort. Given past relationships between Africa and the Global North (and their organizations), African critics have sufficient reason not to support NEPAD. Indeed, NEPAD's neoliberal economic policies and frameworks cannot simply be imposed on African nations and their contexts.

African leaders must actively support the revival of an African Renaissance and take into account the particular issues of the twenty-first century. In the latter case, these leaders must provide for the basic needs (and more) of their people in order to prevent daily issues from undermining the African Renaissance. The Renaissance must also ensure intra-African cultural exchanges, the emancipation of African women, the empowerment of the youth, the support of institutions dedicated to democratic values and sustainable development, and regional cooperation that truly benefits African nations.

## Regional Cooperation: Successes and Challenges

### *Ethnocentrism: The West Does Not Need to /ave Africa*

Ethnocentrism refers to the belief that one's own culture is superior to other cultures, and as such, one can judge another culture based on the standards of their own culture. This sense of superiority is a universal phenomenon among humans and can be based on the culture's values, ways of living, resources, and adaptability. However, as demonstrated by (pseudo)scientific racism, European colonial rule, and other forms of white supremacist systems of domination and oppression, many in the West/Global North have regarded the customs, beliefs, and ways of living of those in the Global South as *uncivilized, backward,* or *primitive*. Despite being a few decades into the postindependence era, there are still those who uphold problematic ethnocentric beliefs towards those they deem inferior to them, including Africans. As a result, Africa is still often seen as the dark continent, a place that lacks creativity and innovation, and a region in desperate need of saving (by the West).

As demonstrated by the failures of Western development strategies in Africa, sustainable development in Africa cannot be measured or judged according to Western standards simply because of the continent's vastly different histories, current contexts, and ongoing overexploitation. Sustainable development in Africa must be developed, implemented, and maintained by Africans themselves, and the continent's indigenous knowledge systems, current technological advances and innovations, natural and human resources, and the potential of its youth must be considered. Besides, political and economic relations between Africa and Western countries have long been exploitative in the sense that African nations and peoples seldom benefit from deals, agreements, and partnerships with the West.

## *The Case of ECOWAS*

On May 28, 1975, the Economic Community of West African States (ECOWAS) was established as a regional economic and political union comprised of 15 West African countries, including Nigeria, Benin, Côte d'Ivoire, Liberia, Mali, The Gambia, Burkina Faso, Niger, Ghana, Cabo Verde, Guinea, Guinea-Bissau, Togo, Senegal, and Sierra Leone. ECOWAS is considered one of the key regional blocs of the African Economic Community (AEC) and it aimed to achieve collective self-sufficiency through the formation of a full economic and trading union. Underpinned by the principles of nonaggression, regional peace, the advancement of human rights, cooperation, equity, social and economic justice, and interdependence, ECOWAS also serves as a peacekeeping force in West Africa. However, the military leaders of Mali, Niger, and Burkina Faso formed a new alliance and severed their ties with ECOWAS in 2024. In the immediate aftermath, these three countries announced their new pact, the Alliance of Sahel States, as a means to put up a united front in the face of external aggression or armed rebellion and to free themselves from foreign influence. It is important to note that Mali faced a coup in August 2021, Burkina Faso in September 2022, and Niger in July 2023—making these countries and their peoples particularly vulnerable to unrest and violence. Since the coups, Mali, Burkina Faso, and Niger have had increasingly strained relationships with the West and, more specifically, their former colonial ruler, France.

While breaking away from ECOWAS has led to the United States and France pulling their troops from the Alliance of Sahel States and the three countries shifting their allegiances to Russia, analysts remain divided on the potential impacts. On the one hand, the post-coup military and political shifts have enabled armed groups to enact rampant violence in these three countries and in broader West Africa. Should Niger, Mali, and Burkina Faso further isolate themselves from the remaining ECOWAS members, the armed groups will be further empowered to exploit the power vacuum.

On the other hand, the withdrawal of Niger, Mali, and Burkina Faso from ECOWAS could lead to relative stability as the Alliance of Sahel States has confronted and ousted the colonial power and influence of France and the United States. Besides, these two Western countries are known to create instability in African nations even after withdrawing from them. Moreover, there is growing frustration with ECOWAS among West African countries as the union has failed to ensure peace and security in the region. ECOWAS instead tends to support political leaders who are amenable to or aligned with the former colonial powers, exacerbating poverty in the region and impeding development efforts.

Indeed, the many criticisms against ECOWAS, including ignoring illegal term extensions by political leaders, have contributed to many people's increasing lack of trust in and support of ECOWAS. Of course, any member withdrawal from ECOWAS will impact economic development, trade, and the movement of people within the bloc, but ECOWAS must serve West African peoples rather than their leaders. As ECOWAS endeavors to reintegrate Niger, Burkina Faso, and Mali into its fold, the true impact of the Alliance of Sahel States on the peoples of West Africa remains uncertain.

## The African Union: A Manipulation Tool?

Formed in 2002 to replace the Organisation of African Unity (OAU), the African Union (AU) is yet another organization that is under fire for its many failures and weaknesses. In fact, from 2022 to 2023, 93% of the AU's decisions have not been implemented, and its assembly (composed of heads of state and governments) has failed to exert legislative power and authority over noncompliant member states (Fagbayibo & Staeger, 2024). This compliance requires member states to willingly give up some of their sovereignty for the sake of continental integration, but it is also worth noting that member states have little trust and confidence in the AU. Indeed, the AU is only as strong as its member states, but regional or continental integration in Africa must be prioritized. In 2017, Paul Kagame submitted a report on how to reform the AU and better coordinate between the member states and African economic communities, but this has yielded very little results—further illustrating the structural weaknesses in the AU.

Furthermore, the AU's budget is largely funded by external partners, including the United States, the European Union, China, India, South Korea, and Turkey, while its member states only pay the AU 80% to 90% of what they owe. The AU is also lacking strong leadership, with the current Chairperson, Mohamed Ould Cheikh Al-Ghazouani, remaining silent on significant atrocities in Tigray, Ethiopia, among other criticisms. The weaknesses in and failures of the structure of the AU and its leadership have all contributed to the member states' ever-increasing frustrations with the organization, but the willing member states, in turn, must actively enable the AU parliament to impose supranational legislative powers on noncompliant member states as well as speed up the decision-making processes in the AU—processes that should also include wider civil society.

## *When ECOWAI and the AU Failed Niger*

On July 26, 2023, a coup d'état occurred in Niger following long-standing tensions between the president, Mohammed Bazoum, and the commander of his presidential guard, General Abdourahamane

Tchiani. The ECOWAS and AU were quick to respond and condemn the coup, and after two summits regarding the appropriate approach to the coup, nine sanctions were levied against Niger. They also made the decision to deploy standby forces. The coup happened amid relative economic progress and political stability in Niger, and while the coup may have come as a shock to some, it is worth noting that there were signs of unease prior to the coup. In fact, those in regional and continental policy circles raised concern over the risk of an imminent coup, and some AU actors, too, tried to draw attention to the military interference in Niger's political sphere. Bazoum, however, dismissed such concerns and attempts by various actors to assist with the situation in Niger.

This is a common occurrence among AU member states. Whether it is based on nationalist pride or ignoring the possibility of losing political power, these states ignore the early warnings of AU representatives. But the AU itself seldom initiates preventative measures, nor does it use its non-indifference provisions to maintain political stability. Armed with diplomacy tools and preventative responses to such situations, the AU had the capacity to broker peace between Bazoum and Tchiani (despite Bazoum's rejections of help). Indeed, the AU's African Charter on Democracy, Elections, and Governance framework was developed to prevent conflict and to enable the AU to intervene when democracy and legitimate exercises of power are threatened.

The sanctions imposed on Niger by ECOWAS were incredibly strict, and the latter bloc also issued an ultimatum to the junta to reinstate Bazoum and restore constitutional order — or face further measures, including military intervention. However, the sanctions and other forms of external pressure backfired on ECOWAS and instead exacerbated humanitarian issues, crippled the cross-border Nigeria-Niger economy, disrupted the lives and livelihoods of Nigerien citizens, and harmed major gas and rail projects meant to improve regional trade and cooperation. ECOWAS' sanctions should have jeopardized the direct interests of the junta (and its leaders) rather than punishing the Nigerien (and northern Nigerian) populations. Indeed, the sanctions have worsened food security among the country's most vulnerable populations. This occurred together with shortages in medicine and staple foods, such as sugar and powdered milk. ECOWAS did not exclude electricity, food, and petroleum products from their punitive restrictions imposed on Niger (exclusions that were granted to other nations undergoing a coup and political unrest).

Perhaps ECOWAS should have instead developed realistic plans to return Niger to constitutional rule; working towards a constitutional transition rather than trying to reverse the coup; reviewed the sanctions and related policies that mainly punish civilians instead of junta or coup leaders; and pushed for dialogue and diplomatic efforts rather than unrealistic ultimatums. ECOWAS' initial response to the 2023 coup in Niger was understandable, but their stringent sanctions have had unintended yet terrible consequences on the Niger economy, existing humanitarian issues, security, and the livelihoods and well-being of Nigerien citizens. In fact, ECOWAS' sanctions have negatively impacted its own interests and regional cooperation efforts.

# Economic Diversification and Intra-African Trade

*Economic Diversification to Mitigate Exogenous /hocks*

European colonial rule forced many African countries to have one-commodity economies — making these countries particularly vulnerable to drastic fluctuations in global markets. Africa is, in fact, home to eight of the world's fifteen least economically diversified economies, and this, in turn, significantly weakens the foundation of

Africa's economic growth and the potential for regional or intra-African trade and cooperation (Usman & Landry, 2021). The lack of economic diversification also makes these countries vulnerable to external shocks, such as the disruption of tourism-dependent economies during the COVID-19 pandemic. Efforts towards economic diversification generally include the expansion of economic sectors that positively contribute to GDP and employment diversification, as well as fiscal diversification.

The latter form of diversification entails expanding the government's sources of revenue and public expenditure targets and, as such, prioritizes the expansion of activity within specific sectors and industries. The expansion of existing sectors and the establishment of new ones also entail effective measures to ascertain the extent to which the economic goal or objective is being achieved. Of course, plans to diversify the economy are all good and well, but they need to be translated into practice.

Given the varying political and socioeconomic contexts across Africa, economic diversification may look different in each country. For example, low-income and resource-rich African countries tend to be undiversified. Interregional inequality also plays a major role in economic diversification efforts. In Africa's coastal countries, the coastal areas and islands are usually more productive and diversified than the inland areas. In non-coastal African countries, the national capital and its surrounding urban areas tend to be more productive and economically diverse than the hinterlands, which largely consist of subsistence farming.

## *Examples From Kenya and Tunisia*

While it may take a few decades, and the progress may be hindered by both internal and external factors, African countries have the potential to diversify their economies. Mauritius, for instance, transformed from a commodity-driven economy that was reliant on the sugar cane industry to an economy that received significant contributions from certain services and processed products, such as tourism, financial services, and textiles. In another example, Kenya has long had a diversified economy that was largely composed of agriculture (and, more specifically, tea) and the tourism industry.

These industries, however, are not well insulated from external economic crises, and as seen in 2008, Kenya's tourism industry declined, and agricultural growth slowed down. Consequently, Kenya took steps towards building on its existing capacities to boost economic diversification, and owing to its strategic geographical position on the Indian Ocean and access to important shipping lanes, the country established a 17,000km underwater fiber optic cable to link south and East Africa to India and Europe. The cable system, Seacom, greatly expanded Kenya's broadband services, connected local industries to international customers, and the lower costs of telecommunications enabled more Africans to connect to the internet and digital technologies.

Kenya has also bolstered its economic diversification by developing its horticultural sector and its financial services. The regional economy in East Africa (namely Kenya, Uganda, and Tanzania) is relatively diverse, strong, and well-integrated largely because of regional coordination efforts.

Since the late 1980s, Tunisia has adopted macroeconomic policies and structural reforms to transform the country into a market-driven economy — to the extent that it is now considered a middle-income country with a stable inflation rate, a high GDP per capita (compared to other African countries), and numerous social services accessible to the large majority of its citizens. This is quite an achievement for a country that lacks many natural resources. However, Tunisia has several advantages compared to other African countries: Its geographic position allows for easy access to Middle Eastern, African, and

European markets, and the country boasts a highly skilled workforce. As such, the economy is rather resilient to internal and external shocks. Since Tunisia has a robust private sector and can compete on the world stage, it is not surprising that many West African governments send delegations there to study Tunisia's policies and programs.

## Continental Trade Partnerships: The AfCFTA

During the African Union's 12th Extraordinary Summit on July 7, 2019, the operational phase of the African Continental Free Trade Area (AfCFTA) was officially launched. With 27 countries ratifying the AfCFTA, the operational phase includes a few salient instruments.

Firstly, the Rules of Origin refer to the governing of the conditions under which a product or service can be traded duty-free across the region and, secondly, tariff concessions that allow for a 90% tariff liberalization with an additional 7% for "sensitive products" over the course of a decade. Online tools to track, report on, and remove nontariff barriers (NTBs), which could potentially impede intra-African trade, will support this.

Another instrument of the AfCFTA is the Pan-African payment system, in which payments will be facilitated on time and in full, and the payments are made in local currency.

Fourthly, the African Trade Observatory will serve as a trade information portal to address and remedy any awareness or information obstacles to trade, such as lack of trade statistics, lack of information on exporters and importers in member countries, and lack of data on trade opportunities. The African Continental Free Trade Area is the largest free trade project since the establishment of the World Trade Organization, and according to the AU, the AfCFTA will help increase trade among African countries, develop regional value chains to stimulate production, boost the capacities of African businesses to access and supply global markets, and strengthen Africa's commercial and economic diplomacy.

Importantly, the AfCFTA is also expected to boost Africa's economic diversification through these regional value changes and the development of the manufacturing sector. In turn, economic diversification has the potential to increase productivity, employment opportunities, and higher value-added exports among African nations.

As such, the AfCFTA also entails provisions for the development of transport, telecommunication networks, energy, and infrastructure to better facilitate the transport of goods and services across the continent.

The AfCFTA is harnessing the economic potential and regional cooperation efforts of the African continent, but as with all ambitious plans by the African Union, only time will tell if the AfCFTA translates into practice (and truly benefits African governments, businesses, and peoples).

## Practical Tools and Frameworks

| An African Renaissance: Political Aspects | An African Renaissance: Sociocultural Aspects |
|---|---|
| • Indigenize democratic systems and processes to serve the needs of Africans.<br><br>• Utilize the positive aspects of globalization.<br><br>• Eradicate the overreliance on foreign aid through intra-African economic and trade partnerships.<br><br>• Ensure African people are included in important decision-making processes.<br><br>• Translate the salient ideas or elements of the African Renaissance into tangible policies.<br><br>• Incentivize political actors to develop, implement, and measure policies and efforts that promote an | • Foster a sense of African pride through educational curricula and performances (such as exhibitions or festivals).<br><br>• Ensure that the arts (film, music, dance, theatre, etc.) are included in the African Renaissance.<br><br>• Support large-scale, grassroots movements and support for an African Renaissance in each African nation.<br><br>• Include the African diaspora in efforts to boost African pride.<br><br>• Leverage African talent (such as art, writing, music, and dance) to write, paint, move to, or compose about African histories and |

| African Renaissance. | cultural practices. |
|---|---|
| **Regional Cooperation: Political and Economic Aspects** | **Regional Cooperation: Sociocultural Aspects** |
| <ul><li>Bolster existing institutions and develop new institutions dedicated to democratic values and sustainable development in Africa.</li><li>Avoid measuring development strategies, policies, or efforts by Western standards or metrics.</li><li>Encourage strong, transparent, and accountable leadership in intra-African blocs, unions, or partnerships.</li><li>Boost civic participation in the decision- and policymaking processes of these blocs and unions.</li><li>Exert legislative power and authority over</li></ul> | <ul><li>Develop programs to boost intra-African cultural and intellectual exchanges.</li><li>Identify ways in which better-resourced African countries can host students, workers, and professionals from lesser-resourced African countries.</li><li>Tackle regional or intra-Africa xenophobia.</li><li>Establish learning and resource centers that focus on preserving and sharing traditional languages, cultural expressions and practices, knowledge systems, and values.</li></ul> |

| | |
|---|---|
| noncompliant member states.<br><br>• Ensure that unions and blocs take preventative measures when it comes to conflicts, coups, and unrest. | |
| **Economic Diversification and Intra-African Partnerships: Political and Economic Aspects** | **Economic Diversification and Intra-African Partnerships: Sociocultural Aspects** |
| • Identify and expand the economic sectors that make significant contributions towards each country's GDP.<br><br>• Establish new and profitable sectors and trade agreements that prioritize collaborations with other African nations.<br><br>• Improve telecommunication networks among African countries.<br><br>• Implement comprehensive | • Identify the key skills, talents, and expertise among the country's labor force and youth.<br><br>• Establish entrepreneurial programs and initiatives for the country's promising youth.<br><br>• Involve African civilians and community leaders in the efforts towards intra-African partnerships and economic diversification. |

| | |
|---|---|
| tools and systems to monitor, measure, and address the obstacles in continental or intra-African trade agreements and partnerships. | |

# Chapter 9:
# The Role of the African Diaspora

> *Africa is our center of gravity, our cultural and spiritual mother and father, our beating heart, no matter where we live on the face of this earth.*
>
> –John Henrik Clarke

To study human history is to study diaspora, or the movement or dispersion of a people from their original homeland. The African diaspora refers to those of African descent who reside outside of their ancestral continent, and their mass movement out of Africa (at different times and for different reasons) happened in five major streams. The first stream can be traced back over 100,000 years, and it is believed that early humans traveled within and outside of the continent.

However, some scholars argue that this exodus should not be seen as part of the diasporic process, as it was vastly different in character (compared to later movements). The second diasporic stream occurred circa 3,000 B.C.E. when Bantu-speaking peoples from modern-day Cameroon and Nigeria spread to other parts of Africa and the Indian Ocean, while the third stream entailed the movement of merchants, soldiers, traders, and slaves to the Middle East, Asia, and parts of Europe in around the 5th century B.C.E.

The latter stream led to the formation of African communities in Portugal, Spain, Italian city-states, and India, constituting what can be described as the premodern African diaspora. It is the fourth and fifth major streams, the transatlantic slave trade and contemporary migration of Africans, that are relevant to our modern-day understandings of the term "African diaspora."

## Who Is the African Diaspora?

Our modern understanding of the term "African diaspora" acknowledges that diasporic identities are historically and socially constituted, reconstituted, and reproduced, and paradoxically, collective identities and cultures among the African diaspora are diverse and always changing.

Moreover, the modern African diaspora emerged from systems of domination and white supremacy in which Black Africans were enslaved, oppressed, and disenfranchised in recent history. Because it is based on lived experiences, feelings of alienation, outsiderness, and isolation, and is both a process and condition, "diaspora" connotes differences and discontinuities.

More specifically, the African diaspora exists within the context of global race and gender hierarchies that are established and expressed along different lines across the world.

For example, the enslavement, exploitation, and denigration of Black Africans in the Americas served the economic interests of the colonial economies and plantations. During the Jim Crow era in the United States, race and gender hierarchies existed along social and economic lines as Black Americans were forced to exist in racially segregated spaces.

Race and gender hierarchies were enforced by the European colonial powers, who created structured definitions of race, gender, national identity, and citizenship in their own countries and in their colonies.

While the arrangement of such hierarchies varies from country to country, it remains a gendered racial hierarchy that persists in the 21st century.

## *The Transatlantic Slave Trade*

From the 16th to 19th centuries, between 11 and 12 million Africans were captured, enslaved, and transported across the Atlantic Ocean to the Americas—constituting the largest long-distance coerced movement of people in history (Lewis, 2024). This slave trade was the second of three stages of the triangular trade: Textiles, wine, and weapons were shipped from Europe to Africa, enslaved people from Africa were shipped to the Americas, and the Americas produced coffee and sugar to be shipped to Europe.

These millions of enslaved Africans were forced to replace the labor of the declining Native American population, and as such, over two-thirds of the slave population toiled on the sugar plantations. The voyage to the Americas was, in itself, horrendous as European traders captured African men, women, and children along the African coast and led them onto the slave ships. The captives were chained and packed tightly together, and the low ceilings made it impossible for them to sit upright.

The heat and low levels of oxygen in the slave quarters were only remedied when the African captives were allowed a few hours on the upper decks of the ship. This respite, however, emerged from the ship crew's fear of an insurrection by the captives (and not for altruistic reasons).

In addition to the terrible conditions on the ship, the African captives also faced starvation, diseases, and physical and sexual violence during the voyage. Only 11 million people survived the journey, but the conditions on the slave plantations were no solace from the death and despair of the slave ships.

*Life on the Plantations*

The plantations in the Americas produced sugar, molasses, rum, and other byproducts from sugar came to be exported to Europe and elsewhere in the Atlantic world. The profits generated from the slave trade and the sugar plantations supported the development and advancement of industries and institutions in North America and Europe, but this came at a harrowing human cost. Indeed, Africans were enslaved on small farms, in transportation and industry, on large plantations, inside the slaveowner's home, and in the towns and cities.

Yet, no matter where they were enslaved, African slaves were considered property and were subject to many forms of violence throughout the slave trade era. In the American South, for example, most slaves lived and worked on cotton plantations where they were forced to plant and harvest cotton, clear new land, kill livestock, cut and carry wood, and dig ditches. Some slaves worked as domestics in the slave owners' homes, and women slaves, in particular, had to care for the slave owners' children as well as sew, weave, and spin for the white families. Skilled slaves were able to work as drivers, carpenters, and mechanics.

Whether skilled or unskilled, a house servant or field slave, the enslaved Africans lived in quarters that made them vulnerable to disease and bad weather, their diets did not meet the demands of their heavy workloads, and their illnesses were not met with medical care or treatment. Life on the rice plantations was particularly deadly, as slaves were forced to stand in water and under the unforgiving sun for hours at a time. Slaves were also under constant threat of being sold. Because they were treated as property, their owners or masters would send them to the auction block as a form of punishment or for financial reasons—separating immediate families and slave communities.

In addition, women slaves were faced with sexual exploitation on the plantations, with some being used as long-term concubines by their masters. No matter how benevolent their masters seemed, far too many slaves were subject to regular whippings, mutilations, torture, rape, and sexual violence and were sold away from their families.

*/lave Resistance and Resilience*

Of course, the slaves resisted in numerous ways: They sabotaged machinery, destroyed crops, faked sicknesses, stole livestock and food, burned buildings and forests, poisoned their masters' food, learned to read and write, or would mutilate their bodies or commit suicide to ruin their own property value. Some slaves successfully or unsuccessfully fled the plantations, while others remained and formed a sense of community with their fellow slaves.

It is in the latter's case that slaves could teach each other skills, share herbal remedies and medicines, and teach their children to escape the punishment of the white masters. Here, some slaves practiced African religions and tried to hold on to their traditional African cultural practices. Indeed, they had been ripped away from their families, ancestral lands, cultures, traditions, and beliefs when they were captured and loaded onto the slave ships.

*Back in Africa*

The transatlantic slave trade also had several negative consequences for the Africans who evaded capture or were able to remain in Africa.

Firstly, the slave trade had a disproportionate impact on the African male population, as male slaves were sought after for plantation work. As such, around two-thirds of the slaves taken to the Americas were male, while one-third were female (Hardy, 2020). Women, children, and the elderly were forced to rebuild what was left of their communities. With this depopulation in mind, it is unsurprising that the poorest regions in modern-day Africa are also the regions from where the largest number of slaves were taken.

Secondly, by the 18th century, slaves were Africa's main export, and this had disastrous consequences on African economies: The slave trade stagnated Africa's economic systems and severely hindered its development. This was exacerbated by the fact that African rulers were cashing in on the prosperous slave trade and, therefore, competed over the control of slave capture and trading.

In some cases, this competition snowballed into conflicts and wars — fostering a culture of violence and sharpening divisions along social and ethnic lines.

Thirdly, the acute focus on the slave trade meant that resources were diverted or allocated away from industrial and agricultural development and innovations and were instead poured into the slave trade. Fourthly, the slave trade also resulted in a massive "brain drain."

One can only imagine the economic development of Africa if the continent's strong and productive labor force was allowed to develop its own communities, farmlands, and broader societies.

## Later Migrations

While most international migration from Africa occurs within the continent (that is, Africans move from one African country to another), there has been a significant increase in the number of African migrants living and working outside of the continent. According to the World Migration Report (2024), the number of African-born migrants living outside of the continent has doubled since 1990, and in 2020, it was reported that most of these migrants were residing in Europe (around 11 million), Asia (almost five million), and Northern America (an estimated three million). In these examples, the proportion of male migrants and female migrants is similar, except in the case of Libya and Egypt (the male migrants outnumber their female counterparts). There are countless reasons for this migration, and the key features of migration out of specific African regions are listed below.

### *North Africa*

Migration out of Africa is notable in North Africa as its geographical proximity to the Mediterranean routes, and Europe makes it a transit point for many African migrants. This has also enabled North African countries to develop and operate extensive trafficking, smuggling, and slave networks. Indeed, there have been numerous reports of torture, forced labor, and violence in this region, and women and girls, in particular, are vulnerable to gender-based and sexual violence. Crossing the Mediterranean is also incredibly deadly, with tens of thousands of migrants dying or disappearing while en route to Europe.

In addition to residing in or near a transit point, North Africans are fleeing via the Mediterranean route for the following reasons: North Africans are escaping human rights abuses, racist violence and xenophobia, a lack of economic (education and employment) opportunities, and regional violence and conflicts. In terms of xenophobia and racism, there have been instances of harassment and violence against sub-Saharan Africans (residing in Tunisia) and Black Tunisians.

Echoing the anti-migrant sentiments and discourses in European countries, some Africans have been unwelcoming or outright hostile and aggressive towards African migrants. North Africa is also vulnerable to the adverse impacts of environmental degradation and climate change. Coupled with a decline in rainfall during the wet season and an increase in warming over the past few decades, North Africa is seriously impacted by climate change while also being considered some of the least prepared.

It is important to note that environmental factors impact all spheres of life, including agriculture and food production (and contribute to food insecurity), and increased water scarcity can escalate existing tensions, conflicts, and violence. As a result, many North Africans are moving within or outside of their countries. The many droughts and wildfires in Morocco and Algeria have exacerbated internal migration and displacement. In conflict-ridden North African countries, such as Sudan, the ongoing violence has killed many civilians and has forced thousands to flee for their own safety — mainly fleeing to other parts of Sudan or to neighboring countries, such as Ethiopia, Chad, and Egypt.

## West and Central Africa

As another hotspot for conflict, violent extremism, and insecurity, the Sahel region of Africa is marked by significant migration flows. The region faces desertification, environmental degradation, lack of access to basic needs and services, and ongoing conflicts between the nomadic farmers and herders. More extreme forms of violence include armed conflict and military clashes between various Islamist groups, as well as military coups in Mali, Niger, and Burkina Faso. In 2022 alone, there were over 2.9 million refugees and internally displaced people in Niger, Mali, and Burkina Faso (World Migration Report, 2024). As seen in other cases in Africa, such violence and clashes tend to spill into neighboring countries. The violence in Niger, Mali, and Burkina Faso has had a ripple effect on Benin, Togo, and Côte d'Ivoire, for example.

Part of this violence also includes the abduction of children, and more specifically, girls. This, coupled with food insecurity, climate change, and natural disasters, makes West and Central Africa prone to internal displacement as well as those trying to flee the region and, in some cases, the continent. Similar to migrations out of North Africa, migrants from West and Central Africa face many dangers as they undertake the voyage to Europe. The abuse and violence against and smuggling and trafficking of migrants is rife along the routes between West and Central Africa, the Saharan desert, and the Mediterranean Sea crossing.

There were almost 2,800 disappearances and deaths recorded along these routes in 2022 — owing to the sheer length of the journey and being stuck at sea on inadequate boats. These are only the recorded deaths and disappearances, and considering the limited search and rescue operations for migrants, it is safe to assume that the actual death and disappearance toll is much higher.

Intra-regional migration also poses many risks to migrants, refugees, and the citizens of the destination country. Indeed, those fleeing conflict in their home countries arrive in countries with high rates of unemployment, high levels of poverty, massive gender pay gaps, and a lack of access to adequate healthcare facilities and services. Many migrant workers' only or main options for employment involve temporary and seasonal jobs, with only a few African countries allowing migrants to settle. Furthermore, the ECOWAS free trade protocol enabled labor mobility in West Africa, and here, the citizens of ECOWAS member states had the right to enter, live in, and engage in economic activities in another member state. This protocol, however, is not without its challenges, as poor infrastructure, different national interests among member states, political unrest, and Burkina Faso, Mali, and Niger leaving ECOWAS have all impeded the potential of the protocol.

## Southern and Eastern Africa

Due to various free movement agreements or arrangements, East Africa has seen an increase in intra-regional migration, including economic migration. For example, the East African Common Market Protocol of 2010 enables the free movement of people, capital, labor, goods, and services, and while it has not been fully implemented across all nations, the citizens of the EAC have the right to enter and work in the participating nations and have access to the free processing of work permits.

In another example, the protocol on the Free Movement of Persons was adopted in 2021 and is the first of its kind to address the migration of people as a result of climate change. Similarly, the Protocol on Transhumance facilitates the safe, free, and cross-border movement of transhumant herders and livestock – acknowledging the importance of pastoralism as a livelihood in the region.

Of course, displacement in and movement out of East Africa are also due to longstanding and newer armed conflicts.

## /earching for a Better Life?

There are many Africans who flee their country or the continent owing to conflict, war, ongoing violence, and climate change, but there are others who leave because of underdevelopment, economic decline, and poverty. Indeed, they travel to Europe, Northern America, Asia, or the Gulf States in search of a better life for themselves and their families.

Of course, those who make it to their destination or the receiving countries are not necessarily safe from harm as they may experience marginalization, legal issues, poor housing conditions, police targeting, racial discrimination, and lack of recognized human rights in the receiving country. Young migrants who reside in Europe, North America, and elsewhere may also be providing for their families back in their home country. Whether they are funding food, housing, and basic needs for their families back home or assisting their families with post-civil-war reconstructions, their remittances to Africa have increased in the past few decades. Remittances support millions of families in Africa, and for many of these families, remittances are the difference between survival and extreme poverty and destitution. In 2023, Africa received $100 billion in remittances, making up almost 6% of the continent's GDP (Fliss, 2023). Remittances demonstrate the generosity and resilience of the African diaspora and community outside of the continent, but also significantly contribute to advancing development in Africa. Here, remittances provide a stable income that improves food security, addresses basic needs, and offers access to healthcare and education to those who remain in the sender's home country.

However, some African governments (and their partners) are struggling to leverage the full potential of remittances for economic growth and sustainable development. Here, high transfer costs, rigid regulatory barriers, inadequate financial sectors, lack of technological infrastructure, and overreliance on informal channels are all obstacles to both the remittance process and African governments' leveraging of it. Moreover, increased remittances mean the increased loss of skilled labor—exacerbating the 'brain drain' in Africa.

## Draining Africa

From the coerced migration of African slaves to the Americas during the transatlantic slave trade to the many skilled African professionals fleeing conflict and war, economic collapse, and worsening living conditions, Africa is suffering from a "brain drain." This term refers to the loss of highly skilled professionals (such as educators, medical professionals, engineers, academics, and scientists) from one country to another, and in the case of Africa, many of its nations are left with a shortage of key skills and expertise.

When a brain drain occurs from lower-income and overexploited countries to wealthier countries, the former countries lose the skills needed to address the challenges of sustainable development and economic growth in Africa.

There are, however, numerous reasons why African professionals leave their countries and, more broadly, the African continent. As mentioned earlier, some may be fleeing persecution, violence, or war, while others may be seeking better education and employment opportunities in the Global North.

Whatever the reason, the brain drain from Africa demonstrates a vicious cycle: The underdevelopment and economic stagnation brought on by colonialism have — to a certain extent — led to skilled Africans leaving the continent to enter and work in the former colonial powers.

The brain drain is not unique to Africa, as several countries in the Global South have lost their young, productive, and skilled workforce. This, in turn, leaves the countries with a shortage of skilled professionals despite the countries having invested resources into training and educating these professionals. But, in many cases, African professionals migrate to the former colonial powers because they know and can identify with the culture and language enforced on them and the previous generations.

For example, it is not surprising to find migrants from Tunisia and Morocco migrating to France or migrants from Angola and Guinea Bissau settling in Portugal. Other receiving countries, such as the United States and Canada, may not have direct colonial ties with African nations, but they do offer migrants strong economies and employment opportunities. Ghana, Nigeria, and South Africa are some of the main African countries that have lost skilled professionals to the United States, for instance.

## The "Greener Pastures"

The receiving countries have several pull factors or favorable conditions for African migrants, including greater economic upward mobility, higher salaries, relatively safer environments, and a higher standard of living. Importantly, these receiving countries may be lacking in skilled professionals and have subsequently eased up on their immigration regulations. For example, the early 2000s saw Australia modifying its restrictions on student visas to allow skilled professionals to stay in Australia's areas of need, mainly rural and remote areas, once they have completed their studies. Tracking the brain drain from Africa is rather challenging, but there are some estimates that paint a picture of the loss of skilled professionals:

In 2020, migration out of Africa increased by 30% since 2010, and highly educated and skilled Africans are pushed or pulled towards the United States, Canada, the United Kingdom, or France (Firsing, 2023). Another report found that seven million immigrants residing in France now make up around 10.3% of its population—with over 12% originally from Algeria, 12% from Morocco, and 4% from Tunisia (Rouhban & Tanneau, 2023).

The healthcare industry is especially impacted by this brain drain, as 80% of the continent (around 40 countries) are experiencing notable health staffing shortages. The World Health Organization (WHO) reports that an average of 500 nurses leave Ghana for Western countries each month; 65% of the 9,000 medical students that graduate from Egyptian universities every year go to work abroad; and between 2016 and 2018, around 9,000 Nigerian doctors moved to the United States, Canada, and the United Kingdom. Since 2017, over 75,000 nurses have left Nigeria. Of course, we need to balance this with the increase in financial remittances that result from this brain drain, and currently, these remittances have surpassed the level of funds received via foreign direct investment and development assistance.

## *The Brain Drain and Remittances as Developmental Assistance*

Financial remittances have the potential to advance Africa's sustainable development and growth goals, but the brain drain that underpins these remittances, too, can promote development—but in the receiving country. African countries are playing a zero-sum game in which the receiving countries become wealthier thanks to the migration of highly skilled professionals out of Africa. In doing so, the African countries receive very little return on their investment in the education and training of their young Africans. This contrasts with the receiving country, which benefits from the labor of these migrants without having to bear the costs of training or educating them. Once again, Western countries are unfairly benefiting from Africa's (human) resources, as African countries are unintentionally providing development assistance to the receiving countries.

In terms of political impact, some scholars have argued that the brain drain has adverse effects on the sociopolitical well-being of African countries. This is because migration deprives Africa's civil societies of important organizational and political skills (that are usually present in middle-class professionals and intellectuals). The brain drain thus makes it challenging to build a strong middle class of engineers, academics, and medical professionals in African countries—leaving the wealthy and corrupt elite and the unskilled and poorer citizens to support African nations and their development goals. It can also be argued that the brain drain hinders the collective brainpower needed to challenge and weed out corruption and mismanagement in African governments and institutions.

Another argument that can be made is that skilled professionals from Africa who migrate to the Global North are usually faced with doing unskilled or even dangerous work. For example, the deskilling of migrants prevents them from learning new technical or industrial skills and experiences to implement in their home countries in Africa.

This is especially nefarious in cases where African migrants are relegated to low-grade or low-status positions or are made to work in unhealthy and exhausting jobs that are usually shunned by the citizens of the receiving country. Coupled with xenophobia and other forms of discrimination, the unequal power imbalances between Western employers and African migrant workers enable the exploitation and deskilling of African migrants.

## The Brain Gain and Returning to the *Motherland*

Addressing the negative impacts of the brain drain on Africa requires African governments and institutions to implement retention strategies. This greatly depends on the African country's infrastructure, economy, available resources and services, as well as safety (in terms of violence and conflict), so it is in Africa's best interest to prioritize peace and security, sustainable development, and economic growth to ensure its young, productive, educated, and skilled human resources are not compelled to leave the country or continent. But, in more extreme cases where African professionals are fleeing conflict, the source and receiving countries need to have viable agreements and solutions in place to mitigate the brain drain from Africa.

This entails taking into account the needs of all countries concerned, monitoring and managing the migration of professionals, and implementing realistic measures to encourage the return of these professionals. For example, African medical professors (who reside and work in non-African countries) can spend their sabbaticals training medical students in African medical schools and/or identify collaboration opportunities with their African counterparts to advance medical research.

The relationship between the source and receiving countries needs to be symbiotic, but given the fact that source countries tend to be overexploited and poor and receiving countries are usually wealthy, achieving symbiosis is easier said than done. In response to the 'brain drain,' researchers have argued for the possibility of a 'brain gain' – or the ways in which this drain can be leveraged and developed into an intellectual resource for the African continent. In our globalized and technologically advanced world, distances and geographical borders are no longer a major obstacle to the exchange of knowledge and information.

So, African professionals have all the more reason to make their skills, expertise, and networks conducive to sustainable development efforts in their countries of origin. This brain gain can occur by enabling African professionals (no matter where they are in the world) to engage in research and training with their African counterparts; transferring technology to African institutions; making research findings and information available and accessible to Africans; and facilitating business, research, and commercial networking between Africans and the relevant stakeholders.

Here are a few measures that can be developed and implemented to remedy the brain drain and facilitate this brain gain.

## *Economic Measures*

- Establish and maintain a productive and healthy economic environment with strong economic management.

- Develop and implement comprehensive anti-corruption strategies, policies, and procedures to encourage accountability and transparency.

- Introduce incentives for Africans working abroad to invest in their country of origin.

- Prioritize the fair and equal distribution of national resources, especially in the education sector.

- Develop viable, long-term development projects that require the skills and expertise of African professionals so that they are deterred from leaving the country or continent.

## *Political Measures*

- Promote good governance, the consolidation of peace, stability, and security, and the respect for human rights to curb the brain drain.

- Develop strategies and policies to enhance Africans' pride in their identity, cultures, and traditions.

- Make African professionals aware of the imperialist machinations of receiving countries in the Global North. Indeed, the 'greener pastures' narrative is undermined by the possibility of being subjected to xenophobia and racism in the receiving countries.

- Exert pressure on Western receiving countries to modify their policies on the immigration of professionals from Africa. African migrants supply the receiving countries with much-needed skills and expertise, and as such, the receiving countries have a responsibility to ensure that there are strong brain gain measures in place and that their human resources demands do not come to the detriment of African countries.

- Strengthen intra-African partnerships and cooperation so that skills and expertise stay within Africa.

- Ensure that labor recruitment agencies and systems are open, transparent, and accountable and that they adhere to immigration policies and labor laws.

## *Social and Technological Measures*

- Develop, maintain, and regularly update the database(s) for professionals migrating out of Africa. This not only helps decision- and policymakers develop strategies or programs to turn the brain drain into a brain gain, but it also helps researchers identify trends and patterns in migration, the shortage or surplus of certain skills, and the potential areas of collaboration.

- Leverage the database(s) to identify the needs and conditions of migrant workers, their families, and their communities.

- African governments must advance gender-responsive economic development programs to provide educational opportunities, employment, and professional development to their female workforce. This will respond to the increasing feminization of labor migration.

- Strengthen the protection of labor and workers' rights via awareness-raising initiatives and civic education to help combat xenophobia and racial discrimination. African migrants working in non-African countries must also be allowed the right to join trade unions and to form community organizations.

- Boost technical cooperation initiatives with the relevant international agencies, such as the International Organization for Migration (IOM).

# Leveraging the African Diaspora

## The Case of Medics2You

Advancements in digital technologies and communication networks have enabled skilled professionals who have left Africa to bridge the talent gap and shortage of skills in their source or home countries through digital platforms. The United Kingdom is home to thousands of Nigerian nationals (some of whom are second or third-generation migrants) working in the National Health Service (NHS), and the United States, United Arab Emirates, and Saudi Arabia, too, benefit from the brain drain of medical professionals from Nigeria. In the meantime, Nigeria is facing a shortage of medical professionals, and according to WHO, there is only one doctor per 5,000 people. Instead of criticizing the skilled professionals who have migrated to other parts of the world, we should identify ways to mitigate the impact of brain drain and leverage the skills and expertise of these migrants via digital platforms.

Medics2You is a tech startup designed to harness the potential of mobile technology and artificial intelligence to connect patients with more than 18,000 doctors. Largely composed of the Nigerian diaspora in the UK, these doctors are available for video consultations and are allowed to prescribe medication to be delivered to the patient's door via local partners. These doctors work according to international standards and guidelines—demonstrating the potential of technology to leverage the skills of the African diaspora while still operating within legal frameworks.

Moreover, Nigeria's generation of digital natives is one of the fastest-growing markets for smartphones and unique mobile subscriptions, and as such, they are adept at using technology and mobile devices to circumvent their country's limited infrastructure.

It is also important to note that the Medics2You application was developed by medical doctors, innovators, and scientists in Nigeria, and this further demonstrates the potential for collaboration between Africans and the African diaspora in their efforts towards sustainable development in Africa.

## *The African Diaspora and Africa's Development*

Whether they are first, second, or third-generation Africans, the African diaspora and their specialized skills and unique experiences are invaluable to sustainable development and economic growth in Africa. African governments, however, need to effectively tap into this potential through viable, long-term strategies, policies, and initiatives.

This does not necessarily entail forcing the diaspora to return to Africa but rather finding ways to promote collaborations between African professionals across the world. In 2013, the UN General Assembly adopted resolution 68/237, which proclaimed the period between 2015 and 2024 to be the International Decade for People of African Descent.

Under the theme of "People of African descent: recognition, justice, and development," the resolution aimed to boost national, regional, and international cooperation for the full enjoyment of social, civil, economic, political, and cultural rights of all people of African descent; advance the respect for and knowledge of diverse cultures, heritages, and contributions of people of African descent; and ensure the effective and full implementation of the legal frameworks in adherence to the Durban Declaration and Programme of Action and the International Convention on the Elimination of All Forms of Racial

Discrimination. As part of this resolution, the Door of Return Initiative sought to bring those of the African diaspora back to the African continent. The initiative is led by the Maroon community of Accompong, Jamaica, in partnership with Ghana, Zimbabwe, and Nigeria, and is underpinned by the principles of African Renaissance and Pan-Africanism. On August 24, 2017, the first symbolic Door of Return monument was erected as part of the Diaspora Festival in Badagry, Nigeria—a cultural event that commemorates the homecoming of the African diaspora (that is, the descendants of the enslaved Africans of the transatlantic slave trade) and that seeks to advance economic development in the tourism and renewable energy sectors and in terms of infrastructure.

On a more emblematic level, the Door of Return monuments represent Africa's openness to the African diaspora. As the CEO and founder of Most Influential People of African Descent (MIPAD), Kamil Olufowobi (2017. para. 10) writes, "Our ancestors left Africa bound and chained through the doomed 'doors of no return,'" but "I firmly believe that reconciliation and prosperity can offer a 'door of return' for people of African descent back to Africa."

## Practical Tools and Frameworks

The skills and knowledge of the African diaspora, paired with their understanding of African cultural practices, place them in a unique position to develop and implement sustainable development efforts that are suited to Africa's economic, political, and sociocultural needs. Here are salient ways in which to tap into the African diaspora's potential and leverage their skills, experiences, and knowledge for the betterment of African nations. In Guinea, for example, a professional and social data bank and diaspora network were created and established across 110 countries and across 50 states in the United States, while Morocco has increased the political and civil rights of

Moroccans living and working abroad. In the latter's case, the Hassan II Foundation for Moroccans Residing Abroad and the Mohammed V Foundation for Solidarity were formed as nongovernmental organizations dedicated to the coordination of the country's diaspora engagement.

In another example, Kenya created a database and diaspora skills inventory of Kenyans living and working abroad — enabling fast and easy communication with Kenyan migrants in other countries.

## *Harnessing and Managing Remittances*

1. Identify and address the ways in which the large inflow of remittances can adversely impact the exchange rate in African nations.

2. Implement microeconomic interventions to ease the rigidity of the labor market.

3. Strengthen the monthly or quarterly tracking, monitoring, and reporting on the inflow of remittances. There is inadequate data from banks and other providers of remittance services, and this makes it especially challenging to ascertain the true extent and potential of remittances. This also requires greater transparency and efficiency in remittance service providers.

4. Adopt strategies to decrease the costs of remittance transfers. Here, governments in both the source African country and the receiving country should deter migrants from forming exclusive agreements with international money transfer agencies and remittance service providers.

5. Enhance financial literacy among African migrants and encourage them to use formal channels of remittance transfer.

6. Increase access to financial services and open bank accounts in rural regions of Africa so that Africans may fully benefit from the remittances they receive from family members.

7. Further develop and enable greater access to mobile phone networks to facilitate the easy and less expensive transfer of money between the migrant and their family or community in Africa. Here, African governments must improve their telecommunications infrastructure and enforce anti-money laundering regulations.

## *Diasporic Partnerships and Engagements*

1. Connect the African diaspora through trade partnerships and agreements. Whether they have direct or indirect ties to the continent, the African diaspora exists in every part of the world, and therefore, there is an economic potential of capital flow, innovation, spending power, and emerging technologies once the connections between those of the diaspora are deepened.

2. Establish people-to-people connections for members of the African diaspora through conferences, business meetings, summits, and other such events. When African businesses and the businesses of the African diaspora connect, there is potential for greater capital and business relationships. Those of the African diaspora can also be encouraged to invest in local African businesses and institutions.

3. Boost diaspora participation in Africa's development policies, frameworks, initiatives, and efforts. This requires strengthening the operational capacity of African organizations and institutions, such as the AU.

4. Strengthen existing or create new government departments, entities, or institutions to promote and coordinate the harnessing of or tapping into the diaspora's potential and to oversee diaspora affairs.

5. Create and implement the provision of dual citizenship for the African diaspora so that they can easily access and be actively involved in their country of origin's development efforts. Indeed, in not allowing dual citizenship for members of the diaspora, African countries may isolate these members and discourage them from contributing to development plans. Considering the diversity of diasporic communities, plans for dual citizenship need to be comprehensive, clear, and created in consultation with civil society.

## *Intra-African Freedom of Movement*

The Berlin Conference of 1884 created the physical and political borders and territories on the African continent and, as such, defined where Africans could move. But if we want to retain skilled professionals, attract the African diaspora to the continent, and leverage the innovations, expertise, and talents of Africans, we need to enable greater freedom of movement within the continent.

To do so, African governments and institutions must:

- Make freedom of movement a salient pillar of sustainable development and economic growth.

- Ensure that national sovereignty, peace and security, and public order and health will not be compromised in this freedom of movement efforts.

- Reduce tariffs on intra-African goods trade to enable the formation of large-scale businesses and corporations that will be able to compete with those from Western countries.

- Prioritize initiatives and policies to mitigate the impacts of climate change and environmental degradation, especially as these are some of the major reasons for the internal and regional displacement of many Africans.

- Tackle issues of xenophobia and discrimination through cultural awareness programs, workshops, and other education initiatives. This is significant, as we cannot encourage the freedom of movement of Africans across the continent if they are subjected to harassment and violence based on their nationality.

## Chapter 10:
# Building From Within—Why Self-Reliance Is the Key to Africa's Future

> *Governance is everything. Without governance we have nothing.*
>
> –Mo Ibrahim

Good governance in Africa goes beyond corruption and wasted money—it is about the lack of trust African citizens have in their leaders and representatives, the erosion of the social contract, and African governments' inability to grow the economy in ways that truly and fully benefit African citizens. Corruption is, of course, a longstanding issue in Africa, but as the continent experiences ongoing conflict and war, climate change, food insecurity, displacement, and numerous socioeconomic issues, the need for good governance becomes all the more important.

As seen in the aftermath of the Rwandan genocide, ambitious reforms and stronger institutions were paramount in rebuilding the nation. In another example, countries such as Senegal and Gambia have adopted fiscal governance reforms, while Ghana, Botswana, and Mauritius have developed anti-money laundering frameworks. Indeed, instead of looking to the West for inspiration, we need to adopt an endogenous approach and look to our very own countries to learn how we can strengthen good governance in Africa. Countries with good governance often have high levels of political commitment to transparency and accountability. This is seen when they provide open access to their proposed policy actions, free their central finance institutions from internal and external political pressures, and declare the assets of government and public officials. This disclosure is also coupled with regular audits to hold both organizations and individuals accountable.

Good governance also requires a deep respect for the rule of law, and relatedly, citizens must be empowered and informed enough to hold their governments accountable for their actions. No government official or political leader is above the law. Another pivotal element found in countries with good governance is the leveraging of technology to improve the efficiency of government processes and to allow for greater transparency in these processes. From integrating new technology in the management and monitoring of natural resources to using chatbots to mitigate the spreading of misinformation during the COVID-19 pandemic, technology can transform African governments for the better.

## The Power of Good Governance

The term "governance" does not have a fixed or specific meaning but is often used to describe the role of three key players in the functioning and well-being of a society: civil society, the market, and the state. Governance can refer to the management of a country's social and economic resources, and relatedly, good governance is based on the efficient management of the public sector, accountability, the free flow and transparency of information, and legal frameworks for development (such as human rights and justice).

Good governance also relies on the eradication of corruption, fostering civic participation and public debate, enabling the freedom of the press and media, fostering grassroots organizations, and addressing the needs of the most marginalized. Of course, these elements and their implementation depend on each country's historical context and current socioeconomic and political landscapes.

Governance is broader than governance as it includes the relationship or synergy between the state and non-state actors that produce beneficial or acceptable outcomes. The term 'good governance' is often used in discourses on transformation, social justice, and human rights in Africa, but it is worth noting that international financial institutions have co-opted this term to encourage or enforce economic reforms based on capitalism and neoclassical economic theory. In these cases, development and growth in Africa are based on boosting the economy and making markets efficient.

At first glance, these economic reforms appear to aid in achieving good governance and generally improving government capabilities, but in reality, the reforms can actually hinder Africa's development. This is because they are based on the standards or guidelines of international finance institutions that have their own agendas and interests. As seen in previous chapters, we must build a continent that is self-reliant and free from the pressures of international organizations.

## *Governance in the African Context*

It is imperative to explore the concept of good governance with the African context in mind. This is because good governance has long been espoused by African leaders and organizations, such as the AU and NEPAD, and it is usually a condition of foreign aid. It also resonates with millions of Africans who experience the adverse effects of poor governance in their everyday lives and, as such, yearn to hold their leaders accountable through truly democratic systems and processes. While many economists and scholars argue that good governance is a prerequisite for economic growth, case studies of development in poor countries have demonstrated that economic transformation was the key to achieving good governance. Taiwan and South Korea in the 1960s and Malaysia and Thailand in the 1980s are significant examples of this.

The African Development Bank, more specifically, argues that good governance should be founded on effective states, mobilized civil societies, and an efficient private sector while still acknowledging the importance of transparency, accountability, fighting corruption, and enforcing judicial and legal frameworks. Several African countries have continued to build on the governance successes they achieved in the early 1990s by adopting institutional reforms that have contributed to improving government infrastructure and through peaceful transitions of power.

Ghana, for example, underwent significant governance reforms in which emphasis was placed on the separation of powers and checks and balances were employed to transform its political landscape.

These reforms began in the early 1990s, and as a result, Ghana is still frequently seen as an inspiration for the institutionalization of democratic rule. More recently, countries such as Kenya and Morocco have been leading the way in terms of overall governance. Yet, other African countries are struggling to develop and implement strong reforms to eradicate corruption, remedy economic decline, and prevent the formation of a dictatorship or one-party state.

Whether this is due to weak leadership, ongoing violence, and conflict, or the lack of political will, nations such as Somalia, the Central African Republic, and South Sudan continue to be plagued with ineffective and poor structures of governance.

*The Plague of Corruption*

Without good, strong, and inclusive governance, African countries will struggle to achieve their social, economic, and sustainable development goals. As always, the most marginalized peoples and communities will suffer the most. Poor or weak governance is also apparent in countries where the political elite are empowered to embezzle public resources (that should instead be used for improving healthcare, education, technology, and infrastructure) without facing legal consequences.

These elites are less likely to promote anti-poverty policies and programs and without the full and productive participation of the poor, economic growth will be severely limited. Corruption can be described as a pandemic across numerous African countries as numerous high-ranking civil servants and their relatives, as well as business and industry leaders, cannot seem to stop themselves from shamelessly stealing public resources.

South Africa, for example, has a strong constitution and state institutions dedicated to strengthening and supporting constitutional democracy. However, the country has been marked by allegations that the former president, Jacob Zuma, and numerous former government ministers and CEOs of state-owned enterprises strategically planned and executed state capture. The reason? To help the wealthy Gupta family and, in turn, line their own pockets.

Here, the term "state capture" refers to systemic political corruption in which private, influential actors and their interests greatly impact or influence a country's decision-making and legal processes. On June 22, 2022, the country's Chief Justice, Raymond Zondo, released the last installment of the Judicial Commission of Inquiry into State Capture – an inquiry that concluded that the African National Congress, under the leadership of Jacob Zuma, supported and enabled state capture and corruption. This comes at a time when South Africa is struggling to account for millions of dollars lost through dubious contracts that formed part of the national campaign to fight COVID-19.

Other African countries, too, are plagued with shady deals where money goes missing, and the political elite become richer. In Namibia, for instance, the former Justice Minister, Sacky Shangala, and former Fisheries Minister, Bernhardt Esau, are both accused of accepting bribes from a fishing company from Iceland.

Another case of alleged corruption can be seen in Angola, where the daughter, Isabel dos Santos, of the country's former president, is accused of acquiring billions of dollars through unlawful activities.

The damage to systemic corruption not only calls into question the legitimacy of government officials and political leaders but also places a further burden on struggling economies in African countries. When government officials, bureaucrats, and business and industry leaders engage in corruption, they tend to fail to serve the most basic needs or provide basic services to their citizens. Without access to services, including adequate healthcare and education, citizens will be hesitant to fully and actively engage in their country's political landscapes and democratic processes.

Several organizations and blocs, such as ECOWAS, the AU, and the Southern African Development Community (SADC), boast protocols on corruption, but these protocols seldom translate into practice, nor do they deliver tangible gains. Many African leaders, too, highlight their anti-corruption stances, policies, and efforts during the electoral campaign, but few of them prioritize such policies and efforts once they are in office.

# Civil Society as a Watchdog

The constitutions of many African countries include a special provision for civil society to play a role in overseeing the progress of democratic institutions. Some constitutions further encourage civil society to monitor its government, measure the government's ethics and adherence to constitutional principles, and keep an eye on human rights. Of course, this largely depends on citizens knowing and understanding their rights: Citizens can only be a watchdog if they have the knowledge and tools to identify corruption and weak governance.

This makes capacity training workshops and education campaigns all the more significant in Africa, as civil societies must identify the government's deficiencies in delivering public services and defend the human and civil rights of the country's most marginalized groups. Indeed, civil society is a cornerstone when it comes to good, strong, and inclusive governance, so they must be educated and empowered to exert their power as watchdogs.

Good governance greatly relies on civil society engaging in decision-making processes, especially processes concerning the allocation of public and development resources. It is not enough for civil society to sign petitions or show up at the ballot box (although these actions are incredibly important); civil society must demand more from their political actors.

Africa's civil societies have long played a role in decision-making processes, in issues of land redistribution, in challenging corruption and government policy, in protecting human rights, and in positively contributing to the development of their countries and the betterment of their communities. While the role of civil society in political and socioeconomic landscapes cannot be dismissed, we must also acknowledge that the funding for civil society organizations (CSOs) in Africa has been and still is a major concern.

CSOs in Africa tend to be funded by Western nations and are therefore seen as an extension of exploitative countries in the Global North. Considering the West's ongoing interference in African affairs and regime changes, the skepticism and hostilities towards CSOs are not completely unfounded. Nevertheless, we cannot discount the role played by civil society in pushing for new laws, policies, or programs and in acting as a watchdog—a role that holds governments to account for their promises and commitments.

This, in turn, can improve the quality of public services and the overall effectiveness of their government. Active citizenship and civic participation depend on civil society's awareness of their civil rights and responsibilities and how they may hold their government accountable. For example, individuals or community leaders may have concerns over governance and service delivery, but may not be aware of the channels or tools available to them to make their voices heard. This is especially problematic in countries where civil society is suppressed, human rights are severely lacking, and when political elites and problematic donor relations supersede the basic needs of society.

## *Protests: A Pillar of Democracy?*

For civil society to act as a watchdog, they need to have viable institutional capacity, a functioning legal framework, and a safe political environment. So, how can civil society exert their role as a watchdog? Firstly, civil society can voice their concerns through protests and demonstrations. These actions have long been criticized by governments, the media, and by fellow citizens. Protests (and those who participate in them) are often seen as unreasonable, destructive, and unlawful, but they are also a notable way to speak truth to power.

Historically, protests have been the driving force behind social justice and activist movements and have helped many marginalized groups fight against injustice and dehumanization. They have also been a key factor in helping marginalized peoples attain basic human and civil rights—rights that many of us may take for granted today.

Moreover, when human rights and freedoms are suppressed or restricted, protesting is usually the first tool citizens use to make their voices heard. Given the nature of protests, they are also powerful in demonstrating the importance of mass mobilization, community, and national or even transnational solidarity. This is one of the main reasons why governments and other political actors are quick to silence protests and critical voices, to outright ban demonstrations, or to misuse law enforcement to target protestors. Numerous protests reveal the flaws in *good* governance, the vulnerabilities of political actors, and the fragility of policies, frameworks, and tactics.

This makes protesting all the more important for a healthy and functioning democracy and for sustainable development. Significantly, protests also make clear to governments that civil society can (and will) mobilize to challenge the state when it misuses its power, prioritizes the desires of foreign donors over the needs of citizens, and lacks accountability and transparency.

This is not to say that protests cannot be destructive or counterintuitive at times, nor should we ignore the imprisonments and deaths of protestors, but we must acknowledge that protests are impactful when governments refuse to include civil society in pertinent socioeconomic policies or strategies or refuse to engage with civil society on various issues. Besides, there are countless examples of protests forcing governments to reconsider decisions, policies, or laws and instead have a dialogue with their citizens. In the early 2000s in South Africa, for example, the Treatment Action Campaign (TAC) mobilized South Africans and protested in the streets to force the government to provide treatment for HIV/AIDS. The TAC has largely been credited with successfully pressuring the South African government to make antiretroviral medication available to South Africans.

### Africa's Youth Demonstrations

Youth demonstrations have had a powerful impact on African governments. Young people comprise the largest proportion of the African population, but they are rarely well represented and are notably excluded from development processes across the continent. This motivates them to engage in protests and demonstrations to have a say in and transform the systems of governance that affect their day-to-day lives. Since the Arab Spring in the early 2010s, young Africans have taken to the streets to challenge dictatorships, unpopular socioeconomic policies, corruption, class inequality, and unfair elections.

While these protests and demonstrations usually fail to initiate systemic economic, social, and political change, we cannot (and should not) discount the quick and efficient mobilization of Africa's youth. Various youth movements in Egypt, Burkina Faso, and Senegal, for instance, have helped end the long-term rule of certain presidents, including Hosni Mubarak (Egypt), Blaise Compaoré (Burkina Faso), and Abdoulaye Wade (Senegal). In other examples, youth protests or demonstrations have challenged constitutional amendments that would extend presidential term limits. This was evident in the cases of Pierre Nkurunziza (Burundi), Joseph Kabila (DRC), and Alpha Condé (Guinea). Such protests tend to be popular and concentrated in urban areas of African countries, as a significant amount of Africa's youth who reside in these areas are subjected to high cost of living, high unemployment rates, and other socioeconomic issues. In addition, the youth in Africa's urban areas are generally easier to mobilize as most of them have access to mobile phones, the internet, and social media.

Africa's youth can express their frustrations with their governments by joining (or forming) political parties, voting in local and national elections, or establishing their own civil society organizations. Many of them deem protests and demonstrations as more effective, quicker to produce results, and less likely to allow manipulations from political actors. In fact, even when they engage in elections, they may still feel unheard, unrepresented, and marginalized.

This is exacerbated by pre- and post-election violence and by the fact that Africa's youth may be deterred from joining political parties as they lack the wealth and status of established political party members. As Africa's youth forgo traditional political channels and criticize the hierarchical structure of political parties, they continue to challenge socioeconomic issues through the platforms they find to be more inclusive of their demographic.

### The 2019 Sudan Protests

The power of protests and the quick and efficient mobilization of Africa's youth are greatly demonstrated in the 2019 protests in Sudan. Beginning towards the end of 2018, the protests were sparked by price increases of basic needs, such as fuel and bread. The protests soon gained momentum, and by April 2019, President Omar al-Bashir had been removed from office. Al-Bashir had been in power for 30 years, but his deposition was followed by the establishment of a Transitional Military Council.

As a result, protests continued with a keen demand for a civilian democracy—leading to the formation of the Sovereignty Council of Sudan. Largely composed of members of the Transitional Military Council and members of the protest movement, this Council took over the leadership of Sudan on August 4, 2019. Soon, the former political system was disbanded, a draft constitution was developed, and the path to the next election was established. Unlike several other youth demonstrations in Africa, the 2019 protests in Sudan successfully forced the military to form a coalition government, and protesters remained strong in their demand for a civilian government.

Several youth protests and demonstrations across Africa struggle with the aftermath of protests. This is because the military is deployed to quell protests but also tends to serve the interests of the political elites. In many cases, the military uses excessive force and live ammunition—leading to the severe injuries and even death of protesters. This occurred during the protests in Sudan, but the protesters were determined to bring about meaningful change. They regrouped and continued even while experiencing military brutality. Once the protesters gained international support, the military had no choice but to give in to their calls for a civilian government.

The strong leadership, clear plans, and relentless work of these protesters illustrate the power of youth movements and demonstrations that are able to maintain momentum, even in the face of military oppression and violence. We should not underestimate this power and determination. It is also worth noting that the protests in Sudan included the active participation of women. They had long been oppressed under al-Bashir's leadership and used the protests as an opportunity to demand equal rights. It is often the case that men dominate the coordination, planning, and performing of protests, and women are discouraged from or fail to participate in such protests. Of course, safety is a concern, as sexual violence has long been used as a weapon against women protesters.

Nevertheless, the protests in Sudan not only included the active participation of women but were also led by young women. From occupying the spaces in front of military headquarters to mobilizing more protesters through graffiti, youth movements and demonstrations in Africa should not be underestimated. The power of young women, too, should not be dismissed.

## *The Role of the Media*

Civil society can only serve as a watchdog if the public has access to information. Several governments across the globe place restrictions on the media, rely on propaganda, and spread misinformation to serve their own interests. Yet, the media is dependent upon the public to expose corruption, the misuse of public resources, and bad governance, and as such, some civil society organizations have even created their own media houses to monitor and report on these issues.

The media also includes social media platforms, and as seen in the Arab Spring protests, social media not only mobilized citizens but also helped in the overthrow of governments. Whether mainstream media or social media (or both) is employed for the organizing and mobilizing of civil society, the media, when yielded responsibly, has the power to transform societies and governments.

Drawing from the example of state capture in South Africa, the media served as a platform for civil society to voice their discontent and frustrations regarding systemic corruption in the country. Here, the media's gathering of facts and information and reporting on state capture was heavily aided by civil society – placing even more pressure on the South African government and law enforcement to take action against the perpetrators. The media can only function as an agent of political and socioeconomic change and can only hold the government accountable in countries where media operations are free from restrictions.

Indeed, in countries where it is highly regulated and censored by the government, the media is less likely to be a credible source of information for civil society. It is, therefore, unsurprising that countries that violate human rights tend to have many restrictions on the media—severely hindering civil society's access to accurate and unbiased information and, in turn, impeding their efforts to hold their governments accountable for any wrongdoing.

## Self-Reliance Is Not Self-Isolation

The term "self-reliance" refers to one's ability to rely on their own resources and capacities instead of relying on those of others. In the context of African development and progress, self-reliance connotes the continent's capacity and willingness to use its own human and natural resources, talents, and unique features to boost its sociocultural, economic, and political landscapes. Africa's recent history is dark. The transatlantic slave trade subjected African slaves to horrendous abuses, destroyed African families and communities, and drained the continent of millions of its people. The advent of European colonial rule, too, exploited the continent's resources, forced Africans to toil for the betterment of European economies, and saw the demise of once-prosperous African kingdoms and empires.

Achieving independence from the colonial powers, however, was only the first step. Precolonial Africa boasted advancements in mathematics, science, astronomy, and literature, had sophisticated trade networks that reached all the way to India and China, and its peoples and lands lived together as one. The death and destruction that came with colonial rule lives on in contemporary Africa: Foreign countries continue to exploit the continent and its resources, interfere in Africa's democracies and anti-imperial efforts, and target Africans in the consumption of Western goods and services. For Africa, economic, sociocultural, and political self-reliance is not a pipe dream; it is the only way for the continent to finally break free from colonial shackles and prosper.

While African nations can and should build their political, social, and economic landscapes from within, this does not necessarily mean that they should isolate themselves from the wider international community. This is especially significant as African nations are still expected to compete in global markets. The COVID-19 pandemic placed immense strain on African economies, but it also demonstrated the dire need for African countries to ensure that their economies are more resilient to external shocks. Whether this occurs through the development of more conducive legal frameworks that support investment flows and trade into African countries or the revitalization of intra-African partnerships and collaborations, the resilience of governments, economies, and societies in Africa must be fostered.

## The Value of Economic Self-Reliance

Economic self-reliance (ESR) refers to an individual's capacity to gain and maintain economic resources that go beyond their basic needs. This theory's focus on individuals remains Western and capitalist in its approach, but we argue that economic self-reliance can be achieved by entire African countries. This does not entail African countries completely isolating their economies from global markets; rather, it promotes the idea of these countries building their economies from within so that they can eradicate their foreign debt and become less dependent on foreign aid and investment.

Importantly, African economies can still be open to foreign investments, but a strong sense of self-reliance will aid these economies in avoiding buckling under the pressure of a foreign state or corporation's exploitative terms and conditions. In other words, African countries can enter into economic agreements on equal footing with their Western partners. When an economy is self-reliant, it is more likely to mitigate or even avoid the consequences of negative external and internal economic shocks. Africa's vast natural resources and untapped potential are key to overcoming socioeconomic challenges and achieving self-reliance.

For example, Africa has significant potential to ensure continent-wide food security and to dominate global food markets, yet it continues to be dependent on external or foreign markets for its food needs. In fact, the African continent spends around $50 billion per annum on food imports—increasing Africa's dependency and vulnerability and impeding any efforts towards economic growth and development (Njiwa, 2023). As of 2023, regional trade (within Africa) comprises a mere 14.4% of all African exports, but this statistic can increase to 33% should the continent leverage regional trade opportunities. Regional or intra-African trade can reduce import costs, boost local economies, maximize local production, and increase the resilience of food systems.

Another benefit of economic self-reliance and intra-African trade is the development of supply chains that can adapt to local needs and contexts. Indeed, the needs of an African country differ from those of a European or Asian country, and as such, we need economic strategies that are locally responsive and not simply copied and pasted from other countries. Of course, this is easier said than done, and to boost economic self-reliance in Africa, post-harvest losses must be reduced, the distribution of agricultural products must be efficient and fair, and farmers must be incentivized to produce high-quality crops (and meet market needs). As discussed earlier, the African Continental Free Trade Area (AfCFTA) acknowledges the multi-faceted nature of economic self-reliance and, therefore, includes provisions to address local needs. Yet, regional organizations, African governments, and all relevant stakeholders must also play an active role in promoting regional trade and integration, establishing and maintaining an environment that enables economic growth, and investing in infrastructure. Should African governments fail, civil society must hold them accountable.

The cycle of economic dependency, debt, and underdevelopment has long plagued Africa, but as seen during the fight for liberation, resilience, too, is rife among African nations. Debt, for example, must be suspended or renegotiated to allow African countries to instead focus their repayments on social expenditures, but ultimately, the need for foreign aid must be completely eliminated. To escape this foreign aid and debt trap, African countries should find other financing options and expand these financing options to meet local needs and demands. Here are a few options for alternative financing.

*Reforms in Pension Fund Mandates*

According to the regulations of many African governments, pensions are invested quite conservatively to protect the savings of the pensioners. While this protection is important, an overly conservative strategy can hinder economic growth and even punish future generations. African governments can, therefore, reform pension mandates to allocate a fraction of these funds to go towards investments that will almost certainly guarantee economic growth and development. Examples of such investments include business start-ups and improvements in infrastructure—but these investments must not come at the cost or safety of pensioners and their funds.

Some African countries have already initiated such reforms: Nigeria, for instance, introduced the Pension Reform Act of 2014 to strengthen fund management and administration, expand coverage, increase accountability, and remedy malpractices. The Act also featured stricter penalties concerning violations of its provisions, the inclusion of the informal sector, and the accessing of benefits in the event of job loss. Bolstered by the flexible nature of investment options and more efficient payment processes, among many other provisions, the past decade has demonstrated notable progress in Nigeria's pension system owing to the Pension Reform Act of 2014.

*Alternative Lending Options*

Traditional banking institutions often have strict security requirements and regulations that can make it challenging for small businesses or start-ups to acquire loans. If commercial banks or financial institutions cannot be drivers of economic growth, then we must support alternative lending options that are responsive to the needs of African businesses and business owners. The African Guarantee Fund (AGF), for example, is a specialized guarantee provider that seeks to facilitate economic development and reduce poverty in Africa. This is achieved by providing access to funds to small- and medium-sized businesses, assisting these businesses with capacity development, and boosting intra-African partnerships. In the latter's case, the AGF partners with 250 financial institutions across 43 countries on the continent to reclaim Africa's fiscal sovereignty, pave a path determined by aspirations instead of debt, and boost self-reliance and innovation.

## The Creative Economy

African cultural pride and creativity were on full display during the 2023 Africa Cup of Nations hosted by Côte d'Ivoire: The opening ceremony was marked by traditional songs and dances and sports players and audience members clad in traditional attire. The views of kente (Ghana) and bògòlanfini (Mali) are a significant representation of Africa's cultural diversity and unique spirit and energy, but they also remind us of the potential of African-made goods and Africa's creative economy. From African fashion designers weaving together traditional fabrics with trendy clothing designs and cuts to homegrown music genres, such as Amapiano, gaining international recognition and awards, Africa's economic self-reliance (and cultural pride) can also be driven by its creative economies and arts and cultural sectors. These industries not only introduce the rest of the world to African talent, goods, and diversity, but the industries also create employment and generate income.

Africa's creative economy only accounts for $58.4 billion (or 2.9%) of global exports of creative goods (Kaba, 2024). This is relatively low in comparison to other countries across the world, and as such, the creative economy only makes up less than 1% of the continent's GDP. This does not mean that Africa is lacking in its creativity; rather, the continent has yet to fully and truly capitalize on its creative industries. As seen during the African Cup of Nations and in other similar events, Africa's creative industries can only reach their potential once we have increased the demand for related goods. The regular continental and international consumption of African-made products can significantly boost and diversify local economies, while also fast-tracking the development of value chains at both national and regional levels. In turn, this can increase domestic revenue and strengthen efforts towards African cultural pride and unity.

To achieve this diversification of the African economies, political leaders and cultural icons, such as musicians, sports players, and actors, must show a high level of commitment to elevating Africa on global creative markets. Even an African actor donning traditional attire on the red carpet can inspire Africans (and others) to consume cultural, African-made goods and support local designers, brands, and businesses. The commitment from political leaders and cultural icons must also coincide with alleviating any and all obstacles that make it challenging for African entrepreneurs to access markets in other regions of Africa and outside of Africa. This requires flexible financing options, boosting manufacturing infrastructure, and implementing more practical measures to support small and medium businesses. In doing so, we can advance more sustainable and inclusive economies, reignite Pan-African unity and solidarity, and make the continent less dependent on foreign aid in the future.

## The International Community's Responsibility to Africa

When the Ghanaian diplomat, Kofi Annan, served as the Secretary-General of the United Nations (1997 to 2006), he challenged the international community to develop and agree on basic principles and processes concerning when intervention is necessary to protect humanity against the violation of human rights. As such, during the 2005 World Summit, the UN General Assembly endorsed the Responsibility to Protect (R2P) as a means to establish international norms for the prevention of genocide, war crimes, ethnic cleansings, and crimes against humanity. While this seems like a great framework to reduce violence, the implementation of R2P is not without criticism. In 2011, in Libya, for example, the UN Security Council approved Resolution 1973 to highlight the responsibility of Libyan authorities to protect the country's population. The resolution also demanded an immediate ceasefire, an end to attacks on civilians, a ban on flights in Libya's airspace, and stricter sanctions on Gaddafi's government. The resolution passed with 10 member states in favor of the resolution and five member states, including Russia and China, abstaining.

Nevertheless, it is alleged by critics of the resolution that NATO's forces went beyond their mandate to act in ways that led to the overthrow of Gaddafi's government. Moreover, it was also reported that Libyan civilians had been supplied with weapons, and the no-fly zone was selectively implemented. It is unsurprising that many began to question the actions of the West (via the UN and NATO) in intervening in Libya's sovereignty. As discussed earlier, the West had significant interests in overthrowing Gaddafi and installing a government that was more amenable to the West's agenda and economic exploits. The R2P was further criticized when, in that same year, the West put forward proposals to the UN to intervene in Syria.

Here, the United States government made numerous attempts over 2011 to 2013 to pass UN Security Council resolutions to justify their military intervention in the Syrian Civil War. Again, Russia and China challenged these resolutions and accused the United States of abusing R2P for their own interests.

Considering that the United States evoked R2P to support a regime change in Libya, there were valid concerns surrounding these proposed resolutions. Indeed, the demand for a ceasefire in Libya resulted in a civil war, and the political, military, and humanitarian consequences had a ripple effect on nearby countries. Coupled with the fact that humanitarian intervention can be underpinned by the intervening country's self-interest, the insufficient evidence of R2P's successes, and the inconsistent application of R2P, the legitimacy of such commitments and Western-dominated international organizations is still being questioned.

## African /olutions to African Conflicts

Despite the failures and criticism of the R2P, it is worth noting that intervention to prevent or end war crimes, human rights violations, genocide, and crimes against humanity remains a strong pillar of conflict resolution. As Africans, we have a responsibility to intervene when a neighboring country is committing atrocities against its civilians. Similar to building economic resilience, African countries should also revise their responses to peace and security threats on the continent. This is pivotal, as conflicts and violence in one African country tend to spill over into neighboring African countries.

To ensure peace and security, African countries must not only be represented in global decision-making and governance processes, but it must also foster intra-African cooperation to alleviate conflicts and security concerns. That is, African governments build their capacities and proactively engage in continental peace, security, and development efforts.

Africa's recent history is teeming with examples of regional unity and solidarity, but the continent is still plagued by ongoing conflicts, ethnic tensions, and violent extremism. The human cost of conflict is devastating, and international organizations must expand their scope to be pro-Africa, legitimate, accountable, inclusive, responsive, and democratic. The UN, for example, should not only intervene in African conflicts when Western interests and agendas are threatened. Similarly, African countries must strengthen their sustainable peace and security initiatives according to local contexts, needs, and priorities, and engage in regional partnerships where possible. Besides, no one understands Africa better than Africans themselves, and while we must find African solutions to peace and security threats, the international community is not absolved of its responsibilities to Africa.

Should Africa partner with international organizations, such partnerships must still be based on African contexts and needs rather than on the vested interests of the UN's most powerful member states. Africa also needs to be able to enter these partnerships on an equal footing so as to not collapse under the pressure of Western influence and interests. And if Africa continues to be denied a seat at global negotiating tables, then it needs to release itself from the shackles of neocolonialism, foreign aid, and Westernization and instead, create its own tables. This is all the more important as peace and security issues cannot be separated from development issues.

## *Bringing an End to Economic Exploitation*

Mngomezulu and Fayayo (2019, p. 13) write that while "it is true that the international community has invested time and resources in addressing African conflicts, it is equally true that most of the African conflicts could have been avoided if the international community was not covertly and overtly involved." The international community and, more specifically, Western countries have intervened in African political affairs and governance when the former's vested interests were threatened. But a similar dynamic can be seen in mostly Western multinational corporations (MNCs).

### *Oil in the Niger Delta*

When crude oil was first discovered by the Shell Petroleum Development Corporation (SPDC) in Nigeria in 1956, it did not take long for oil drilling to commence. In fact, drilling began in 1958 but being one of the biggest oil-producing countries in Africa has done little to ensure peace and security in the country. It is not a coincidence that resource-rich regions in Africa are also the most conflict-ridden.

The international community has vested interests in these regions, so it is unsurprising that tensions between multinational oil corporations and the Niger Delta's ethnic minorities soon turned into conflict. While we cannot attribute all of Nigeria's security problems to the international community, the competition for oil remains one of the major reasons for ongoing conflict in the Niger Delta.

The United States of America, more specifically, has fueled much of the conflict in this region. Using the justification of "constructive engagement" the Clinton administration ignored the atrocities committed by Sani Abacha and his government to protect their own oil interests in the region.

In 1998, Clinton even endorsed Abacha's candidacy for the presidency. With the assurance that the international community would not challenge the United States' endorsement, Abacha continued his repression of political rivals and his violence against civilians. Yet, even after Abacha's death, the United States still directly or indirectly fueled conflict in Nigeria, and when the local communities in the Niger Delta expressed their frustration with the fact that they were not benefiting from the local oil industry, the United States supported the Nigerian government's violence against the civilians.

Moreover, when the local communities tried to demand control over the oil reserves, the United States supplied the Nigerian army with Chevron boats and helicopters to help the army terrorize the local communities. The United States' actions were supported by oil companies, including Shell, Mobil, and of course, Chevron.

## Coltan Mining in the DRC

The Democratic Republic of Congo (DRC) is rich in resources such as diamond, cobalt, zinc, and gold, to name a few examples, that are estimated to be worth $24 trillion (Ojewale, 2021). Yet, it is the country's coltan that has made it a target for Western MNCs. The DRC is the world's largest producer of coltan, derived from the name columbite-tantalite, a metallic ore that is refined into tantalum powder. This powder is then used to manufacture heat-resistant capacitors in electronic devices, such as cell phones and laptops. With a global market value of $1,504.81 in 2019 and a growth rate of 5.58% per annum, coltan is a high-demand commodity. The mining of coltan, however, has come at a terrible human cost.

In addition to causing immense environmental damage, coltan mines are rife with child labor, violence, and human rights abuses. A recent report by ENACT Africa (Ojewale, 2021) revealed that the exploitation of coltan is destroying ecosystems and wildlife habitats in the DRC. That is, animals are being displaced—making them susceptible to being poached—and the chemicals used in the washing of coltan pollute the water systems in the DRC. The mining of coltan requires miners to dig craters in streambeds, remove the soil from the surface, and collect the coltan underground. But what seems like a relatively simple process is far more dangerous and nefarious. The DRC's Ministry of Mining recommends that miners dig no deeper than 30 meters but many of them dig as deep as 200 meters and these holes are seldom covered after the mining has stopped—leading to landslides that have trapped coltan miners underground.

Without proper regulations and laws, coltan mining can also be fatal. In September 2020, 50 miners died in Mwenga, Shabunda, owing to coltan mining, while tensions between mining cooperatives and coltan mining corporations have escalated into deadly violence. Despite anti-child-labor laws, most of the DRC's coltan is mined using child labor, and here, more than 40,000 children dig in very dangerous conditions (Ojewale, 2021). These children are also subjected to harassment, abuse, and numerous mining-related illnesses, and of course, their labor in the mines prevents them from receiving an education. However, it is challenging to ascertain the true quantity of coltan mined by children, as much of the DRC's coltan is traded in an underground economy and then smuggled into a global supply chain.

The lack of regulations in these mining sites also means that miners are exposed to radon, a radioactive substance, on a daily basis. The mines are also rife with rape, prostitution, sexually transmitted diseases, and child trafficking. The numerous international certification protocols, such as the Dodd-Frank Act, the Regional Certification Mechanism of the International Conference of the Great Lakes Region, and the Organisation for Economic Cooperation and Development Due Diligence Guidance, have not prevented or significantly reduced the use of children in the coltan mines.

Addressing and mitigating the human and environmental cost of coltan mining in the DRC entails the government reforming and expanding the Congolese Environment Agency, civil society training others to monitor and report on labor violations and abuses in these mining sites, and forcing coltan companies to lessen the environmental risks related to their operations. But, if we consider the high demands of tech products, the electronics industry requires a large and steady supply of coltan—making it near impossible to force coltan and tech companies to prioritize humans and the environment over massive profits.

To address and eliminate the exploitation of MNCs in Africa, we need to boost intra-African trade, promote ethnic tolerance, strengthen political leadership, eradicate corruption, and grow local economies. Indeed, an Africa that is self-reliant and united will make it challenging for the international community and MNCs to continue their exploitation of the continent's resources and people. While it may seem challenging, it is not insurmountable.

## Practical Tools and Frameworks

*The Cornerstones of Good and Inclusive Governance*

- Prioritizing peaceful coexistence (and this entails remedying internal conflicts and violence).

- Mitigating the impacts of climate change and health pandemics.

- Boosting regional cooperation.

- Addressing socioeconomic inequalities and inequities.

- Ensure the freedom of independent press and media.

- Promote the full and active participation of civil societies in economic and political systems. This is especially relevant for marginalized populations, such as women, the youth, the poor, and ethnic or religious minorities.

- Engage in robust national dialogues (with input from civil societies) on institutional reforms.

- Ensure the clear separation of powers and adopt effective checks and balances to boost accountability and transparency among political actors.

- Address and remove all obstacles that hinder voter registration and turnout.

- Encourage the participation of civil societies in the constitution-making process.

- Make sure that the constitution is protected from and against abuses of power.

- Promote a constitution amendment process that is robust and free from the influence and manipulations of opportunistic political actors and leaders.

- Develop and implement education projects and programs that aid citizens in understanding the constitution and its provisions. African countries' citizens and their diaspora must play an important role in the shaping of legal and institutional environments.

- Ensure that development needs are being met at the pace expected by African citizens—to make it less challenging to implement or adopt social reforms and to engage in transformation efforts.

## Civil /ociety and Holding Governments Accountable

As daunting and dangerous as it may be in more repressive and authoritarian African contexts, civil society can still play a major role in holding their governments and political actors accountable (and pressuring them to boost transparency).

This can be achieved by:

- Eradicating laws that deliberately suppress civil society and replacing them with those that encourage civil society to grow within their environments.

- Collaborating with relevant stakeholders to fight corruption, improve the standard of living, and advance development goals.

- Involving civil society in matters related to governance, such as consulting CSOs on policy development and implementation.

- Fostering robust and constructive debates and discussions between civil society and democratic leaders.

- Prioritizing nonviolent protests, demonstrations, and other measures to maintain social order while also voicing concerns.

- Addressing misinformation and disinformation in the media, especially in news media.

- Encouraging the formation of internally funded civil society organizations (CSO's) to prevent foreign interests and agendas from being prioritized.

- Establishing formal and informal platforms for civil society to engage in socioeconomic and political affairs.

- Developing and implementing a clear and comprehensive strategy to protect civil society and encourage their participation in decision- and policymaking.

- Leveraging education and awareness-raising campaigns to educate citizens on their rights and responsibilities. This must work hand-in-hand with making information more accessible to civic groups and citizens.

- Supporting the formation of coalitions, collaborations, and networks for collective impact.

- Adapting social accountability strategies and tools so that community members, leaders, and activists can constructively engage with local government and authorities.

- Ensuring the inclusion of underrepresented or marginalized groups in civil society, including women, people with disabilities, and religious and ethnic minorities.

## *Reducing the Exploitation of MNCs in Africa*

| Who Is Responsible? | What Can Be Done? |
| --- | --- |
| African Governments | - Identify weaknesses in existing laws, regulations, and procedures.<br>- Reform labor laws and recruitment practices so that they are fair, ethical, transparent, and protect vulnerable Africans from the exploitation of MNCs.<br>- Boost transparency in the supply chain to prevent and stop the trafficking of miners.<br>- Reform public procurement processes to prevent labor exploitation |

| | |
|---|---|
| | and trafficking.
• Establish independent agencies or organizations dedicated to monitoring and reporting on coltan mining sites.
• Enforce the existing laws that ensure fair and safe working conditions and decent wages.
• Regulatory institutions must have the capacity to respond to concerns over the exploitation of labor and the environment on coltan mining sites.
• Force MNCs to self-regulate their operations through tax inducements and nonfinancial incentives.
• Enforce penalties on MNCs that do not comply with labor and environmental laws and |

|  |  |
|---|---|
|  | regulations. |
|  | • Develop a legitimate and productive coltan industry and economy with fair wages and safe working conditions. |
| Civil Society | • Place pressure on MNCs as those that sell well-known brands may be quick to respond should they want to avoid negative publicity. |
|  | • Disseminate information and awareness on the dangers of artisanal mining and labor exploitation to local communities. |
|  | • Organize and mobilize local communities for protests and demonstrations against child labor and unsafe conditions in the mines. |
|  | • Work with the government to develop and adopt a globally binding certification |

|  |  |
|---|---|
|  | system. |
|  | • Develop action plans to record and investigate corruption, labor violations, and human rights abuses by MNCs. |
|  | • Exert pressure on the AU and other such organizations to hire rapporteurs dedicated to reporting on the criminal trading of coltan and, more generally, of African resources. |
|  | • Collaborate with NGOs and NPOs that are dedicated to improving ethical, environmental, and social issues in local and global supply chains. |
|  | • Work with environmental organizations and groups to identify ways to address the issues of landslides, loss of habitat, soil erosion, and water pollution as a result of coltan mining and other |

| | |
|---|---|
| | forms of mining. |
| The International Community | - A global watchdog institution dedicated to setting regulations for, monitoring, and investigating coltan (and other forms of mining) MNCs must be established. The institution must be independent and free from vested interests.<br><br>- Hold MNCs accountable for their exploitative practices in African nations.<br><br>- Challenge large tech companies through protests, boycotts, and demonstrations. |

# Chapter 11:
# Towards a Solution—African Unity and Economic Prosperity

> *We are pro-Africa. We breathe, we dream, we live Africa because Africa and humanity are inseparable.*
>
> C-Robert Sobukwe

Contemporary discourses on development in Africa struggle to find a balance between dependence and self-reliance. Despite decades since its independence from colonial rule, Africa continues to be manipulated to remain dependent on the Global North. The alternative, self-reliance, is also tricky as it stands in contrast to our globalized world and the need for Africa's greater integration into the global economy. As globalization and digital technologies render physical borders insignificant, how can Africa imagine a liberated and prosperous future?

The AU's Agenda 2063, titled *The Africa We Want,* includes a focus on the mobilization of African people and their ownership of Africa's programs; self-reliance and the continent funding its own development; the need for continental unity (including island and land-locked states); inclusive and accountable governance and institutions in all spheres; and African people and people of African descent serving as agents of change and transformation.

These are ambitious ideals to which a continent should aspire — still grappling with ongoing conflicts and wars, economic and social inequality, corruption, poverty, and displacement. The prosperity of Africa greatly depends on the strength of its governments, institutions, and populations.

For example, strong democratic processes are needed to force a generation of incumbents to relinquish political power, civil society must be empowered to challenge governments, institutions, and MNCs, and African people must have their basic rights and needs met to fully participate in the betterment of their local communities, societies, and countries.

## The African Way: Pan-Africanism and Development

Pan-Africanism refers to the idea that people of African descent have common interests and should, therefore, be unified. Throughout history, this idea has been expressed through cultural or political movements, and like many other philosophies, there are numerous variants or schools of thought in Pan-Africanism. In the political context, Pan-Africanists envision an African nation that is unified and in which those of the African diaspora can live.

Such ideas emerged in the mid-19th century in the Western world, and early Pan-Africanists highlighted the many commonalities between African people and Black people in the United States. Some of these Pan-Africanists promoted the idea that Black Americans should separate from white America and form their own nation, while others believed that Black Americans should return to their homeland and create this new nation in Africa.

## A Brief History

*20th Century Pan-Africanism*

Exploring the beliefs of the early Pan-Africanists is important for understanding how and why Pan-Africanism developed and evolved throughout history. But it is worth noting that the 'father' of modern Pan-Africanism is the American sociologist, historian, and civil rights activist W. E. B. Du Bois. Du Bois (cited in Kuryla, 2024, para. 4) was a strong advocate for the study of African history and culture, and based on his own studies, he made the following famous statement: The "problem of the twentieth century is the problem of the color line." The color line is not only applicable to the context of the United States but also to the suffering of Africans (owing to European colonial rule) on the African continent. As the years went on, Pan-Africanism garnered more and more thinkers, including Marcus Garvey, who believed in the cause of African independence; Senegalese politician and cultural theorist Léopold Senghor; Martinican author and politician Aimé Césaire; and Kenyan anti-colonial activist and politician, Jomo Kenyatta.

Many modern Pan-Africanists drew inspiration from and exchanged ideas about African nations and the United States — to the extent that Pan-Africanists formed a Black Atlantic intellectual community in which commonalities were highlighted, and geographical distance (and forced migration via the transatlantic slave trade) was relegated to the background. Césaire and Senghor, for example, were influenced by Du Bois and many Harlem Renaissance writers, such as Langston Hughes and Claude McKay. Yet, by the 1940s, the intellectual leadership of African Americans had subsided, and Africans had now led the Pan-Africanist movement. One of the most influential leaders was Ghana's Kwame Nkrumah, who argued that European colonial rule in Africa would come to an end if Africans could politically and economically unite. As more and more African nations gained independence in the 1960s and 1970s, countless African Americans celebrated the new era for Africa.

Africa's independence from colonial rule coincided with the reemergence of Pan-Africanist thought in the United States. Indeed, the 1960s and 1970s in the United States were marked by the civil rights movement and the Black Power movement. It was not uncommon for African Americans to adopt African cultural practices and dress styles to connect to their African roots. Leading Pan-Africanist thinkers of this time included Senegalese anthropologist, historian, and physicist Cheikh Anta Diop and American activist, professor of Africana studies, and creator of Kwanzaa, Maulana Ron Karenga. As an iteration of Pan-Africanism, Afrocentrism grew in popularity in the United States during the 1980s, and African culture and thought were adopted as a means to correct the intellectual and cultural dominance of Europe.

During the 20th century, many Pan-Africanists attempted to institutionalize Pan-Africanist thought and create formal organizations to operate alongside the intellectual contributions of Pan-Africanist thinkers. The first meeting focused on discussing Pan-Africanist ideas and occurred in London in 1900. Organized by Trinidadian lawyer and activist Henry Sylvester Williams, the meeting was attended by Black intellectuals from Great Britain, the West Indies, Africa, and the United States.

The following decades saw a few more Pan-Africanist meetings, and by the 1940s, focus was placed on Pan-Africanists from Africa, including Kenyatta and Nkrumah, and their hopes for independence. Here, the idea of African unity was mainly limited to the African continent as anti-colonial movements were gaining more prominence. While much of the Western world scoffed at the idea of African unity, the regional alliances that had been formed among African countries united to fight for Africa's independence. In 1963, for example, Kwame Nkrumah (Ghana), Emperor Haile Selassie (Ethiopia), and Gamal Abdel Nasser (Egypt) held a meeting with 32 new independent African nations, and this led to the formation of the Organization for African Unity (OAU). The OAU was established to advance the political, economic, and social integration of Africa, promote the solidarity of African states, eliminate all forms of colonialism, defend African independence and sovereignty, and boost their cooperation efforts for the betterment of African peoples. The OAU was succeeded by the African Union in 2002.

*The /uppression of Pan-Africanists*

Pan-Africanist intellectuals, academics, writers, and students have not always been welcomed in African countries. In the immediate aftermath of independence, some African countries followed in their former colonial power's footsteps and reproduced their oppressive structures and machinery. Soon, Pan-Africanists found themselves at odds with the ruling elites, especially in newly independent African countries that were moving towards authoritarianism. Facing the possibility of imprisonment, hundreds of Pan-Africanists, such as Ngũgĩ wa Thiong'o (Kenya), Nawal El Saadawi (Egypt), Ama Ata Aidoo (Ghana), and Bessie Head (South Africa), went into exile.

However, some of them, including Ama Ata Aidoo and Mĩcere Gĩthae Mũgo, still experienced imprisonment and torture. Mũgo, for example, remained stateless and was forced to leave Kenya in 1982, but was still a target of harassment from her government. She was stripped of her Kenyan citizenship and found refuge in the newly independent Zimbabwe, where she remained until the 1990s. Mũgo only regained her Kenyan citizenship in 2009, and most of her literary works and writings remained banned in Kenya until only a decade ago. Like many other Pan-Africanists and activists, the banning of her work meant that many Africans were unaware of Mũgo's incredible contributions to decolonization and democratization in Southern Africa and Kenya, respectively. Many Pan-Africanist thinkers believed that national liberation is a continuous process that requires people to understand and transform their oppressive governments and build strong democracies. That is, liberation is not necessarily achieved with formal independence, and instead, citizens must exert agency and vigilance and hold their leaders accountable should they falter or not serve the interests of their people.

This idea of a people-oriented Pan-Africanism was slowly but surely institutionalized through various projects, conferences, and spaces of learning across Africa. The University of Nairobi, for instance, supported the democracy movement in Kenya during the country's transition from a dictatorship. However, this came at a deadly cost, as several university professors and students were regularly detained, killed, and/or exiled in the 1990s.

## Pan-Africanism Today

While the OAU and later the AU have taken significant steps to boost economic growth in Africa (as seen with the African Continental Free Trade Agreement), there have been several challenges in the adoption of related policies and programs. The COVID-19 pandemic, for example, delayed the implementation of the African Continental Free Trade Agreement, and ever-increasing globalization and connectivity enabled foreign countries to politically and economically influence African countries. Coupled with the exploitation by MNCs, the "new Scramble for Africa" is well underway. Despite this, there have been several instances of Africans leveraging globalization and digital technologies to express pride in their African identities. The ability of social media platforms to connect people from all over the world, including the African diaspora, has led to more and more Africans and people of African descent attempting to create a collective African identity online. From the sharing of memes to trending hashtags, the Pan-African idea of a united Africa or African identity has had to adapt to new contexts.

Pan-Africanism can also be applied to current development and democratization strategies on the African continent. Here, an-Africanism sees human rights and democracy as a bottom-up struggle in which African people have agency, hold their political leaders accountable, and contribute to reforms in governance structures. That is, governance must serve the needs and interests of citizens, and instead of governments offering human rights, citizens must exercise vigilance to ensure that their rights are being honored. Pan-African scholars and intellectuals are included in this endeavor, and as seen over the past few decades, many of them have worked towards decolonizing the academic sector and transforming it into an intellectual hub of democratization.

The influence of Pan-Africanist ideals can also be seen in governance institutions and norms in Africa: The Casablanca group of the Pan-African movement called for a borderless Africa and a united federation of African states, while the Monrovia group supported economic cooperation based on the nation-state. The latter group's approach prevailed and formed the basis of the OAU and then the AU. Agenda 2063, for example, seeks to create a federation of African states and to establish the African diaspora as the African Union's 6th region.

This will enable Pan-Africanists in the Americas and Caribbean, for example, to engage with the AU's structures, programs, and decision-making processes. Unfortunately, the people-orientated approach of Pan-Africanism still experiences many setbacks in contemporary Africa, as in many cases, the idea of democracy and citizen agency as a bottom-up process is still sometimes regarded as radical or subversive. This is especially challenging in countries where the ruling elites have used the ideology of Pan-Africanism to legitimize their oppressive governments. This was exacerbated by the control and restrictions placed on national universities. As the hub of Pan-Africanist thought, oppressive governments planted informers in these universities, impeded the formation of academic unions, removed tenure for certain professors, and promoted academics that were amenable to the government. It is unsurprising that the relationship between public (and private) universities and oppressive governments continues to be marked with suspicion, tension, and hostility.

## *Pan-Africanism to Achieve /ustainable Development*

Similar to the approach to national liberation, Pan-Africanism sees democracy as a continuous or ongoing process in which citizens must collectively engage in the transformation of governance structures and institutions. This means that democracy is not limited to multiple political party options and voting in local and national elections; rather, it requires global solidarity, non-indifference, and the responsibility to protect. Because Pan-Africanism does not equate freedom with statehood (because governments can and *do* violate the rights of their citizens), the emphasis on citizens embracing the struggles of their fellow Africans is a clear step towards continental and even global solidarity.

As stated by Mĩcere Gĩthae Mũgo (cited in Nantulya, 2024):

> I am a border crosser, defying geographical containment. I am Zimbabwean, I am African, I am Pan-African, I am Nigerian, I am Jamaican, I am an internationalist, I am a Black American, I am trans-nationalist. I am a citizen of the world. (para. 23)

Pan-Africanism influenced the norms of numerous African norms institutions and their norms, but it must be strengthened and maintained to ensure African unity, the empowerment of African citizens to exert agency, and enable African citizens to keep a keen eye on their governments. Indeed, Africans can use the intellectual foundations of Pan-Africanism, adapt them to their current and specific contexts, and leverage these foundations to address obstacles in the democratization process. A survey by Afrobarometer (2023) revealed that almost 70% of Africans prefer democracy to other systems of governance, and over three-quarters of them reject one-party and military rule. The survey also found that the African youth have a stronger commitment to democracy, but still experience resistance from those who quell citizen agency and who present fraudulent elections under the guise of democracy.

Importantly, only 43% of African citizens are satisfied with the way democracy operates in their countries. The dissatisfaction with their governments' use or implementation of democratic principles and processes is perhaps why so many young Africans are increasingly drawn to adapting Pan-Africanism and leveraging it as a tool for nonviolent resistance and democracy.

Grassroots organizations, too, are challenging the ruling elites' appropriation of Pan-Africanist ideology to protect their own interests and to portray people's movements as agents of imperialism. It is important to note that these grassroots organizations, youth groups, and related social and activist movements see their struggles as connected and, as a result, have made solidarity a core principle of their work.

Indeed, the repression of citizens in one country will not be met with indifference or inaction from the citizens of another country. It is through these connections that Africa can achieve deeper integration of its societies and the greater representation of Africans in key decision-making processes. As more and more Africans form Pan-African youth groups and grassroots organizations, the rebirth of Pan-Africanism and an African Renaissance can pave the path towards sustainable development, economic growth, and the well-being of Africans.

# The Importance of Continental Unity

African nations and peoples can develop and strengthen continental unity and solidarity through building intra-African trade partnerships, collaborating on innovative development projects, policies, and efforts, and establishing peace and security in conflict-ridden countries. Establishing peace and development on the African continent is an onerous process, but we can (and should) leverage African Indigenous Knowledge Systems (AIKS) and traditional approaches to conflict resolution.

## *Identifying the /ources of Conflict*

Most conflicts and wars in Africa are underpinned by the desire to secure power and resources for a group of elites or for an ethnonational population, and this often comes at the expense of the rest of the population. Moreover, these conflicts often lead to the outflow of refugees and internally displaced persons (IDPs) — further demonstrating the need for continent solidarity as no African country is unaffected by the conflicts happening in other African countries — and the breakdown of society.

With infrastructure being destroyed, people dying, being imprisoned and tortured, further damage to the environment, and healthcare and education services suffering, conflict breaks the ties that hold people together. Development and growth efforts, too, are severely hindered.

The link between peace and development cannot be undermined as conflicts and wars deplete the resources that could rather be used to build infrastructure, schools, and clinics. To understand the sources of conflicts in Africa, we must also explore the leaders of these countries: Military and political elites use the legacies and structures of colonialism to exert power and control over their people and to serve their own interests. Besides, it is easier to control and oppress people who are struggling with their African identities, sense of self and belonging in Africa, and who valorize Western cultures, norms, and values over African ones. Social solidarity was already fragile in many African countries, and military and political elites have leveraged this for their own political and economic gains.

The process of modernization has also hindered efforts towards social solidarity as African populations residing in rural areas are often excluded from benefiting from the resources and wealth of their countries. Since educated and skilled citizens flock to the capital cities and their contributions to the economy are respected, many of those in rural areas lack resources for adequate healthcare, education, and other services, causing African societies to fragment further.

### /ocial /olidarity and AIK/ for Achieving Peace

Social solidarity is a key element for achieving long-term peace in a society or country. This type of solidarity entails not only the absence of violence but also an environment where members of society recognize each other as human beings and, consequently, support each other's common well-being.

As claimed by AIKS, the recognition of the interconnectedness of each human being and of humans to nature is a significant foundation on which to base conflict resolution strategies.

To create a framework for achieving peace and security, we must interweave AIKS and modern principles to ensure the inclusion and dignity of all Africans.

Cultural values and a sense of community influence the ways in which Africans treat and interact with each other, and as such, we can re-establish social solidarity in conflict-ridden communities or countries by:

- Emphasizing the similarities between cultural values, traditions, and practices.

- Reinforming members of the community about these values, traditions, and practices (especially if these factors were eroded during colonialism).

- Highlighting the need for sharing and equitable distribution of resources.

- Reviving progressive cultural attitudes and norms and adapting them to modern contexts.

In Mozambique, for example, traditional healing and reconciliation practices were employed in the aftermath of conflict to help combatants, and more specifically, child soldiers, to re-integrate into their communities. Child soldiers often endure higher casualty rates than their adult counterparts because they are young and have limited life and combat experience, but even if they survive the conflict or war, they are often left with psychological trauma, injuries, and/or disabilities, and desensitization to brutal violence.

Some child soldiers are even expected to enact atrocities upon their own families and communities — deepening their trauma and hindering any hopes of them returning to or re-integrating into their communities. In addition, conflict tends to interrupt or delay the education of child soldiers, and without adequate support, learning, and rehabilitation, their future prospects are limited, and they are likely to fall into the cycle of poverty (or being re-recruited into armed groups).

Transformative justice goes beyond punishing child soldiers and, instead, promotes their rehabilitation and reintegration and prevents their future engagement in armed conflicts. Because the challenges faced by child soldiers are multi-faceted, their rehabilitation, too, must use different angles and approaches, including combinations of trauma counseling, skills development and education programs, vocational training, and therapeutic interventions.

The multipronged approach can address the many rehabilitation needs of child soldiers as it bridges the education gap, offers them new skills, and increases their chances of employment—all while assisting them with their trauma. Community dialogues and community-based psychosocial support are also important for the reintegration of child soldiers into their communities, as such efforts can help rebuild understanding, trust, and a sense of belonging.

## *Re-Instilling a /ense of Ubuntu*

The cultural worldview of *Ubuntu* is seen in societies across East, Central, and Southern Africa, and it attempts to articulate what it means to be human. That is, a person who has Ubuntu is someone who is friendly, caring, generous, and compassionate and is a person through other people. Indeed, we are human because we live through others, we share with others, and we do not feel threatened by the achievements of others because we belong to a greater whole.

This worldview can be applied to peace-building efforts as it promotes inclusivity, reciprocity, and a shared destiny between peoples. It also uses peace-building and reconciliation as a foundation for legislation. Because it also promotes communal life and maintains positive relations with others, Ubuntu can also be woven into efforts or strategies for maintaining law and order in a society. For example, each community member is linked to each other, and when one of them breaks the law, the entire community becomes a law-breaking group. Relatedly, if a community member is wronged, then the whole community has also been wronged, and the community will need to work together to remedy the wrong.

Depending on the nature and severity of the wrongdoing, Ubuntu can be used to resolve disputes and promote reconciliation at the family level, village, or community level or between inter- and intra-ethnic groups. In Southern Africa, for instance, disputes were resolved through the institution of *inkundla* in which the entire community or society was involved in finding a solution to the dispute. Usually led by the chief or a council of elders, the process entailed identifying the wrongdoing or dispute, finding a resolution based on the inputs from the victim and the victim's and perpetrator's family members, and finding a solution to achieve justice and maintaining peace and social cohesion.

The resolution would often include the perpetrator being encouraged to show remorse or to repent, ask for forgiveness from their victim or the victim's family, and offer some form of compensation or reparation for the harm that they caused. The process comes to an end when the various parties are encouraged to commit to reconciliation, to coexist in the community, and to restore peace within the community.

Here, other members of the community or society are also allowed to provide their inputs or opinions as the dispute or wrongdoing affects the community or society as a whole. Of course, the proceedings and outcomes of *inkundla* depended on whether there was resistance to the elders' or chief's recommendations, if the perpetrator did not show remorse, or if the victim or their family was not willing to forgive the perpetrator.

The process is not always straightforward, but we can still learn from its underpinning principles and apply them to modern-day peace-building efforts.

These principles include:

- The community's or public's participation in reconciliation and peacemaking processes.

- The supporting of victims (and/or their families) and encouraging perpetrators to repent, show genuine remorse, and make peace.

- The acknowledgment of guilt and remorse and the granting of forgiveness to achieve social harmony and reconciliation.

- The interdependence and interconnectedness of human beings and the need to share resources and cooperate with each other to maintain a sense of community and belonging.

## /olidarity and Ubuntu in the 21st Century

In the African context, solidarity is generally practiced among family members, but there is a need to institutionalize solidarity efforts through adopting new or rethinking existing civil protection mechanisms. Such mechanisms are vital for guaranteeing basic rights and freedoms, offering social security to cover individuals in case of risk or illness, and for assuring the security of the individual and property within legal frameworks. But, this presents an interesting paradox: As more and more Africans realize that their needs and interests may not align with those of the community, they may become socially isolated from their communities and detached from their civic responsibilities. This is increasingly relevant in a globalized world where Western norms and values dominate (and prioritize the individual over the community). Numerous African scholars and authors have argued that practicing solidarity can also limit one's individual freedom.

Here, the "foundation pact" that outlines the rules of behavior that preserve and maintain harmony within a group or community may be rejected by some of the youth of Africa.

For example, when African youth from rural regions flock to the urban areas for education and employment opportunities, it makes it easier for them to forget or neglect this foundation pact. Perhaps they no longer see why they should care for their elderly family members, or become more focused on maximizing their earning potential than on active civic participation. Having individual or personal interests, goals, and mindsets is not inherently a negative trait, and the African youth *should* have access to greater education and employment opportunities. But this does not mean that they have to rid themselves of their family and community ties and their responsibilities to their people. Instead, we need to find a balance and adapt the idea of solidarity to suit modern contexts and conditions. This is a struggle for many postcolonial societies that live at the crossroads of African and Western cultures and value systems.

As echoed by Boni (2012, p. 79), we are "witnessing societies in the midst of change" but despite the hybrid nature of these societies, "forms of social solidarity, whether distorted or not, persist within them in the form of two-way relationships binding individuals together." These relationships may be experienced or imagined, may involve obligation and dependency, and may also require Africans to give up some of their individual freedoms.

Moreover, this moral obligation to one's family (and community) can very quickly become an economic obligation. Many of these obstacles to social solidarity, however, can be addressed and remedied when the state adequately fulfills its role and duties to its people. The economic obligation to support one's family and/or community can be eased if the laws protecting the rights and duties of citizens are translated into practice if families and communities live in less precarious conditions, and if the state provides a degree of protection to those who bear the obligation to care for others. Social security policies and programs are only as strong as the government or institutions providing them, and as such, we must first ensure the strength, accountability, and inclusive nature of the government and/or institutions.

In functioning and relatively peaceful societies, the social security interventions that are aimed at risk pooling and sharing among individuals and communities are, by nature, based on the concept and practice of Ubuntu. However, because Ubuntu focuses more on kinship and community, it must be adapted to respond to the types of risks experienced by Africans living in a globalized world.

This can be seen when globalization shifted subsistence agriculture to cash crop production by agricultural-industrial businesses or industries. The advent of this undermined community-based labor agreements and instead led to the proliferation of formal, paid work. As a result, social security interventions or programs are now funded by the employer and the employee's set contribution.

Formalizing Ubuntu and, more generally, AIKS can be challenging as it requires sharing some of the risks and responsibilities with governments and institutions, and this, in turn, greatly depends on the transparency, accountability, and efficiency of these entities.

Nevertheless, doing so is a key step towards integrating Ubuntu and AIKS into various sociocultural, economic, and political spheres in African countries. Social security is an essential part of addressing socioeconomic vulnerability, especially for those not receiving remittances or other forms of support from their family members. African governments are becoming more conscious of their duty to expand social security coverage, but what is incredibly important is these governments' acknowledgment and integration of AIKS in social security interventions and the inclusion of rural regions.

# Africa by Africans and for Africans

*Education and Amareness Programs for AIK/ and Peace-Building*

To integrate AIKS and other traditional practices in structures of governance and efforts towards attaining long-term peace and security, African officials and civil society actors must be educated on progressive African cultural values and principles. These are values and principles that promote human dignity and the welfare of African peoples and their broader communities. As more and more African elders die, we lose important wisdom and traditional practices, so there are numerous strategies that can be employed to ensure that we do not completely lose such knowledge systems. Firstly, we must engage with the elders, perform interviews with them, and document their experiences, wisdom, and traditions. Secondly, teaching and training materials must be developed to inform curricula across different levels of education.

The revised curricula should highlight the importance of traditional knowledge and practices and explore how AIKS can be leveraged to address sociocultural, economic, and political issues. The latter is especially relevant for high school and university students. Relatedly, teachers, trainers, and lecturers should also be trained on African history and AIKS so that they may better educate their students on these topics.

Thirdly, educational institutions should collaborate with organizations, such as the AU and the United Nations Educational, Scientific and Cultural Organization (UNESCO), to ensure the comprehensive dissemination of educational and training material and curricula frameworks. At the core of these strategies is the inclusion of young Africans from across the continent, as they are Africa's future teachers, intellectuals, artists, leaders, and policymakers. Given the importance of recording the wisdom of elders and training the youth on AIKS, multigenerational dialogues, discussions, and debates must be encouraged across African societies. We live in a globalized and digital world, and as such, a media strategy is needed to raise awareness of AIKS and its potential for peace-building, conflict resolution, and reconciliation. This strategy needs to include both traditional and digital media: Many Africans residing in rural regions have better access to radios and newspapers, while those in urban areas are more likely to have access to smart devices and the internet. To avoid the exclusion of rural Africans and to ensure the extensive dissemination of information and awareness on AIKS and traditional practices, all forms of media should be leveraged.

## Africa Rising: Building a Resilient Continent

Coined in 2011 to describe the rapid economic growth across sub-Saharan Africa since 2000, the term "Africa Rising" also refers to the new narrative about Africa—a narrative that moves away from the

"Dark Continent" and towards democratization, peace, greater access to digital technologies, and the increase in entrepreneurship. The term soon gained popularity when the IMF used it as a title for a 2014 conference held in Mozambique and when the BBC, The Economist, and Time featured it on their front pages. Because 'Africa Rising' was coined by and gained popularity thanks to Western media outlets, it has faced some criticism for stereotyping Africa as a continent teeming with consumerism, rapid social change, and big businesses. Critics also claim that these stereotypes starkly contrast and undermine the ongoing conflicts and socioeconomic issues in Africa.

There are others, however, who have defended "Africa Rising" and argue that this narrative is nowhere near dead. Supporters of the term claim that critics should not omit Africa's largest economies from calculating the aggregate growth rate, nor should they focus on each country's growth rate. Instead, when we look at Africa as a whole, it is clear that the Africa Rising narrative can still be used to describe the continent's current economic growth.

This, coupled with better macroeconomic management, efforts towards good governance, and rising entrepreneurship, demonstrate that economic expansion is a reality for many African countries. Besides, African countries are not the only ones that experience setbacks in their economies. The oil price shock of 2014 and the COVID-19 pandemic, for example, had negative impacts on economies around the world.

## *The Post-COVID-19 Recovery*

In addition to the high infection and death rates, the COVID-19 pandemic brought development and economic growth to a standstill and demonstrated the need for countries across the world to strengthen their resilience to unexpected economic shocks and threats to human health and safety. As COVID-19 eased and the infection and death rates declined, there was a clear need for the strategic re-opening of economic and development activities. In fact, the pandemic presented an opportunity for African countries to revise their development policies and focus on building more equitable, sustainable, and inclusive economies.

For example, as evidenced during the pandemic and lockdown(s), African governments need to invest in the digitization of important economic sectors, such as education, health, and agriculture, reform labor laws to better protect workers and their jobs, and adopt policies to boost public-private sector participation. More specifically, the pandemic highlighted the need to increase investments in disease profiling, research, and public healthcare infrastructure and services.

This also includes further investments in Africa-led institutions, such as the Africa Centers for Disease Control and Prevention, to better prepare the continent's readiness for future external shocks. While there is no one-size-fits-all policy for alleviating the consequences of COVID-19 and helping African economies recover from the shock, policymakers need to acknowledge the local economic, social, political, and environmental realities of Africans to make more informed decisions.

This process also entails productive engagements with local experts and civil society leaders so that policy design and implementation respond to local realities rather than politics. The consequences of COVID-19 are urgent, globalized, and far more devastating on national, regional, and global economies, trade, health systems, societies, and cultures than any other event in recent history.

These consequences were also exacerbated in the Global South as even before COVID-19, many of these countries did not have a strong enough standing in the global order. That is, countries in the Global South were disproportionately adversely impacted by the pandemic. The impacts of COVID-19 also include economic, social, and environmental trade-offs that policy and decision-makers also need to consider for future development plans and strategies. The COVID-19 lockdown led to a decline in carbon dioxide emissions, less littering, and better air quality, but it also destroyed economies and livelihoods. Small- to medium-sized businesses did not have the resources to recover, and the poorer segments of African society were disproportionately affected by the negative impacts.

Moreover, the pandemic and subsequent lockdowns pushed marginalized groups further into the periphery, forced millions into poverty, and even led to hunger pandemics. Recovering from the pandemic, therefore, requires development efforts to be more resilient, efficient, and inclusive so that future economies leave no one behind. Indeed, conserving and protecting nature and increasing the GDP cannot be celebrated if people are still hungry and lack access to basic needs.

# Practical Tools and Frameworks

## *Building a Resilient Africa: Key /trategies*

| Political | Socioeconomic |
|---|---|
| Improve risk governance structures to better address external shocks and natural disasters. | Promote resilience through ensuring equitable and inclusive access to basic services and employment opportunities. |
| Include AIKS in disaster preparedness processes and plans. | Increase resilient investments of national governments. |
| Strengthen state capacities and ensure the productive and effective functioning of institutions. | Include civil society in dialogues and discussions surrounding policy, laws, and strategies. |
| Ensure the full economic participation of marginalized groups, including women, the youth, and religious and ethnic minorities. | Support grassroots, bottom-up approaches from civil society groups. |
| Establish justice, peace, and security as a precondition for progress and development. | Fight income inequality by increasing women's access to financial services and digital technology. |

| | |
|---|---|
| Develop progress and development frameworks or strategies through the lens of fragility and resilience. | Build sustainable infrastructure to address the growing population in urban areas, while also improving education and employment opportunities in rural regions. |
| Implement tools and institutions to track, monitor, and measure strategies regarding resilience. | Enhance transport, sanitation, and waste management services. |

## Developing a Pan-African Framemork for the 21st Century

*Questions to Ask*

- How does neocolonialism undermine African political autonomy?

- How do international monetary institutions promote Western hegemony in Africa?

- What are the key obstacles preventing or hindering African unity and solidarity?

- How do we balance state sovereignty with intra-African cooperations, partnerships, and unity?

- How do we address and eradicate xenophobia among African ethnic groups and countries?

- How do we manage the balance between nationalism and Pan-Africanism?

## What to Consider

| Factor | Actions |
|---|---|
| Human Rights | - Make development a human right as the right to development is part of the human condition and, therefore, necessary.<br><br>- Mainstream human rights into economics to ensure that development programs implemented by foreign powers, international relations, and MNCs truly benefit African citizens. |
| Government Responsibilities | - African governments must act collectively in regional and global partnerships.<br><br>- However, African governments must act individually when creating national development policies that affect their citizens and that are specific to national |

contexts and issues.

- Governments must adopt the principle of non-indifference when there is conflict and war in neighboring African countries.

- Develop the call for the right to self-determination along the lines of international law so foreign organizations, powers, and corporations have to adhere to this law *and* right.

- Enforce African countries' sovereignty over their natural resources and wealth.

- African governments must rely on each other for regional integration and development, rather than looking to foreign powers and institutions.

- These governments should

|  |  |
|---|---|
|  | adopt policies, constitutional amendments, and strategies based on Pan-Africanism. A constitution informed by Pan-Africanism, for example, ensures the separation of powers between the three branches of government. In addition, this can prevent African leaders from clinging to political power far beyond their terms.<br><br>• Create and establish independent constitutional institutions (such as a human rights commission) to enforce the right to development. |
| The International Community's Responsibilities | • International institutions and MNCs must acknowledge Africa's right to development.<br><br>• International development policies must be revised to |

serve African development objectives as developed by African civil society, policy and decision-makers, community leaders, and local business leaders.

- International bodies must also address and remedy unfair and inequitable trade rules and practices.

- MNCs must not loot natural resources, destroy the environment, and engage in land-grabbing when operating in African countries. Their approach needs to be based on human rights.

- Develop new or revise existing trade partnerships and agreements so that they do not infringe on the independence and regional integration of African economies.

- International financial institutions should not

|  |  |
|---|---|
|  | impede the development efforts of African countries. Moreover, their development programs in African countries must not adversely affect the rights, well-being, and livelihoods of local communities. |
| Civil Society | • Keep an eye on not only their own governments but also the governments of other African nations.<br><br>• Lead campaigns to promote human rights at local and international levels.<br><br>• Build Pan-Africanism from the bottom by actively engaging in decision-making processes and nonviolent protests (when human rights are violated) and serving as a watchdog.<br><br>• Collaborate with other CSOs to advance socioeconomic justice |

|  | initiatives. |
|---|---|

## Checklist: Promoting /ocial /olidarity in African /ocieties

| Item | Completed |
|---|---|
| Promote power-sharing: This includes inclusive governance and the equitable distribution of resources. | |
| Integrate the concept and practice of Ubuntu into policies, strategies, and education curricula. | |
| Support AIKS and indigenous practices by recording and preserving them, creating education and training materials based on AIKS, and forming partnerships with other stakeholders to ensure the extensive merging of AIKS into all spheres of society. | |
| Integrate human rights norms into healthcare policies and programs and ensure that access to healthcare is based on equality, inclusion, dignity, and nondiscrimination. | |

| | |
|---|---|
| Build trust and cooperation between communities, civil society, the private sector, and the private sector with the government. | |
| Promote transformative justice and reconciliation efforts at small-scale community levels to address minor disputes and crimes, such as family squabbles and petty theft. | |
| Design and implement effective social protection policies, programs, and interventions and pressure African governments to enforce these efforts. | |
| Create more programs and offer more services centered on childcare, elder care, and other forms of caregiving to alleviate some of the obligations on family and community members. | |
| Provide greater employment and education opportunities in rural regions so that Africans residing in these areas are not pressured or forced to move to the cities. | |
| Leverage traditional and new media platforms to spread | |

| awareness and disseminate information regarding human rights, social security laws and policies, and the duties of local and national governance to communities. | |

## *Building Resilience to Pandemics and Climate Change*

| Recommendation | Details |
| --- | --- |
| Build inclusive, green, and equitable economies. | This entails investing in decentralized, green energy solutions and ensuring that all Africans have equitable access to affordable and reliable energy sources. |
| Fast-track the digitization process. | This includes increasing access to digital technologies and the internet and subsidizing high-speed internet and broadband services. Costs can be reduced through corporate partnerships. |
| Address digital poverty. | This can occur through integrating information and communications technology skills in the curricula of schools, universities, and adult education programs. |
| Leverage smart grids and internet access to boost youth employment opportunities. | This entails using digital technology to connect Africa's youth with employment opportunities, increasing e-commerce in existing businesses, boosting access to e-health services and telemedicine, and improving digital finance services. |

|  | These initiatives are especially important in vulnerable and rural communities. |
|---|---|

# Conclusion

> *The strange thing about Africa is how past, present and future come together in a kind of rough jazz, if you like.*
>
> –Ben Okri

## Rewriting History

By studying the origins of the human race and precolonial African history and culture, Cheikh Anta Diop's works are considered the foundation of the theory Afrocentricity: He posed questions concerning cultural biases in scientific research, argued that there was a shared cultural continuity among African peoples, and his works greatly contributed to the postcolonial research on African civilizations. As a researcher, Diop studied in Paris, where his 1954 publication, *Nations nègres et culture* (*Negro Nations and Culture*), sparked controversy in academic circles. This book featured comprehensive research by Diop to restore the history of Black Africa—a history that has long been misconstrued, misrepresented, obscured, or outright falsified by European explorers, writers, and colonists.

*Negro Nations and Cultures* (1954) claimed that Ancient Egypt was populated by Black people, and this not only made Diop a controversial figure during this time, but his writings also contradicted the theories and beliefs of scientific racism that were popular among Western scientists, academics, and political figures. Through his study of Pharaonic iconography, linguistics, blood groups, and skin pigmentation, Diop asserted that Egypt had a prehistory, was a hub of science, history, and art, and that all classes of its society belonged to the same black race. Much of Diop's research and works came at the turning point of African independence, and these nations were in need of reclaiming their own African histories, cultures, traditions, and identities. Indeed, scientific racism and European colonial rule denied and deprived Africans of their heritages.

At the time, Diop's research forced some scientists, academics, Orientalists, and others to reconsider their ideas about Africa and its ancient civilizations, yet even today, many academics, writers, and so on try to discredit Diop's research and writings. In 2017, for example, a conference at the University of Toulouse II, themed "France in the mirror of Egypt. Cultural imperialism, heritage and scholarly knowledge" (1880-2015), revealed that even the curricula on Ancient Egypt were heavily diluted and reduced. Moreover, a survey (De Saint Perier, 2023) found that one in five French people (between the ages of 18 and 24) believed that the pyramids in Egypt were built by aliens and not by the Egyptians themselves. This demonstrates not only the continued misrepresentation of African history, but also the undermining of the intellectual and scientific advancements of Ancient Egypt.

As Pan-Africanist historian, Amzat Boukari-Yabara (cited in De Saint Perier, 2023, para. 35), writes, Diop "was a pioneer in the decolonisation of history and the revaluation of the African historical narrative. However, he remains banned from school curricula, and universities refuse to discuss his work." Western historians and academics still struggle to recognize the Africanness of Ancient Egypt and, in doing so, refuse to attribute its advancements in agriculture, science, mathematics, and astronomy to Black people. Coupled with the banning of Diop's writings, it is no wonder that many still see

Egypt as separate from Africa or as the exception to the rule of African primitiveness and lack of civilization. So, before we focus on the future of Africa, we need to address the ills of its past. The history of Africa and its peoples, as documented by Western explorers, writers, and colonists, was teeming with stereotypes of Africa and, in contrast, the valorization of European culture. It is, therefore, unsurprising that African scholars and intellectuals are tempted to rewrite African history according to its realities in favor of African cultures and traditions. Yet, even when they do so, Westerners continue to deny Africans their history, identity, and culture and even defend or eulogize colonial rule. The term "historicism" was initially used to describe a form of philosophy that placed importance on history, but in this context, historicism can be used to refer to significant world achievements that are falsely or erroneously attributed to the Western world.

The reason for this attribution is to justify and maintain the structure and culture of white supremacy and Western dominance in our postindependence and globalized world. And, more nefariously, it dismisses the very real intellectual, artistic, and technological contributions of African civilizations and peoples—further illustrating the need for Africans to be the narrators of their own histories.

## Neocolonialism and Western Interference

When European explorers, missionaries, and colonists arrived in Africa under the guise of civilizing and saving the savages, they plundered the continent's natural resources, seized the land, enslaved and exploited its peoples, spread diseases, enacted violence, tortured, and genocides, and looted Africa of its art and artifacts. Indeed, if Europeans truly had considered Africans as savage, primitive, and uncivilized, they would not have burnt its libraries, snatched its sophisticated trade networks, and stolen its art to display in their own museums. A similar pattern can be found in African countries in the years after independence: Western countries intervene in African political affairs and systems of governance under the guise of spreading democracy and freedom, promoting human and women's rights, and saving African peoples from their so-called dictators. It is no coincidence that those the West labels as *dictators* are usually the political leaders who are anti-colonial, anti-West, and pro-African independence and unity. Through the use of foreign aid and/or outright overthrowing African leaders and governments, it is in the West's best interests to continue the oppression and subjugation of African human and natural resources. This makes building a stronger, more resilient, and more self-reliant Africa all the more necessary.

## The Future Is African

Attempting to reproduce Western economic models and development strategies does not work in Africa owing to the continent's diverse political, economic, and sociocultural contexts and needs. Coupled with the potential of integrating AIKS into different spheres of African life, it is clear that future development work, policies and strategies, peace and security initiatives, and boosting of African pride must be developed by Africans and for Africans. Paradoxically, this requires us to look into our recent histories to explore the ways in which precolonial African societies progressed and prospered, identify and address the colonial values and ideals built into our political and economic systems, our institutions, and our cultural identities and mindsets; learn from the Pan-Africanists who strove for a united Africa. As we have seen throughout history and even today, Africans are resilient, have the capacity to resist and challenge colonialism and its legacies, and are willing to fight for their rights and freedoms. Africa is rising, and it will continue to do so until all Africans have broken free from the shackles of colonialism, cultural inferiority, and Western domination.

# Glossary

- **African Renaissance:** A political, cultural, and economic vision for the African continent that seeks to achieve African unity, renewal, and development.

- **Apartheid:** A policy or system that promotes discrimination and segregation on the basis of race.

- **Bloc:** A group of countries with similar interests that form an alliance to achieve political and/or economic objectives.

- **Brain Drain:** The emigration of highly educated, trained, or skilled people from a country (usually their country of birth).

- **Chiefdom:** A political organization or territory ruled over by a chief.

- **City-State:** A political system in which an independent, sovereign city is the political, economic, and cultural center in its continuous territory.

- **Civic Participation:** This is when individuals or groups engage in activities that benefit the well-being and health of their communities. Activities can include voting, engaging in political organizing or activism, volunteering, and engaging in community projects.

- **Colonialism:** The practice of acquiring full or partial power over another country, usually entails the exploitation of the colony's human and natural resources.

- **Colonial Settlers:** The population of nonindigenous peoples who reside in a settler-colonial state.

- **Coup d'état:** A sudden and unlawful means of seizing power from a government.

- **Cultural Globalization:** The expansion of a culture's beliefs, values, ideas, experiences, and customs across the world.

- **Cultural Products:** Any goods and services that are economically, politically, or socially significant to a particular culture. Such products can include the performing arts, visual arts, architecture, festivals, cultural industries, and heritage conservation efforts (such as museums and galleries).

- **Decolonization:** The process by which a colony gains political, economic, cultural, psychological, and educational independence from its colonial power.

- **Democratization:** The process of introducing the systems and principles of democracy to a government regime or country.

- **Diaspora:** The forced or voluntary dispersion of people from their original homeland.

- **Dictator:** A ruler with complete power over a country.

- **Digital Poverty:** The inability to access or fully interact with and in online spaces and the lack of or limited access to digital technologies.

- **Digitization:** The conversion of images, sound, and text into digital forms or mediums.

- **Economic Diversification:** The process in which a country's economy shifts away from its traditional sectors and towards a greater range of products and services. The aim is to not only boost economic growth but also protect the country or economy from external shocks.

- **Empire:** A group of countries or states under the power of a single sovereign state or monarch.

- **Endogenous Development:** The process of improving the quality of life in a local community or area through the community building its own values and resources.

- **Eugenics:** Beliefs and practices related to selective breeding and forced sterilization to improve the genetic quality of humans.

- **Expropriation:** When the government claims privately owned land (often without the permission of the landowner) for the public's benefit and use.

- **Foreign Aid:** This refers to any form of assistance, such as a loan, grant, or gift, that one country voluntarily transfers to another country.

- **Foreign Intervention:** When a country uses force to interfere with another country's political affairs, often to the detriment of the target country's population and territory. Interferences can include economic boycotts and sanctions, blockades, or the overthrow of the target country's government or ruler.

- **Gacaca Court:** A traditional system of criminal justice used in the aftermath of the Rwandan genocide.

- **Genocide:** The deliberate and systematic killing of a large number of people from a particular nation or ethnic group. Oftentimes, the aim is to completely eradicate the nation or ethnic group.

- **Global North:** A term that refers to the world's wealthy and industrialized countries, which are largely located in the Northern Hemisphere.

- **Global South:** These are countries that are seen as having lower levels of economic and industrial development and are usually located to the south of the countries in the Global North.

- **Global Village:** A term that describes the world as a single community connected by telecommunications and digital technologies.

- **Globalization:** The global spread of technology and trade that facilitates the increasing interdependence and interconnectedness of economies and societies from across the world.

- **Good Governance:** The process of managing public institutions and resources in ways that advance human rights and the rule of law, decrease corruption, boost accountability and transparency, are efficient, and that serve or address the needs of the population.

- **Historicism:** The theory that cultural phenomena and philosophies are determined by and/or based on history.

- **Humanitarianism:** An ideology underpinned by the value of human life and in which humans or governments provide assistance to other humans or countries to alleviate suffering, poverty, or natural disasters.

- **Humanitarian Intervention:** A strategic plan or action to prevent or stop the violation of human rights in another country or state.

- **Imperialism:** A policy in which a country's power and influence are expanded through colonization, the use of the military, or other means.

- **Indigenous:** This term refers to people originating from or existing in a land prior to the arrival of colonists.

- **Indigenous Knowledge System (IKS):** This refers to the collection of practices, knowledge, and beliefs that have been developed by a group of people or a community over many generations.

- **Individual Freedoms:** This describes political rights that cannot be violated or infringed upon by other people, organizations, and governments. This generally includes freedom of speech, freedom of assembly, and freedom of religion, to name a few examples.

- **Intra-Continental:** Being or occurring within a continent.

- **Militia:** A military group or force that emerges from a civil population to supplement the country's usual army in an emergency.

- **Multi-National Corporation (MNC):** This is a company that operates in multiple countries, often with its headquarters in one country and its subsidiaries or branches in other countries.

- **Nationalism:** Identifying with and taking pride in one's own nation and its interests.

- **Neocolonialism:** The process of exerting political, economic, and cultural power to control or influence other countries, especially countries that were once colonies.

- **Pan-Africanism:** An ideology and movement that seeks to unite African people and the African diaspora from across the globe.

- **Pastoralism:** A form of animal husbandry where domesticated animals (usually livestock) are free to graze on large, vegetated lands. This technique has historically been employed by nomadic people who travel with their herds.

- **Precolonial:** Existing before colonial rule.

- **Psychosocial:** This describes the social aspects or factors that influence a person's mind or behavior.

- **Regional Cooperation:** This term refers to the collaborative effort between countries in a particular region to work together towards achieving common goals, sharing information, facilitating cultural and intellectual exchanges, and developing joint projects.

- **Remittance:** A term used to describe money being sent as a gift or a form of payment. It is usually used in the context of (economic) migrants who send money to their families in their country of birth.

- **Reparations:** The act or process of making amends for one's wrongdoings, usually through offering financial compensation or other forms of assistance to those who have been wronged.

- **Scientific Racism:** The now-discredited theory or belief that different ethnic and racial groups have innately different levels of physical, intellectual, and moral development.

- **Social Solidarity:** A sense of unity, connection, or moral obligation to others within a group or community.

- **Sustainable Development:** A term that refers to projects, investments, policies, and efforts towards benefitting humans and nations without harming the environment or human welfare.

- **Totalitarianism:** A system of government that is highly centralized and dictatorial, and that requires its citizens to be fully obedient and subservient to the state.

- **Transformative Justice:** A framework that aims to respond to, prevent, or transform harm, abuse, and/or violence.

- **Ubuntu:** A term, philosophy, and practice used to describe humanity to others. It is often signified by the phrase, "I am because we are."

- **Veto Power:** The legal power to cast a negative vote, reject a decision or proposal, or stop an official action.

- **Westernization:** The process by which non-Western countries and peoples adopt the ideas, cultures, customs, and institutions of Western countries, namely those in North America and Europe.

- **Xenophobia:** The prejudice against people from other countries.

# References

*A great Pan-Africanist: 1C Robert Sobukwe Quotes.* (2023, February 27). The Pan-African Institute for Socialism (PAIS). https://paisafrica.org/robert-sobukwe-quotes/

Adebajo, A. (2016, April 24). *Mbeki's dream of Africa's renaissance belied South Africa's schizophrenia.* The Conversation. https://theconversation.com/mbekis-dream-of-africas-renaissance-belied-south-africas-schizophrenia-58311

Afolayan, J. (2020, February 4). *How technology can help combat Africa's brain-drain.* The Africa Report. https://www.theafricareport.com/22917/how-technology-can-help-combat-africas-brain-drain/

*Africa Day and 10 quotes by African popular leaders.* (2018). Indian African Chamber of Commerce & Industry. https://www.indoafrican.org/africa-day-and-10-quotes-by-african-popular-leaders/

*Africa's financial self-reliance is not self-isolation, but a commitment to base development on own resources: Ministers of Finance.* (2022, June 22). African Union. https://au.int/en/pressreleases/20220622/africas-financial-self-reliance-not-self-isolation-commitment-base

*Africans want more democracy, but their leaders still aren't listening.* (2023, January). The Afrobarometer Network.

https://www.afrobarometer.org/publication/pp85-africans-want-more-democracy-but-their-leaders-still-arent-listening/

Agbolo, S. (2022, September 6). *Most African Indigenous Languages are on the Brink of becoming Extinct by 2100*. Kabod Group. https://kabodgroup.com/most-african-indigenous-languages-are-on-the-brink-of-becoming-extinct-by-2100/

Ajala, O., & Ezenwa, O. E. (2024, February 28). *Ecowas: west African trade bloc shaken as three member states withdraw and form their own alliance.* The Conversation. https://theconversation.com/ecowas-west-african-trade-bloc-shaken-as-three-member-states-withdraw-and-form-their-own-alliance-224209

Amoateng, N. (2022, August 19). *Military Coups in Africa: A Continuation of Politics by Other Means?* ACCORD. https://www.accord.org.za/conflict-trends/military-coups-in-africa-a-continuation-of-politics-by-other-means/

Anderson, D. M., & Weis, J. (2018). The Prosecution of Rape in Wartime: Evidence from the Mau Mau Rebellion, Kenya 1952–60. *Law and History Review, 3C*(2), 267–294. https://doi.org/10.1017/s0738248017000670

Annobil, A. (2020). *Top 10 Quotes from Mo Ibrahim*. Africa Business 2020. https://africabusiness2020.com/2015/12/16/top-10-quotes-from-mo-ibrahim/

Apusigah, A. A. (2007, October 7). *Endogenous Development and the New African Initiatives. Working with Indigenous Institutions for Sustainable Natural Resource Management and Poverty Reduction.*

Cikodgh. https://cikodgh.com/wp-content/uploads/2022/01/Endogenous-_Development_and_New_African_I.pdf

Arasli, H., Abdullahi, M., & Gunay, T. (2021). Social Media as a Destination Marketing Tool for a Sustainable Heritage Festival in Nigeria: A Moderated Mediation Study. *Sustainability, 13*(11), 6191. https://doi.org/10.3390/su13116191

Ayoub, J. (2017, November 29). *Slave trade under the walls of "Fortress Europe."* Al Jazeera. https://www.aljazeera.com/opinions/2017/11/29/how-the-eu-is-responsible-for-slavery-in-libya

Bailey, L. (2021, January 25). *Africa in 30 Beautiful Quotes*. Pan-African. https://pan-african.net/africa-in-30-beautiful-quotes/

Beamish, R., & Smith, D. (2024, March 14). *How Africa's diaspora can boost the continent's prosperity.* World Economic Forum. https://www.weforum.org/stories/2024/03/global-black-economy-africa-innovation-prosperity/

Bekele-Thomas, N. (2024, May 5). *Accelerating Africa's journey towards a prosperous future.* Africa Renewal. https://www.un.org/africarenewal/magazine/april-2024/accelerating-africa%E2%80%99s-journey-towards-prosperous-future

Benedict, O. H., & Ukpere, W. I. (2012). Brain drain and African development: Any possible gain from the drain?. *African Journal of Business Management, C*(7), 2421.

Beri, P. B., Mhonyera, G., & Nubong, G. F. (2022). Globalisation and economic growth in Africa: New evidence from the past two decades. *South African Journal of Economic and Management Sciences, 25*(1). https://doi.org/10.4102/sajems.v25i1.4515

Beyer, G. (2023, June 21). *Muammar Gaddafi: The "Mad Dog of the Middle East."* TheCollector. https://www.thecollector.com/mummar-gaddafi-mad-dog-middle-east/

Boddy-Evans, A. (2019, August 2). *Events leading to the Scramble for Africa*. ThoughtCo. https://www.thoughtco.com/what-caused-the-scramble-for-africa-43730

Bohm, A., & Brown, G. W. (2020). R2P and Prevention: The International Community and Its Role in the Determinants of Mass Atrocity. *Global Responsibility to Protect, 13*(1), 60–95. https://doi.org/10.1163/1875-984X-2020X001

Bongmba, E. K. (2004). Reflections on Thabo Mbeki's African Renaissance. *Journal of Southern African Studies, 30*(2), 291–316. https://www.tandfonline.com/doi/pdf/10.1080/0305707042000215374

Boni, T. (2012). Solidarity and Human Insecurity: Rethinking Solidarity from the Point of View of Africa. *Diogenes, 59*(3–4), 72–81. https://doi.org/10.1177/0392192114538921

Boonzaaijer, C. M. S., & Apusigah, A. A. (2008). Endogenous Development in Africa. In *Endogenous Development in Africa: Towards a Systematisation of Experiences* (35–52). COMPAS/UDS.

Bostan, Z. (2011, July 19). *"Another false dawn for Africa?" An assessment of NEPAD*. E-International Relations. https://www.e-ir.info/2011/07/19/another-false-dawn-for-africa-discuss-this-assessment-of-nepad/

*Building on indigenous solidarity models to strengthen the culture of social security in Africa*. (2024, February 26). International Social Security Association (ISSA). https://www.issa.int/analysis/building-indigenous-solidarity-models-strengthen-culture-social-security-africa

Calland, R. (2024, April 26). *South Africa's constitution was set up as the bedrock of its democracy: it's been challenged over last 30 years, but has held firm*. The Conversation. https://theconversation.com/south-africas-constitution-was-set-up-as-the-bedrock-of-its-democracy-its-been-challenged-over-last-30-years-but-has-held-firm-228556

Cartwright, M. (2019a, March 5). *Ghana Empire*. World History Encyclopedia. https://www.worldhistory.org/Ghana_Empire/

Cartwright, M. (2019b, March 1). *Mali Empire*. World History Encyclopedia. https://www.worldhistory.org/Mali_Empire/

Cartwright, M. (2019c, February 22). *Timbuktu*. World History Encyclopedia. https://www.worldhistory.org/Timbuktu/

Cheeseman, N. (2019, July 23). *Democracy in Africa: success stories that have defied the odds*. The Conversation. https://theconversation.com/democracy-in-africa-success-stories-that-have-defied-the-odds-120601

Cheung, J. (2024, March 5). *Negative Effects and Challenges of Globalization on Cultural Diversity.* LinkedIn. https://www.linkedin.com/pulse/negative-effects-challenges-globalization-cultural-dr--6w4kc/

*Colonialism in Africa* (2018, May 31). World Atlas. https://www.worldatlas.com/articles/colonialism-in-africa.html

Cosso, M. (2024, January 24). *Foreign Aid in Africa: More than Meets the Eye.* University of Chicago. http://uchicagogate.com/articles/2024/1/24/foreign-aid-africa-more-meets-eye/

Coulibaly, B. S. (2017, June 27). *In defense of the "Africa Rising" narrative.* Brookings. https://www.brookings.edu/articles/in-defense-of-the-africa-rising-narrative/

*Covid-19: Rwanda has vaccinated over C0% of its population.* (2022, April 8). AfricaNews. https://www.africanews.com/2022/04/08/rwanda-has-vaccinated-over-60-of-its-population/

Daouas, M. (2001, December). *Africa faces challenges of globalization.* Finance and Development. https://www.imf.org/external/pubs/ft/fandd/2001/12/daouas.htm

De Saint Perier, L. (2023, February 18). *Cheikh Anta Diop, the man who gave the pharaohs back to Africa.* The Africa Report. https://www.theafricareport.com/282654/cheikh-anta-diop-the-man-who-gave-the-pharaohs-back-to-africa/

*Desmond Tutu: Quotes.* (2024). In Encyclopedia Britannica. https://www.britannica.com/quotes/desmond-tutu

Diop, C. A. (1997). *The African origin of civilization: Myth or reality.* Lawrence Hill Books.

Dizikes, P. (2022, May 19). *From South Africa, a success story for democracy.* MIT Political Science. https://polisci.mit.edu/news/2022/south-africa-success-story-democracy

Dorn, W. (2024b, April 9). *Rwanda's genocide could have been prevented: 3 things the international community should have done.* The Conversation. https://theconversation.com/rwandas-genocide-could-have-been-prevented-3-things-the-international-community-should-have-done-expert-226970

*Economic Diversification in Africa: A Review of Selected Countries* (2011). OECD/UN, OECD Publishing, Paris, https://doi.org/10.1787/9789264096233-en.

Eltis, D. (2007). A brief overview of the Trans-Atlantic Slave Trade. *Voyages: The trans-Atlantic slave trade database,* 1700–1810. https://resources.saylor.org/wwwresources/archived/site/wp-content/uploads/2013/05/HIST211-1.3.3-TransAtlanticSlaveTrade.pdf

*Eugenics and Scientific Racism.* (2022, May 18). National Human Genome Research Institute. https://www.genome.gov/about-genomics/fact-sheets/Eugenics-and-Scientific-Racism

Fagbayibo, B., & Staeger, U. (2024, March 5). *The African Union is weak because its members want it that way – experts call for action on its* powers. The Conversation. https://theconversation.com/the-african-union-is-weak-because-its-members-want-it-that-way-experts-call-for-action-on-its-powers-224191

Fayemi, A. K., & Samuel, O. S. (2014). Africa Versus the West on Reparation. *Peace Review*, *2C*(3), 380–387. https://doi.org/10.1080/10402659.2014.937997

Fentahun, G. (2023). Foreign aid in the post-colonial Africa: Means for building democracy or ensuring Western domination? *Cogent Social Sciences*, 9(1). https://doi.org/10.1080/23311886.2023.2241257

*Fifteen quotes to celebrate African Liberation Day 201C*. (2019). The Rules. https://therules.org/15-quotes-celebrate-african-liberation-day-2016/

Firsing, S. (2024, March 19). *Africa's migration and brain drain revisited*. Africa at LSE. https://blogs.lse.ac.uk/africaatlse/2024/03/19/africas-migration-and-brain-drain-revisited/

Fliss, L. (2023). *The Transformative Power of Digital Remittances in Africa*. Office of the Special Adviser on Africa. United Nations. https://www.un.org/osaa/news/digital-remittances-africa

Gage, H. (2022, January 28). *A Success Story: 10 Impressive Improvements in Rwanda*. The Borgen Project. https://borgenproject.org/improvements-in-rwanda/

Gathara, P. (2019, November 15). *Berlin 1884: Remembering the conference that divided Africa*. Al Jazeera.

https://www.aljazeera.com/opinions/2019/11/15/berlin-1884-remembering-the-conference-that-divided-africa

Gbadamosi, N. (2021, October 12). *Stealing Africa: How Britain looted the continent's art.* Al Jazeera. https://www.aljazeera.com/features/2021/10/12/stealing-africa-how-britain-looted-the-continents-art

*GDP per capita, PPP (current international $) – Rwanda.* (2020). World Bank. Archived from the original on 29 July 2021. https://data.worldbank.org/indicator/NY.GDP.PCAP.PP.CD?locations=RW

Githui, W., David, N., & Maurice, S. (2015). The role of indigenous knowledge in socio-economic development. *International Journal of Science and Research*, 4(4), 32–37.

Gray, H., & Khan, M. (2010). Good Governance and Growth in Africa: What can we learn from Tanzania? *The Political Economy of Africa* (357–374). Routledge.

Gray, N. (2019, March 16). *Walking a fine line: The pros and cons of humanitarian intervention.* E-International Relations. https://www.e-ir.info/2019/03/16/walking-a-fine-line-the-pros-and-cons-of-humanitarian-intervention/

Gumedze, S. (2019). *Development: developing the bridges between Africa and the diaspora* [PDF]. Dakar, Senegal. https://www.ohchr.org/sites/default/files/Documents/Issues/Racism/Development-STATEMENT-DAKAR-Dr-Sabelo-GUMEDZE.pdf

Gwaradzimba, E., & Shumba, A. (2010). The nature, extent and impact of the brain drain in Zimbabwe and South Africa. *Acta Academica, 42*(1), 209–241.

Gwiyani-Nkhoma, B. (2006). Towards an African historical thought: Cheikh Anta Diop's contribution. *Journal of Humanities, 20*(1), 107–123.

Haque, S. (2023, October 11). *Thief Meets Thief: The British Museum and Colonialism.* Spheres of Influence. https://spheresofinfluence.ca/thief-meets-thief-the-british-museum-and-colonialism/

Harden, B. (1986, April 5). *How Not to Aid African Nomads.* Washington Post. https://www.washingtonpost.com/archive/politics/1986/04/05/how-not-to-aid-african-nomads/df2edbff-7294-46dd-abf1-fc3dc13b36ff/

Hardy, W. (2020, September 25). *Riches & Misery: The Consequences Of The Atlantic Slave Trade.* OpenLearn. https://www.open.edu/openlearn/history-the-arts/history/riches-misery-the-consequences-the-atlantic-slave-trade

Harsch, E. (2013). The legacies of Thomas Sankara: a revolutionary experience in retrospect. *Review of African Political Economy, 40*(137), 358–374.

Harsch, E. (2023, November 12). *Thomas Sankara: How the leader of a small African country left such a large footprint.* E-International Relations. https://www.e-ir.info/2023/11/12/thomas-sankara-how-the-leader-of-a-small-african-country-left-such-a-large-footprint/

Hecht, I. (2020, May 1). *Postcolonial Reconstruction in Ghana, 1952–CC.* Monthly Review. https://monthlyreview.org/2020/05/01/postcolonial-reconstruction-in-ghana-1952-66/

*History of Slavery and Early Colonisation in South Africa.* (2017, June 7). South African History Online. https://www.sahistory.org.za/article/history-slavery-and-early-colonisation-south-africa

Ibrahim, A. A. (2013). The impact of globalization on Africa. *International Journal of Humanities and Social Science, 3*(15), 85–93.

Ighobor, K. (2013, March 20). *Reflecting on the Brutal Transatlantic Slave Trade.* Africa Renewal. https://www.un.org/africarenewal/web-features/reflecting-brutal-transatlantic-slave-trade

Igimoh, I. (2024, March 7). *Examining Italy's Aid Delivery Efforts in Libya.* African Leadership Magazine. https://www.africanleadershipmagazine.co.uk/examining-italys-aid-delivery-efforts-in-libya/

Imoh-Itah, I., Amadi, L., & Akpan, R. (2016). Colonialism and the post-colonial Nigeria: Complexities and contradictions 1960–2015: A post-development perspective. *International Journal of Political Science, 2*(3), 9–21.

*Is the AU failing coup countries?* (2023, September 1). The Peace and Security Council Report ISS Africa. https://issafrica.org/pscreport/psc-insights/is-the-au-failing-coup-countries

Isilow, H. (2024). *"Unity dead and buried": What next as key Sahel states ditch West Africa bloc?* Anadolu Ajansı. https://www.aa.com.tr/en/africa/-unity-dead-and-buried-what-next-as-key-sahel-states-ditch-west-africa-bloc/3275921

Jansen, L. (2024). *Understanding endogenous development in Africa.* LinkedIn. https://www.linkedin.com/pulse/understanding-endogenous-development-africa-lesle-jansen-lawrence-/

Kaba, A. J. (2007). The two West Africas: The two historical phases of the West African brain drain. *Journal of Pan African Studies, 1*(8), 77–92.

Kaba, M. (2024, April 15). *The African Way: the case for economic self-reliance.* African Business. https://african.business/2024/04/trade-investment/the-african-way-the-case-for-economic-self-reliance

Kamga, S. D. (2019). A call for a 'right to development'-informed pan-Africanism in the twenty-first century. *African Human Rights Law Journal, 19*(1), 418–444.

Kasomo, D. (2012). An assessment of ethnic conflict and its challenges today. *African Journal of Political Science and International Relations, C*(1), 1–7. https://doi.org/10.5897/ajpsirx11.001

Kimbap, D. (2017, October 17). *Ghana, Mali, and Songhai, three of the greatest Western African trading states.* About History.

https://about-history.com/ghana-mali-and-songhai-three-of-the-greatest-western-african-trading-states/

*Kingdom of Kongo 1390 – 1914.* (2018, January 25). South African History Online. https://www.sahistory.org.za/article/kingdom-kongo-1390-1914

Kom, Z., Nicolau, M. D. & Nenwiini, S. C. (2024). The Use of Indigenous Knowledge Systems Practices to Enhance Food Security in Vhembe District, South Africa. *Agricultural Research*, 13, 599–612. https://doi.org/10.1007/s40003-024-00716-8

Kuryla, P. (2024, November 19). *Pan-Africanism.* Encyclopedia Britannica. https://www.britannica.com/topic/Pan-Africanism

Lawal, S. (2024, April 7). *What caused the Rwandan genocide 30 years ago?* Al Jazeera. https://www.aljazeera.com/news/2024/4/7/30-years-on-what-led-to-the-rwandan-genocide

*Leaked email by H. Clinton reveals NATO's aim to destroy Libya, says it was to prevent Gaddafi from unifying Africa.* (2023, July 16). Azer News. https://www.azernews.az/region/212351.html

Lewis, T. (2024, October 25). *Transatlantic lave trade.* Encyclopedia Britannica. https://www.britannica.com/topic/transatlantic-slave-trade

Lombardo, A. P., & Howard-Hassmann, R. E. (2005). Africans on Reparations: An Analysis of Elite and Activist Opinion.

*Canadian Journal of African Studies/Revue Canadienne Des Études Africaines*, *39*(3), 517–548. https://doi.org/10.1080/00083968.2005.10751328

Mafu, L. (2019). The Libyan/Trans-Mediterranean Slave Trade, the African Union, and the Failure of Human Morality. *Sage Open*, 9(1). https://doi.org/10.1177/2158244019828849

Maganga, T. (2020, August 20). *Youth Demonstrations and their Impact on Political Change and Development in Africa*. ACCORD. https://www.accord.org.za/conflict-trends/youth-demonstrations-and-their-impact-on-political-change-and-development-in-africa/

Mahlangu, B. (2012, September 12). *Interviewing Bantu Biko - Extracts from his Quotes.* News24. https://www.news24.com/news24/MyNews24/Interviewing-Bantu-Biko-Extracts-from-his-Quotes-20120912

Mahomoodally M. F. (2013). Traditional medicines in Africa: an appraisal of ten potent African medicinal plants. Evidence-based complementary and alternative medicine. *Evidence-based Complementary and Alternative Medicine.* https://doi.org/10.1155/2013/617459

Maiangwa, B., Dan Suleiman, M., & Arthur Anyaduba, C. (2018). The Nation as Corporation: British Colonialism and the Pitfalls of Postcolonial Nationhood in Nigeria. *Peace and Conflict Studies*, *25*(1). https://doi.org/10.46743/1082-7307/2018.1438

Makara, S. (2018). Decentralisation and good governance in Africa: A critical review. *African Journal of Political Science and International Relations, 12*(2), 22–32.

Malunga, C., & Holcombe, S. H. (2014). Endogenous development: naïve romanticism or practical route to sustainable African development? *Development in Practice, 24*(5–6), 615–622. https://doi.org/10.1080/09614524.2014.938616

Marie, A. (2023, September 8). *Building resilience in Africa: Enabling an inclusive digital economy and energy access for all.* The South African Institute of International Affairs (SAIIA). https://saiia.org.za/research/building-resilience-in-africa-enabling-an-inclusive-digital-economy-and-energy-access-for-all/

Maritz, D. (2012, April 7). *Rwandan Genocide: Failure of the International Community?* E-International Relations. https://www.e-ir.info/2012/04/07/rwandan-genocide-failure-of-the-international-community/

Marumo, P. O., & Chakale, M. (2018). Mbeki on African Renaissance: A vehicle for Africa development. *African Renaissance, 15*(4), 179–191. https://doi.org/10.31920/2516-5305/2018/v15n4a9

Mbaku, J. M. (2020, January 8). *Good and inclusive governance is imperative for Africa's future.* Brookings. https://www.brookings.edu/articles/good-and-inclusive-governance-is-imperative-for-africas-future/

Mbeki, T. (1996, May 8). *I Am An African* [Text]. The Constitutional Assembly of South Africa.

http://afrikatanulmanyok.hu/userfiles/File/beszedek/ThaboMbeki_IamanAfrican.pdf

Mhaka, T. (2022, July 2). *Corruption: Africa's undeclared pandemic.* Al Jazeera. https://www.aljazeera.com/opinions/2022/7/2/corruption-africas-undeclared-pandemic

Michalopoulos, S., & Papaioannou, E. (2016). The long-run effects of the scramble for Africa. *American Economic Review, 10C*(7), 1802–1848.

*Migration and Migrants: Regional Dimensions and Developments.* (2024). World Migration Report. UN Migration. https://worldmigrationreport.iom.int/what-we-do/world-migration-report-2024-chapter-3/africa

Mishra, P. (2014, August 30). *Nationalist Scots embody a wider dissatisfaction with our top-down world.* The Guardian. https://www.theguardian.com/commentisfree/2014/aug/30/scotlands-complicity-with-empire-does-not-disqualify-independence

Mlambo, V. H., Zubane, S. P., & Mlambo, D. N. (2020). Promoting good governance in Africa: The role of the civil society as a watchdog. *Journal of Public Affairs, 20*(1).

Mngomezulu, B. R., & Fayayo, R. (2019). The role of the international community in sustaining conflicts in Africa. *Journal of African Foreign Affairs, C*(3), 5–21. https://doi.org/10.31920/2056-5658/2019/6n3a1

Moeti, M. (2022, August 31). *African Traditional Medicine Day 2022.* WHO | Regional Office for Africa. https://www.afro.who.int/regional-director/speeches-messages/african-traditional-medicine-day-2022

Msimang, B. (2024, July 21). *The Role of NGOs in Africa: A Double-Edged Sword?* IOL. https://www.iol.co.za/news/opinion/the-role-of-ngos-in-africa-a-double-edged-sword-0ccf14a6-c971-4084-a342-1b186f989b3a

*Muammar al-Qaddafi - Death, Facts & Life.* (2022, September 15). Biography.com Editors. https://www.biography.com/political-figures/muammar-al-qaddafi

Murithi, T. (2006, September 25). *African Approaches to Building Peace and Social Solidarity.* ACCORD. https://www.accord.org.za/ajcr-issues/african-approaches-to-building-peace-and-social-solidarity/

Murrey, A. (2018). Africa's Sankara: On Pan African Leadership. *A certain amount of madness: The life, politics and legacies of Thomas Sankara*, 75–95.

Mutombo, P. N., Kasilo, O. M. J., James, P. B., Wardle, J., Kunle, O., Katerere, D., & Dhobi, M. (2023). Experiences and challenges of African traditional medicine: lessons from COVID-19 pandemic. *BMJ Global Health*, 8(8), https://gh.bmj.com/content/bmjgh/8/8/e010813.full.pdf

Mwangi, E. (2010). The incomplete rebellion: Mau Mau movement in twenty-first-century Kenyan popular culture. *Africa Today*, 57(2), 86–113.

Namubiru, L., & Wepukhulu, K. S. (2020, October 29). *Exclusive: US Christian Right pours more than $50m into Africa.* OpenDemocracy. https://www.opendemocracy.net/en/5050/africa-us-christian-right-50m/

Nantulya, P. (2024, March 19). *Pan-Africanism reborn?* Africa Center for Strategic Studies. https://africacenter.org/spotlight/pan-africanism-reborn/

Narayanan, N. (2024, March 4). *Exploring the dynamics of child soldiering, transformative justice, and policy mandates in Africa.* Indian Council of World Affairs. https://www.icwa.in/show_content.php?lang=1&level=1&ls_id=10618&lid=6740

Ndiaye, M., & Ajah, A. C. (2020). Agentic Governance in Africa: Managing the Tension between Dependence and Self-Reliance. *Journal of African-Centered Solutions in Peace and Security, 3*(2), 66–86.

Ndlovu-Gatsheni, S. (2019, July 29). *Revisiting the African Renaissance.* Oxford Research Encyclopedia of Politics. Retrieved 18 Nov. 2024, from https://oxfordre.com/politics/view/10.1093/acrefore/9780190228637.001.0001/acrefore-9780190228637-e-720.

Nebe, C. (2021, September 22). *Namibia: A timeline of Germany's brutal colonial history.* Deutsche Welle. https://www.dw.com/en/namibia-a-timeline-of-germanys-brutal-colonial-history/a-57729985

Negedu, I. A., & Ojomah, S. O. (2018). Deconstructing African History from Western Historicism. *Alternation: Interdisciplinary Journal for the Study of the Arts and Humanities in Southern Africa, 23*, 302–325. https://doi.org/10.29086/2519-5476/2018/sp23a14

*Neocolonialism*. (2024). Internet Encyclopedia of Philosophy. https://iep.utm.edu/neocolon/#H2

Njiwa, D. (2023, July 18). *Africa's journey to self-sufficiency: The power of intra-Africa trade.* AGRA News. https://agra.org/news/daniel-njiwa-africas-journey-to-self-sufficiency-the-power-of-intra-africa-trade/

Nnoko, J. (2024, July 31). *"It's Like Killing Culture": Human Rights Impacts of Relocating Tanzania's Maasai.* Human Rights Watch. https://www.hrw.org/report/2024/07/31/its-killing-culture/human-rights-impacts-relocating-tanzanias-maasai

O'Dowd, M. F., & Heckenberg, R. (2020, June 23). *Explainer: What is decolonisation?* The Conversation. https://theconversation.com/explainer-what-is-decolonisation-131455

Obasi, N. (2023, December 5). *ECOWAS, Nigeria and the Niger Coup Sanctions: Time to Recalibrate.* Crisis Group. https://www.crisisgroup.org/africa/sahel/niger/ecowas-nigeria-and-niger-coup-sanctions-time-recalibrate

Obeng-Odoom, F. (2024). Reparations. *The Review of Black Political Economy, 51*(3), 458–478. https://journals.sagepub.com/doi/pdf/10.1177/00346446231162589

Oberle, S. (2022). *Africa Unite*. The Green Forum. https://thegreenforum.org/post/africa-unite-africa-sometimes-nicknamed-mother-continent-due-its-being-oldest-inhabited

Ocheni, S., & Nwankwo, B. C. (2012). Analysis of colonialism and its impact in Africa. *Cross-Cultural Communication, 8*(3), 46–54.

Oirere, S. (2024, June 5). *Senegal proposes review of international fisheries agreements, threatening future of EU access deal.* Seafood Source. https://www.seafoodsource.com/news/environment-sustainability/senegal-proposes-review-of-international-fisheries-deals-to-safeguard-its-marine-resources

Ojewale, O. (2021, October 11). *Coltan child miners: the dark side of the DRC's wealth.* ENACT Africa. https://enactafrica.org/enact-observer/coltan-child-miners-the-dark-side-of-the-drcs-wealth

Okereke, C. (2023, March 19). *How U.S. Evangelicals Helped Homophobia Flourish in Africa.* Foreign Policy. https://foreignpolicy.com/2023/03/19/africa-uganda-evangelicals-homophobia-antigay-bill/

Olaopa, O. R., & Ayodele, O. A. (2021). Building on the strengths of African indigenous knowledge and innovation (AIK&I) for sustainable development in Africa. *African Journal of Science, Technology, Innovation and Development, 40*(2), 1–14. https://doi.org/10.1080/20421338.2021.1950111

Olufowobi, K. (2017, May 25). *Opinion: The "door of return" is open for people of African descent.* CNN.

https://edition.cnn.com/2017/05/25/africa/africans-doors-of-return/index.html

*Operational Phase Of The African Continental Free Trade Area Launched.* (2024, November 21). African Union. https://au.int/en/articles/operational-phase-african-continental-free-trade-area-launched

Osafo-Kwaako, P., & Robinson, J. A. (2013). *Political centralization in pre-colonial Africa. Journal of Comparative Economics,* 41(1), 6-21. https://doi.org/10.1016/j.jce.2013.01.003

Osman, A. (2009). *Indigenous Knowledge in Africa: Challenges and Opportunities.* Lecture Presented at the Inaugural Lecture. The Centre for African Studies, University of the Free State. https://www.ufs.ac.za/docs/librariesprovider20/centre-for-africa-studies-documents/all-documents/osman-lecture-1788-eng.pdf

Oyedokun, O. D. (2023, October 31). *The Real Reason Why Africa Was Called the Dark Continent.* Africa Rebirth. https://www.africarebirth.com/the-real-reason-why-africa-was-called-the-dark-continent/

Oyier, C. (2017). Multinational corporations and natural resources exploitation in Africa: challenges and prospects. *Journal of CMSD,* 1(2), 69-78.

Palmer, C. A. (2000). Defining and Studying the Modern African Diaspora. *The Journal of Negro History,* 85(1-2), 27-32. https://doi.org/10.1086/jnhv85n1-2p27

Patterson, T. R., & Kelley, R. D. G. (2000). Unfinished Migrations: Reflections on the African Diaspora and the Making of the Modern World. *African Studies Review*, *43*(1), 11–45. https://doi.org/10.2307/524719

Polat, F. (2024, August 20). *What is Driving Italy's Policy in Libya?* TRT World Research Centre. https://researchcentre.trtworld.com/featured/perspectives/what-is-driving-italys-policy-in-libya/

Popoviciu, A. (2024, March 30). *Senegal's fishermen pin hopes on new president to help them fill their nets*. Al Jazeera. https://www.aljazeera.com/features/2024/3/30/senegals-fishermen-pin-hopes-on-new-president-to-help-them-fill-their-nets

Ramutsindela, M. (2009). Gaddafi, continentalism and sovereignty in Africa. *South African Geographical Journal*, *91*(1), 1–3.

Ratha, D., Mohapatra, S., Ozden, C., Plaza, S., Shaw, W., & Shimeles, A. (2011). *Leveraging migration for Africa: Remittances, skills, and investments*. World Bank Publications.

Rouhban, O., & Tanneau, P. (2023). *Immigrants and descendants of immigrants*. L'Institut national de la statistique et des études économiques (Insee). https://www.insee.fr/en/statistiques/7342924?sommaire=7344042

Ruhumuliza, G. N. (2019, October 21). *Kagame's Rwanda is still Africa's most inspiring success story*. Al Jazeera.

https://www.aljazeera.com/opinions/2019/10/21/kagames-rwanda-is-still-africas-most-inspiring-success-story

*Rwanda Literacy Rate 1978-2024.* (2024). MicroTrends. https://www.macrotrends.net/global-metrics/countries/RWA/rwanda/literacy-rate

Samuel, A. E., Baines, J. R., Wente, E. F., Dorman, P. F., and Bowman, A. K. (2024, August 22). *Ancient Egypt.* Encyclopedia Britannica. https://www.britannica.com/place/ancient-Egypt

Sayeh, A. M. (2022, June 13). *Governance and Accountability in Africa: Progress and Road Ahead* [Speech]. High-Level Conference on the Promotion of Good Governance and Fight Against Corruption. https://www.imf.org/en/News/Articles/2022/06/13/sp061322-governance-and-accountability-in-africa-progress-and-road-ahead

Sebudubudu, D. (2010). The impact of good governance on development and poverty in Africa: Botswana-A relatively successful African initiative. *African Journal of Political Science and International Relations, 4*(7), 249.

*Security Council calls for strengthening Africa's role in addressing global security, development challenges, adopting presidential statement ahead of day-long debate.* (2024, May 23). United Nations. UN Meetings Coverage and Press Releases. https://press.un.org/en/2024/sc15706.doc.htm

Skibba, R. (2019, May 20). *The disturbing resilience of scientific racism.* Smithsonian. https://www.smithsonianmag.com/science-nature/disturbing-resilience-scientific-racism-180972243/

Slorach, R. (2020, January 10). *From eugenics to scientific racism.* International Socialism. https://isj.org.uk/from-eugenics-to-scientific-racism/

*Tackling Africa's brain drain challenge through smart digital technologies* (2021, April 20). African Union Development Agency - NEPAD. https://www.nepad.org/blog/tackling-africas-brain-drain-challenge-through-smart-digital-technologies

Tesfu, J. (2008, June 29). S*onghai Empire (ca. 1375–1591).* Blackpast.org. https://www.blackpast.org/global-african-history/songhai-empire-ca-1375-1591/

*The History of LGBT legislation.* (2013). South African History Online. https://www.sahistory.org.za/article/history-lgbt-legislation

*The Justice and Reconciliation Process in Rwanda.* (2014). Outreach Programme on the Rwandan Genocide and the United Nations (1–2). The Department of Public Information. https://un.org/en/preventgenocide/rwanda/assets/pdf/BackgrounderJustic202014.pdf

*The Kongo Kingdom* (2024). Royal Museum for Central Africa. https://www.africamuseum.be/en/discover/history_articles/kongo-kingdom

The World Health Organization. (2023). *WHO health workforce support and safeguards list 2023* (pp. 1–8). https://www.who.int/publications/i/item/9789240069787

Thompsell, A. (2019, September 19). *Why was Africa called the Dark Continent?* ThoughtCo. https://www.thoughtco.com/why-africa-called-the-dark-continent-43310

*Transatlantic Slave Trade.* (2022). The Colonial Williamsburg Foundation. Slavery and Remembrance. https://slaveryandremembrance.org/articles/article/?id=A0002

Tunamsifu, S. P. (2022, December 12). *The colonial legacy and transitional justice in the Democratic Republic of the Congo.* ACCORD. https://www.accord.org.za/ajcr-issues/the-colonial-legacy-and-transitional-justice-in-the-democratic-republic-of-the-congo/

*Uganda's Constitutional Court rejects petition against anti-gay law.* (2024, April 3). Al Jazeera. https://www.aljazeera.com/news/2024/4/3/ugandas-constitutional-court-rejects-petition-against-anti-gay-law

Usman, Z., & Landry, D. (2021, April 30). *Economic diversification in Africa: How and why it matters.* Carnegie Endowment for International Peace. https://carnegieendowment.org/research/2021/04/economic-diversification-in-africa-how-and-why-it-matters?

van Nieuwkerk, A. (2024, September 23). *UN security council: African countries face hurdles and dangers in getting permanent seats.* The Conversation. https://theconversation.com/un-security-council-african-countries-face-hurdles-and-dangers-in-getting-permanent-seats-239642

Wane, N. N. (2005). African indigenous knowledge: Claiming, writing, storing, and sharing the discourse. *Journal of Thought, 40*(2), 27–46. https://www.jstor.org/stable/pdf/42589823.pdf

Wane, N. N., & Akena, F. A. (2019). Ancient governance in Africa. *Gender, Democracy and Institutional Development in Africa*, 37–65. https://www.academia.edu/download/88417923/978-3-030-11854-9.pdf

Watson, J. L. (2024, August 18). *Cultural globalization*. Encyclopedia Britannica. https://www.britannica.com/science/cultural-globalization

West African leaders' summit opens as coup-hit countries form alliance. (2024, July 7). Al Jazeera. https://www.aljazeera.com/news/2024/7/7/west-african-leaders-summit-opens-as-coup-hit-countries-form-alliance

## Image References

Abdulaziz, K. (2020). *Bitobolo Village* [Image]. Pixabay. https://pixabay.com/photos/bitobolo-village-hill-landscape-5762542/

Blue Ox Studio. (2019). *Photo of People Walking Outdoors* [Image]. Pexels. https://www.pexels.com/photo/photo-of-people-walking-outdoors-2014342/

Dascal, A. (2019). *The Sphinx, Egypt.* [Image]. Unsplash. https://unsplash.com/photos/the-sphynx-egypt-GXIr_uawluA

De Mer, J. (2014). *Slave cabin, Laura plantation, Louisiana* [Image]. Pixabay. https://pixabay.com/photos/slave-cabin-laura-plantation-440349/

Ehlers, M. (2019). *Brown Map on Map* [Image]. Pexels. https://www.pexels.com/photo/brown-map-on-map-2660262/

Feyissa, S. (2020). *African Union Headquarters in Addis Ababa, Ethiopia* [Image]. Unsplash. https://unsplash.com/photos/gray-concrete-building-under-blue-sky-during-daytime-RJY_nEbG8fU

Fisk, T. (2019). *Aerial Photo of Cargo Ship Near Intermodal Containers* [Image]. Pexels. https://www.pexels.com/photo/aerial-photo-of-cargo-ship-near-intermodal-containers-2231744/

Harrson, D. (2021). *South-African landscape with sun behind the trees* [Image]. Unsplash. https://unsplash.com/photos/green-trees-under-cloudy-sky-during-sunset-ySKrdi4jC44

Ifeoluwa, A. (2021). *Black Star Square, Ghana* [Image]. Unsplash. https://unsplash.com/photos/white-concrete-building-with-flag-on-top-during-daytime--CgUhaShACE

Ifeoluwa, A. (2021). *Kwame Nkrumah statue* [Image]. Unsplash. https://unsplash.com/photos/a-statue-of-a-person-standing-in-front-of-a-building-0qz48eDvNHo

Mart Production. (2021). *Close-up of a World Map* [Image]. Pexels. https://www.pexels.com/photo/close-up-of-a-world-map-8472922/

Odunsi, O. (2018). *Power* [Image]. Unsplash. https://unsplash.com/photos/persons-right-fist-grayscale-photography-e-TuK4z2LhY

Portraitor. (2020). *Kigali, Rwanda, Africa* [Image]. Pixabay. https://pixabay.com/photos/kigali-rwanda-africa-statue-heaven-4811549/

Rotimi, D. (2019). *White arc photo* [Image]. Unsplash. https://unsplash.com/photos/white-arc-LxENUKJXh_k

The Digital Artist. (2018). *Earth Globalisation Network* [Image]. Pixabay. https://pixabay.com/illustrations/earth-globalisation-network-3866609/

Tokluoğlu, F. (2022). *People Walking with Camels on Desert* [Image]. Pexels. https://www.pexels.com/photo/people-walking-with-camels-on-desert-13960856/

Urama, K. C. (2020). *Building Back Better: Policies for Building Resilient Economies in Post-COVID-19 Africa* (pp. 1–12). African Development Bank Group. https://www.afdb.org/sites/default/files/building_back_better_in_post_covid-19_africa-kcu-_31-08-20-final-1sept.pdf

Vesakaran, A. (2022). *Rwanda National Flag* [Image]. Pexels. https://www.pexels.com/photo/rwanda-national-flag-13867737/

Wiseman, J. (2021). *Africa on the globe* [Image]. Unsplash. https://unsplash.com/photos/white-and-brown-desk-globe-IebZAH6kaNw

Xie, K. (2016). *African guarantee fund member spotlight.* Convergence Finance. https://www.convergence.finance/news/3Mu8C08uYPNua9xpCSHliq/

Zam, Q. (2024). *Elderly Man Reading in Traditional Tanzanian Setting* [Image]. Pexels. https://www.pexels.com/photo/elderly-man-reading-in-traditional-tanzanian-setting-29280957/

Ziegler, R. (2023). *People Fence Refugees* [Image]. Pixabay. https://pixabay.com/illustrations/people-fence-refugees-globe-world-8389312/

www.ingramcontent.com/pod-product-compliance
Lightning Source LLC
LaVergne TN
LVHW051037070526
838201LV00066B/4843